Seeds of Treason

Seeds of Treason

THE TRUE STORY OF
THE HISS-CHAMBERS TRAGEDY

by

Ralph de Toledano
and
Victor Lasky

A NEWSWEEK BOOK

Published for *Newsweek*

by

FUNK & WAGNALLS COMPANY · NEW YORK

To

Joseph Stalin

without whose help this book
would never have been written

Preface

THIS IS MORE THAN THE STORY OF A FAMOUS TRIAL. It is more than the account of two men caught in what one of them called "the tragedy of history." It is, in a broad way, the story of an era, an anatomy of that time in American history when communism was a polite word and a fashionable avocation. That era is petering out today—although the sound and fury of the Hiss proponents during the two perjury trials were windy enough to convince us that gilt-edged communism was still a negotiable bond. The moral of the story is obvious—that under cover of the flummery of cocktail parties and fancy front organizations, the real Communists were systematically betraying the United States.

When this book was conceived, we had one goal: to knit into a coherent account the loose threads of a complex but fascinating story. As working newspapermen, both Lasky and I had shared the frustration of telling the story piecemeal and ignoring the long-range significance. The one-dimensional reporting of a daily paper and the two-dimensional recapitulation of a news magazine cease to be effective in what is fundamentally a four-dimensional, organic phenomenon. There is more to a musical score than the trajectory of the first violins and the woodwinds. There is more to this account than an answer to the question—so frequently repeated until an American jury gave its response—"Who is lying, Hiss or Chambers?"

In going about the task of arriving at the sum of the parts, the first problem was to make contact with the protagonists. There was no trouble in getting to Whittaker Chambers. Once he had been convinced that we were interested in him as a man, not as a grotesque fixed by the hostile spotlight of unwanted notoriety, Chambers came forward willingly. In the case of Alger Hiss, the reception was notably different. After stalling over a period of weeks, one of his lawyers told us rudely, "I can't expose Mr. Hiss to redbaiters." Why an innocent man, who protested that he hardly knew what a Red was, should be afraid of redbaiters was slightly puzzling.

Friends of Whittaker Chambers had been eager to cooperate with us. Friends of Alger Hiss were either close-mouthed or hostile. This again was puzzling. College friends and State Department associates were helpful in supplying details of the outer Hiss and of his incredible rise in the government. But that was as far as we could go. Certainly, it was not for want of trying on our part. Lasky, an indefatigable reporter, knocked on many doors in gathering the material for the chapter on Hiss. His conversations with key people, his search through the files, and his correspondence would fill a volume. Boiled down to size, it gives the essence of Hiss, not the lifeblood.

Perhaps it is better that Hiss moves through these pages thinly. For Chambers is the protagonist and Chambers is the symbol. The slanders about the man who attempted to shield Hiss have merged handily with an easy cynicism which accepts base motives where none exist. *Seeds of Treason* is an attempt to set the record straight, to show that the "mystery" of the case is no mystery at all.

There are people named in these pages who have been tempted to break clean from their Communist past. But there are few with the strength and the inner resources to accept consciously an ordeal not by flame but by mire. Perhaps the verdict of twelve Americans in a Federal courtroom will encourage others to step forward, giving us an opportunity to dig up a few more seeds of treason before they have spread their roots too far. This is a large "perhaps," yet in God's own time and God's own way it may become a certainty.

Seeds of Treason has been a difficult and exhausting book to write. But there were helping hands along the way, and

to those who extended them, a heartfelt thanks. There was
Representative Richard M. Nixon who devoted time and
effort to filling in large gaps in the House Un-American
Activities Committee sections; Charles A. Pearce who encouraged when encouragement was needed; Tom Murphy
and Tom Donegan, and Tom Spencer—two United States
Attorneys and one FBI agent; Samuel Shaffer of *Newsweek's*
Washington Bureau, whose week-to-week memoranda on the
House hearings went so far beyond surface coverage; Edward
W. Barrett and Kenneth G. Crawford who gave the manuscript an expert reading; Nora de Toledano, who arranged
chaotic notes, wrote first drafts of several chapters, and spent
hundreds of hours checking over the book; Mary Hood who
cheerfully typed the finished manuscript; and many, many
others whose names can not (or must not) be added hereto.

As *l'envoi*, there is this. Waiting in the press room for the
jury's verdict in the second trial, I remembered some words
from the Book of Jonah: ". . . a gracious God, and merciful,
slow to anger . . ." If we fail to cry treason when we see it,
we sail into the tempest and leap into the belly of the whale.
Look behind you. The whale is there.

R. DE T.

New York
30 January 1950

Contents

Seeds of Treason

It is necessary [for Communists] to use any ruse, cunning, unlawful method, evasion, concealment of truth [to gain their ends].

LENIN

They act like a secret battalion of paratroopers . . . I accept as a fact beyond dispute the devotion of Communists to their party. But in the light of experience I am bound to suggest that devotion so absolute develops in those who are moved by it a power within themselves to make simple truth and plain honesty things of secondary importance to be sacrificed by a coercive casuistry . . . It makes conspiracy endemic in such a party, it makes success the sole criterion of methods . . . The real purpose inherent in the strategy which Communists everywhere are determined to employ is the organization of catastrophe.

HAROLD J. LASKI

1

Of Whittaker Chambers

ONE SPRING DAY IN 1932, THE PHONE RANG IN THE *New Masses* office in New York. Whittaker Chambers, the editor, picked up the receiver. Twenty-four hours later, he was in the Communist underground, a Soviet agent, a "faceless man."

It was as simple and as quick as all that. The phone rang. Max Bedacht, a high-level party functionary, said, "I must see you at once on important business, Comrade Chambers." Chambers hurried out to meet him.

"You are going into the underground," he was told. "If you wish to remain a Communist, you have no choice. If you refuse, you will be expelled from the Party." Standing in the middle of the journey between hell and purgatory, Whittaker Chambers chose hell. Perhaps for a Bolshevik, there was really no choice; perhaps by what he himself would have called the "dialectics of the situation," it had to be hell.

This is the story of the steps which led to that choice. It is the story of the consequences of that choice—for Whittaker Chambers, for a handful of other Communists, and for the United States of America.

In 1924, Whittaker Chambers believed his life was at an end, the world he lived in on the verge of barbarism. He was only twenty-two years old, a sensitive and perceptive young man, but his depression could not be discounted as purely glandular. He had tried and rejected many formulas and

3

ideologies; he had worked as a day laborer and as a bank clerk; he had seen postwar Europe and stepped through the hothouse of collegiate intellectualism. But nowhere had he found a place for himself or a purpose to his existence.

So Whittaker Chambers sat one evening on a cold stone bench in the Columbia College quadrangle, trying to convince himself that suicide was the one logical course. But for him, this was a silly and impossible solution. Nor could he accept the authority of religion. Sitting there, oblivious to the noisy activity of the undergraduates who surged out of the Hartley and Livingston dormitories, he decided to accept the Communist promise of moral order in a world of chaos, to join the Party if he could, and to save the world from what he saw as the imminent collapse of Western civilization. His conviction of impending doom, which he might have shared with priest, scholar, or messiah, had roots in his boyhood and young manhood. It led him away from prayer, contemplation, or prophecy to more direct and violent means.

The man Whittaker Chambers was born J. Vivian Chambers in 1901 of mixed Dutch, German, French, and English—or briefly, American—stock. Shortly thereafter, the family moved from Philadelphia to Lynbrook, a rural Long Island community. Jay Chambers, his father, was a moderately successful, if slightly eccentric, commercial artist. His mother, Laha Whittaker Chambers, had been a stock company actress for several years before her marriage. In an amorphous atmosphere of gentle culture and high, undefined thinking, young Vivian grew up.

He was a quiet, intense boy who lived closely within himself. Most of his free time was spent in long walks in the surrounding countryside and in hours of listening to records or browsing in his father's library. At the age of eleven, he found and read Dostoievsky's *Crime and Punishment*. He understood this grim book well enough to confound his teachers at Lynbrook High School.

Freedom of choice in reading matter was typical of the

elder Chambers' intellectual tolerance toward his children. He was dogmatic only in one respect, and that was his refusal to discuss religion. He was neither atheist nor agnostic but was deeply convinced that religion was a vestigial encumbrance, something which nice people just never discussed. Only under pressure from Mrs. Chambers had he permitted the baptism of his children as Episcopalians, his own nominal faith. It was at this baptism that Vivian was given the name of Whittaker. By the time he reached college, he had understandably dropped the Vivian.

When Mrs. Chambers insisted on sending Whittaker and his younger brother Richard to Sunday School, Jay Chambers did not object too strenuously. But their introduction to Bible readings and Protestant liturgy ended abruptly. After two weeks, a small girl in their class came down with whooping cough, her mother accused Whittaker of having carried the germs, and the two boys were taken out of Sunday School, never to return. This lack of concrete religious belief was always a felt want to Whittaker. It caused him to explore Christian Science (typically, he read *Science and Health* in German) and Fabianism; it led him into and out of Communism; and finally it brought him to the Quaker faith he holds today.

Whittaker is remembered by his high school teachers and friends as brilliant but unconforming. "His hair was combed by the wind," one of his classmates remembers. "He usually wore sneakers. He was a butterball." Another friend recalled, "I don't think Vivian even learned to play marbles." But everyone agreed that intellectually he was head and shoulders above the other students, with a keenness of perception and an early knack for colorful literary expression. In those years, he had few friends. Most of his emotional nourishment came from his mother. It was from her that he got his love of poetry and his feeling for the dramatic in life.

But though in some ways cast in his mother's image, Whittaker also had his father's iconoclasm and his own rebellious-

ness of spirit, both clashing with his mother's domineering
conservatism. A job in the Lynbrook bank, when he was
seventeen, bored him. His mother's insistence that he go to
college irritated him. There was an explosion and he ran away
from home. Prophetically enough, the little money he had
carried him as far as Baltimore. A week-end in a dingy little
hotel convinced him that he needed a job quickly if he was to
remain on his own. Under the name of Charles Adams—he
admired John Quincy Adams—he registered with an employment agency where he was hired with a group of common
laborers to repair the street railway on New York Avenue in
Washington.

For months, he swung a pickax, operated a pneumatic drill,
and laid track, till his bleeding hands toughened as he himself hardened. All day he worked with the Mexicans and
Puerto Ricans in the work gang, picking up their hybrid
Spanish and learning at first hand what the proletariat was
like. When the Washington job was finished, he hitched his
way down to New Orleans, working on farms to pay for food.
Arriving dead broke in the fabulous Crescent City, he was
able to earn enough to pay for a room in a miserable dive in
the French Quarter. Living under the same roof in this room-
ing house were the dregs of the city, including a beaten old
prostitute with the terrifying name of One-Eyed Annie.

From New Orleans, he worked his way west, taking jobs
as an itinerant farm laborer. Somehow, though he never quite
realized what they stood for, he joined the Wobblies—the
Industrial Workers of the World—a brawling, revolutionary
group then on the decline. Eventually, he came to the conclusion that he had seen enough of the working world. He
decided to return to Lynbrook.

Now, by his own choice, he was ready for college. When
his mother suggested Williams, he agreed. But three days of
its sleek, upper-class attitudes and "those young collegiate
faces" was enough for Whittaker. He took the first train back
and matriculated at Columbia College. But his quick reject-

tion of Williams was no sign that he had achieved any degree of social or political sophistication. In his own words, he was still a country bumpkin then, still a staunch admirer of Calvin Coolidge, still neutral on the *status quo.*

It was at Columbia, however, that Whittaker Chambers' dissatisfaction and unmotivated rebellion began to take shape and find a direction. He was thrust into a group of campus intellectuals such as the College had rarely seen before, at a time when the country as a whole was rich with iconoclasm and postwar cynicism. Among his acquaintances were Joseph Freeman, Clifton Fadiman, John Gassner, Lionel Trilling—all young men of high seriousness. His closest friend was Meyer Schapiro, a boy of brilliant and inquiring mind. Under his tutelage, modern art and modern literature began opening to Whittaker.

Teachers like Mark Van Doren, his faculty adviser, chipped away at the old mold, too. The easy solutions implicit in Jay Chambers' nineteenth century humanism no longer applied. In the ferment and turmoil of new ideas, the shallow underpinnings of Whittaker's old acceptances were knocked away. The adolescent urge to remake the world in the image of order and perfection seethed within him. At first, the expression of this struggle between the world as it was and the world as it should be was literary; Whittaker Chambers began writing poetry. By undergraduate standards, it was mature and incisive verse and no more maudlin than it should have been.

Joining the staff of *Morningside,* the campus literary magazine, Chambers quickly became its editor. But this honor was short-lived. The fall 1922 issue carried a playlet by one John Kelly—"A Play for Puppets." Describing Our Lord's third day in the Sepulcher and His Resurrection, it was no more than a manifestation of what Chambers later called his "adolescent atheism"—but it caused a furor on the campus. Two weeks before it appeared, it had been hailed as "brilliant" by Professor Van Doren, a work "conceived in purest profan-

ism and dedicated to the anti-Christ." Other faculty members
were not so ready to share Van Doren's enthusiastic appraisal.
John Kelly was ordered to appear before the student committee on publications. Chambers tore off the disguise and
admitted that he was Kelly. But he refused to apologize for
the play.

"The author sees nothing irreligious in the play," he said
arrogantly to a New York *Tribune* reporter. "He has no
apologies to make. The mistake was made in supposing the
time ripe for the publication of such a play." And with that
haughty blast, he resigned from the editorship. He was not
expelled from Columbia, but henceforward he was definitely
persona non grata with Dean Herbert E. Hawkes.

This joust with authority, and his disgust over what he considered "sentimentality over religion," once more soured
Whittaker Chambers on the collegiate life. Once more, he
decided to get away from a hampering environment. But this
time, he went farther afield than Baltimore; with Meyer
Schapiro, he booked passage on a German steamer and sailed
for Europe. It was this trip which, more than anything else,
pushed young Whittaker into the Communist Party.

To the impressionable student, Berlin was a paranoid city
that summer of 1923. A careening inflation combined with
the psychosis of defeat had struck its inhabitants. People
walked through the streets with tears running down their
faces. Purse-snatching was common on the main thorough-
fares. What little pleasure could be extracted from life was
frenzied and orgiastic; and if a bushel of marks would not
buy a loaf of bread, a cigarette could buy a woman. At night,
while demoralized householders sat listlessly in their homes,
Communist students surged through the streets shouting that
tender Marxist anthem, "Grease the guillotine with the fat of
tyrants . . . Blood, blood, blood must flow."

For a young man seeking a sense of direction and a scale of
values, this was hardly the place for sound orientation. Nor
did Whittaker's subsequent wandering help. Leaving Ger-

many, he made his way through war-devastated France and
Belgium. Here the shock was not in what was but in what
had been: cities and villages in ruins; everywhere the jagged
remnants of prewar living and prewar security; once-fertile
land pitted with shell holes and scarred by trenches; and
the cemeteries with their horribly neat rows of crosses dip-
ping into the horizon. These were pictures of doom for young
Whittaker; this was the twilight of man.

Perhaps he did not think of it in such articulate terms. It
was more a spectacle of humanity crucified and bleeding,
helpless before forces it could not control. Many years later,
testifying in Washington, he said: "I did not understand the
cause of the crisis or know what to do about it. But I knew
that, as an intelligent man, I must do something about it."

Returning home, looking for an answer, Whittaker Chambers had little desire to go back to college. He had even less
desire to merge himself with the jazz age culture of his con-
temporaries. In order to begin his search, he made his peace
with Dean Hawkes and returned to the Columbia campus.
But it was only to live at John Jay Hall and to use the university library; he attended no classes. So as not to be dependent on his family, he took a nighttime job in the New
York Public Library, handing out papers in the newspaper
room. And he sought out his old friends at Columbia to ask
their advice. He had heard about Marxism. Perhaps in the
writings of the socialist theoreticians he might find a solution
to the world's besetting problems. "Where can I learn about
socialism?" he asked his friends.

They offered him the writings of the Fabian socialists.
Taking copious notes, he read the Webbs and R. H. Tawney.
The ideal of a planned economy appealed to him—as far as
it went. But polite Marxism did not satisfy Whittaker. It was
obvious to him that though the Fabians could write glibly of
the socialist state to come, they had not the faintest notion
of how the new society could be achieved. Even a dying
capitalism would not surrender meekly to the Webbs.

The fundamental point to Chambers, as it had been to Lenin, was, "How does a revolutionary movement seize and hold power?" He thought for a while that he had found the answer in *Reflections on Violence,* Georges Sorel's incendiary treatise. But though the French syndicalist called with religious fervor for direct action as a means of overthrowing capitalism, Chambers felt that the book barely arrived at the crucial question. When Clifton Fadiman gave Whittaker a copy of the "Communist Manifesto" of Marx and Engels, he read only the first sentences: "A spectre is haunting Europe the spectre of Communism . . . All the powers of old Europe have entered into a holy alliance to exorcise this spectre . . ."

"What horrible rhetoric," Chambers thought, and he tossed away the pamphlet.

"One evil hour, walking along Fourth Avenue and browsing in the bookshops, I came across a booklet in a fire sale," Chambers recalls. "It was called 'A Soviet At Work' and it was written by Lenin." Its description of a functioning soviet moved Chambers almost as much as it enlightened him. "This is the answer," he thought. "This man Lenin knows the mechanics of power—how to seize it and hold it. This is what I've been looking for." Like Paul on the road to Damascus, he had seen the light. He was converted.

2

The Evil Thing

"NO ONE RECRUITED ME," WHITTAKER CHAMBERS WAS to testify many years later. In Marxism-Leninism, he felt he had found a simple explanation and a program for action— or in terms more suited to his metaphysical temperament, a moral solution for a world of moral confusion.

"The very vigor of the project particularly appeals to the more or less sheltered intellectuals who feel that the whole context of their lives has kept them away from the world of reality," he said. "They feel a very natural concern, a Christian concern one might say, for underprivileged people. They feel a great intellectual concern for recurring crises, the problem of war which in our time has assumed an atrocious proportion and which always weighs on them. They say, What shall I do? At the crossroads the evil thing, communism, lies in wait with a simple answer."

Once he had reached that crossroads, the new convert moved determinedly to implement his conclusions. But this was not as easy as it might seem. The Workers' (Communist) Party was an elusive thing in 1925. Only a year before, a secret convention of the Party at Bridgman, Michigan, had been raided and the Party leaders arrested, on the tip-off of a government agent who had infiltrated the highest echelons of the organization. Now the Party was wary of all new recruits and doubly wary of those with middle-class back-

grounds who came in out of the blue. It was even difficult
to find out where Party branches met.

Then Chambers remembered Sender Garlin, the "campus
radical," who had passed briefly through Columbia. He remembered, too, that Garlin was associated with an outfit
called Russian-American Relief. Chambers sought Garlin out
and asked him naively, "Where's the Communist Party?"
Garlin questioned him closely to determine his sincerity.

"Go see Clarence Miller," he said at last. "He'll take you
to a meeting."

In a midtown loft—a cold, dirty hall in Hell's Kitchen, its
walls draped with faded red crêpe-paper streamers—Chambers got his first view of the revolution in action. The comrades were Greeks for the most part, with a scattering of
other nationalities. Most of the members spoke only their
native tongues; yet this was called the English Speaking
Branch. Among the few English speakers in the branch, however, were Benjamin Gitlow (later to become a top man in
the Party) and Juliet Stuart Poyntz—forceful, brilliant, and
unscrupulous—a Daughter of the American Revolution. (In
the late thirties, Juliet Poyntz was liquidated by the Party
when she broke with the Soviet military intelligence apparatus in this country.)

Chambers had expected to find tough-minded and dedicated Leninists, devotedly working for the downfall of the
capitalist system and for the creation of the proletarian
dictatorship. What he did find, for the most part, was a
squawling group of people, the dregs of discontent, who were
primarily concerned with the Party's intramural political
jockeying.

"I guess the social revolution has to make use of all social
elements," Chambers mused as he looked about him.

Factionalism, not revolution, seemed to be the order of the
day. On the one hand, a group headed by Jay Lovestone
intrigued to retain its leadership. On the other, the Browder-
Foster clique schemed to topple the Lovestoneites by winning

the favor of the bosses in Moscow. The two groups, Chambers realized, were united only in their hate of something called Loreism—a sort of 1925 brand of Browderism—which the angry dialecticians of the Party excoriated as "a right wing deviation from the revolutionary Leninist line of the Comintern." Loreism was obviously a heresy to be "relentlessly combated."

From the very start, Chambers had little respect for these picayune Communists. But he had joined the Party without any reservations, and he was ready to accept them as the feeble instruments which in time could be tempered to the kind of steel which had bored through the corrupt Russian state. He was ready to believe that in time the American party would develop its own American bolsheviks. So he plunged into what Party activity he could find; he joined a study group headed by Scott Nearing.

As his assignment, Chambers was directed to write a paper on the Hungarian revolution of Béla Kun, a fruitful subject for investigation since the bolshevik coup among the Magyars had failed. With his customary thoroughness, Chambers plunged into the subject. He was still a clerk in the New York Public Library, and from this vantage point he systematically plowed through everything he could find on Kun's abortive attempt to set up a soviet Hungary. On the side, he continued studying the mechanics of power, absorbing Lenin's *State and Revolution* and *Imperialism*—as well as Bukharin's *ABC of Communism*.

All this time, Chambers was digesting Lenin's sardonic dicta: the bolshevik is the man who takes power; the socialist is the man who would like to but doesn't take power; the liberal is the man who does nothing. This was a basic and sustaining dogma in the years of heavy underground work.

One night, at his post in the library, his nose buried in a book on the Hungarian soviet "republic," Chambers realized that a dark little man was watching him intently. He had seen the man before and remembered him as someone who came

in frequently to read the Hungarian papers. The two struck
up a conversation about Hungary and then shifted to the
subject of communism. When the library closed that night,
Chambers accompanied the little man to his flat, a small,
bare room containing only a chair, table, and bed. There they
got down to the core of things—the theory of revolution.

Chambers had never met a man so schooled in the Marxist
dialectic, so single of purpose, so direct of intellect. Pro-
foundly interested, Chambers returned to the monastic little
room many times, and the influence on him of the talks he
had there was great. "He was the most thoroughly integrated
human being I had ever met," Chambers says, "and the one
most responsible for turning me into a real bolshevik." But
he never learned the man's name. One night, as Chambers
was leaving, the little man asked him:

"You are a Communist, of course?"

"Yes," answered Chambers. "I am a member of the Party."

"I am the West European representative of the Communist
International," the man told him casually. "You are not to
tell anyone of these visits, not even your fellow Party members." So the seminar in revolution remained secret.

Whittaker Chambers might have remained an "intellectual" Communist, working at the library by night and reading books at Columbia by day. But this life was interrupted
in a singularly unpleasant manner. One day, some Communist pamphlets were found in his locker at the Public Library,
detectives were called in to investigate the dangerous radical, and Chambers was fired. To further damn him, the
detectives went to his home in Lynbrook and there found
some books he had borrowed from Columbia without taking
the librarian into his confidence.

Shortly after this, Chambers turned up at the New York
office of the *Daily Worker*, the Communist newspaper. The
manager, Louis Katterfeld, looked at the young bourgeois-
turned-revolutionary and patronizingly gave him the most

routine assignment he could think up. He sent him out to
pick up unsold copies of the *Daily Worker* from the news-
stands which carried it. Lugging a small suitcase, Chambers
would cover the Bronx, Brooklyn, and parts of Queens every
day, doing the kind of penance the Communists seem to
expect of their novices.

When the *Worker's* main office was moved from Chicago
to East 9th Street in New York, Chambers began getting
writing assignments. The first story thrown at him was about
Sandino, the Nicaraguan rebel, and the would-be newspaperman was lost; he didn't even know how to write a news lead.
In fairly short order, however, Chambers picked up that
simple skill and was turning out "eye-witness" accounts of
such distant events as the riotous American Legion convention in Paris.

On the *Daily Worker,* Chambers got his first good look at
the Party bureaucracy. There was obtuse Louis Engdahl,
Vern Smith, Harry M. Wicks, tough William Dunne, and
Tom O'Flaherty, brother of Liam. None of them was cut to
the heroic bolshevik pattern; all were given to an easy-going,
disconcerting cynicism about the Party and its leaders.

Chambers himself was something out of the ordinary in
that office. Small and unkempt, he was hardly the collegiate
type. But he was markedly an intellectual and therefore suspect. One day Bill Dunne looked pointedly at Whittaker and
said loudly:

"I always look at these new comrades and I wonder which
one will point a finger at me in a courtroom." Dunne was a
good prophet.

In October, 1926, Chambers' sense of social responsibility
was blunted by a personal tragedy when his younger brother
Richard committed suicide. The shock was not unexpected;
Richard had talked frequently of ending his life and had
made several attempts previously. Whittaker had twice
before thwarted suicide attempts, and Richard had tried
hard to convince his older brother to go along with him.

Many years later, Chambers was to recall these discussions: "Dickie read the French rationalists at a time when he was unprepared to understand them. He came to the conclusion that this was an irrational world and he didn't want to continue in it. You know, there are gentle folk unable to cope with this world, and he was one of them." There was another factor; Richard was obsessed with the idea that the Chambers family was somehow doomed.

His brother's death left Chambers in what he later described as "a state of complete immobility." He was able to move about, to use his arms and legs, but all desire of motion left him. He was struck by a paralysis of the will. Living inertly within himself during this period of mourning, Chambers dropped out of the Party completely. Finally Sender Garlin sought him out. By returning to his Party work, Garlin remonstrated convincingly, he would shake off his paralysis.

It was in the ferment of the Sacco-Vanzetti agitation that Whittaker Chambers returned to the *Daily Worker.* But he was not assigned to write the exciting and living stories. Instead he was given the dull job of editing a page called Workers Correspondence—letters from the raw proletariat, many of them semi-literate, reporting on Party work in the shops and factories. Though he did not relish the job, Chambers realized that this correspondence was important. This spadework among the comrades, more than irate polemics, was what built up the sort of organization which could create a soviet America. So he labored late and long in the vineyard.

And his reward came, not from the American party which considered the page a waste of space but from Moscow itself. A letter from the Comintern, analyzing the *Daily Worker,* excoriated the paper. But it praised Workers Correspondence as the only good thing there. Chambers' reward, of course, was to have the page taken away from him; it had become a plum.

The next assignment for Chambers was a promotion to

foreign editor. It was while handling foreign news copy that
Chambers got his first real jolt in the Party. Curiously enough,
what shook him was a trifling piece of copy from Moscow.

Leon Trotsky had just been expelled from the Party. This,
in itself, bothered Chambers. He did not try to understand
the arguments for or against it, but he could not forget that
after all Trotsky had—with Lenin—fathered the revolution.
Trotsky was a master of the *coup d'état*; he had organized
the triumphant Red Army. Yet Chambers could have swallowed the sordid story of Trotsky's political destruction
without too much trouble had there not been a hair in it.

That hair was a brief cable from Moscow describing
Trotsky's journey into exile, to Alma Ata. The Communist
technique is not only to destroy a man but to destroy his
reputation as well. So the cable reported that Trotsky, traveling with "sixty pieces of luggage and his hunting dogs," had
caused wondering peasants to exclaim, "Who is this great
lord passing through our village?" Chambers dutifully
printed the item but he never forgot his sense of outrage.

At about the time the *Daily Worker* moved to Union
Square, Chambers' salary was upped from $10 to $25 a week,
and he became editor in fact though not in title. His routine
consisted of running the copy desk and persuading the lino-
typers, old-line trade unionists bitterly antagonistic to the
Communists, to get the paper out on time. By winning over
the printers, Chambers was able to meet a deadline now and
then, and the *Worker* began making the mail train.

The nominal editor of the *Daily Worker* was Robert Minor.
But he spent most of his time at the national headquarters on
125th Street, rushing down to the *Worker* office at about
9 P.M. when most of the copy was in. "Chambers, I've got to
catch a train," he would say—he lived in Croton-on-Hudson.
"Will you write today's editorial for me?" And Chambers
would, as Minor went galloping off for Grand Central Station.

Whittaker Chambers' first rift with the Party grew out of
his loyalty to Minor. One day, Harrison George, a staff mem-

ber and brother-in-law of Earl Browder, told Whittaker, "If we could only get Bob Minor off this paper . . ." Leaving the sentence unfinished, he added, "And I think it will be arranged."

"They've got the knife out for you, Bob," Chambers warned Minor. And then he indiscreetly expressed his disapproval of Party factionalism and of the current anti-Zionist, anti-Semitic line. (The year was 1929 and William Gropper's cartoons of the hook-nosed Jew, with a star of David on his paunch and whip in his hand, guarding the money bags, were appearing in the Yiddish Communist press.) With typical Communist gratitude, Minor rushed to Charles Durba, head of the all-powerful Control Commission, and informed him of Chambers' heresies.

The results were immediate. Durba phoned Chambers and in a sepulchral voice said, "Chambers, I'd like to see you." Before Chambers had a chance to respond to the summons, another man was assigned to "assist" him. This was *mene, mene, tekel, upharsin* for Whittaker Chambers. He picked up his hat and walked out without bothering to resign. But drastic as this break seemed then, it was with the Communist Party, not with its Leninist doctrine. The evil thing, communism, still held his faith.

3

Writer to Spy

WHEN WHITTAKER CHAMBERS WALKED OUT OF THE *Daily Worker* office in 1929, he still believed firmly in the bolshevik seizure of power and the dictatorship of the proletariat. The right instruments to bring about the revolution would come in time. They would be schooled and dedicated young men, and he would be one of them. In the meantime, he would write.

Chambers knew that he could easily earn more than his *Daily Worker* salary by doing literary translations. Ever since the middle twenties, when he had translated the best-selling *Bambi* by Felix Salten, his reputation in that field had been high. (He found no difficulty in getting another assignment, Franz Werfel's *Class Reunion*.) And he could continue to write the poems which, he must have known, were completely un-Marxist in their reflection of an older and sadder philosophy.

What he wanted most of all was to crystallize his political thinking, to arrive at some conclusions, and to put these conclusions down in the form of stories. Proletarian writing in those days was preoccupied with the more squalid aspects of American industrial life. It was mawkish, self-pitying, and dishonest—pulp fiction in reverse. Chambers had no desire to describe the insides of garbage pails. His aim was at once grandiose and practical; he wanted to create the bolshevik as a figure in American literature. It was this character who dominated the short stories he began to write.

During this relatively calm and productive period in his life, Whittaker Chambers married Esther Shemitz. He had seen her for the first time when he was covering the 1926 Passaic textile strike for the *Worker*. The police had surrounded a hall in which strikers were gathered. Suddenly the doors burst open and the strikers marched out to meet the police. They were led by a slender, dark-haired girl.

"Get that bitch in the brown beret," the police shouted as they moved in on the strikers. The girl, a labor organizer, was arrested in the struggle that followed. Chambers learned then that her name was Esther Shemitz, but it was not until years later that he met her. Never a Party member Esther was one of the multitude of sympathizers who work in Party organizations and accept Party doctrine without formal membership. When they were married at City Hall in 1931, Grace Hutchins, a Bryn Mawr-Back Bay Communist, and Anna Rochester, author of *Rulers of America*, a slashing treatise on United States capitalism, were their witnesses.

After leaving the *Worker*, but before his marriage, Chambers had written as a memorial to Richard, a poem full of moving and romantic despair. Harriet Monroe had published it in her magazine, *Poetry*.

The moving masses of clouds, and the standing
Freights on the siding in the sun, alike induce in us
That despair which we, brother, know there is no withstanding . . .

Only the momentum of the motion of masses,
Being or substance, has any meaning—or their cessation
Upon the perfect turn of the experience motion amasses

We see all about us how, in creation,
Flowers from the dark gathering in their roots, with one motion,
Thrust themselves perfect, O God, perfect, from increation . . .

You know it is the cessation of the motion in me I am waiting
And not the lack of love, or love of the sun's generation
Of bodies, or their stasis, that keeps me—but my perfection for
    death I am waiting.

Now, married to Esther and with the security which a good marriage brings, Chambers imposed on himself the more rigid discipline of his political stories. The Communists have tried desperately to obscure Chambers' impact on left-wing writing. Yet his importance in the very early thirties is there on the record, ready to be measured. Chambers wrote five stories for the *New Masses* in this period, working at them in the cold-water flat, on New York's East Side, which he and Esther had rented. At least two of the stories, "Death of the Communists" and "Can You Make Out Their Voices," had world-wide repercussions in left-wing literary circles.

"Death of the Communists," a first-person account by a seemingly antagonistic prisoner, described the imprisonment of five Communists and their execution for attempting to foment mutiny among a garrison of soldiers. It was a story hardly American in character, reading almost like a skillful translation from the Russian. But in its balanced, unhurried sentences, it did portray the heroic bolshevik, it did set up a criterion of behavior for the Leninist fighter, and it did characterize the bolshevik's steely dedication to an ideal.

In the story, as the Communists waited to be shot, they took turns at explaining their doctrine to the half-savage inmates of the prison:

"[Thompson—one of the Communists] made the convicts understand . . . their position, not only as individuals, but as part of a social whole, of a social process, in the light of a universal philosophic theory . . . But it was from the uncommon persuasiveness . . . of the Communist, Kubelik . . . that I became conscious of a feeling which has little to do with reason . . . To the convicts his labored phrases seemed to strike like blows against their bars . . . He spoke once of his doctrine's having been invented by no one, but as a method disclosing the reality of things . . . Communism is the emery that clears away the dirt and moss and lets you see the meaning of the stone imprisoning you [Kubelik told the convicts], a meaning that is underlined with bars of steel."

After the Communists had been executed—a rifle volley cut
them down as they sang the "Internationale"—the narrator
described how he felt borne away on the wave of the future.
"I had a feeling, singularly light and unsorrowful, that their
deaths made no essential difference to themselves, to what
they were effecting, or to that for which they stood. Indeed
I felt as I have felt only once before in my life, when I was
lying on my back in a small boat . . . and a swell and a
strong tide carrying me along with no effort on my part."

From there on, "Death of the Communists" was all
crescendo, powerful enough to stir an aging journalist in
California.

My dear Whittaker Chambers (*he wrote*)

My hat came off while I was reading today a story of yours.
How you can write! And your stuff—
Whenever I hear people talk about "proletarian art and litera-
ture," I'm going to ask them to shut their minds and look at you.
I hope you are very young, though I don't see how you can be. I
hope, too, that you are daring, that you have no respect for the
writers of my generation and that you know as well as I do that
you can do it.
Now I'll put on my hat again.
(*The letter was signed*) LINCOLN STEFFENS.*

Hallie Flanagan, then director of Vassar College's experimental theatre, read "Can You Make Out Their Voices"—she
later described it as "one of the great American short stories"
—and wired Chambers for permission to dramatize it. Produced by the students at Poughkeepsie, the play was taken
up by Communist groups all over the world. An enthusiastic director of the Shanghai People's Theater wrote Miss
Flanagan that it had been put on "before the working
class of Shanghai as a part of our protest against Japanese
imperialism."

* From *Letters of Lincoln Steffens,* copyright 1938, by Harcourt, Brace,
and Company, Inc. Reprinted by permission of the publishers.

What Moscow thought of the story was considerably more important to Chambers' future in the Communist movement. And Moscow went all out. A critique published in *International Literature* pitilessly criticized the *New Masses* but praised Whittaker Chambers as the find of 1931. "For the first time in American literature ['Can You Make Out Their Voices'] gives a revolutionary exposition of the problem of the agricultural crisis and correctly raises the question of the leading role of the Communist Party in the revolutionary farmers' movement." Then the imprimatur was placed on Chambers' writings: they correctly interpreted "the task of presenting the image of the Bolshevik" as set forth by Comrade Stalin.

This remote laying on of hands by Moscow convinced Party leaders that Whittaker Chambers must be brought back into the Party as soon as possible. Early in 1932, two of the cultural commissars, Joseph Freeman and Mike Gold, were assigned to win him back. The lure they held out to him was the editorship of the *New Masses*.

For three months then, Chambers edited the *New Masses*, handling the copy of important left-oriented writers like John Dos Passos, Charles Yale Harrison, Josephine Herbst, Langston Hughes, and Theodore Dreiser—all of them contributing to the Communist magazine in those days. For three months he was absorbed in his new job. Then, in the midst of the fourth issue under his editorship, the phone call came from Max Bedacht. The instructions from Bedacht were typically mysterious. Chambers was to meet John, a man he knew in the open Party as Robert Mitchell. John, who had once helped organize a subway strike in the twenties, was now operating under various first-name aliases—Mike, Arthur, and Don.

Without any explanation, John took Chambers up-town where the two men strolled casually along Riverside Drive near Grant's Tomb. A cruising limousine picked them up, and there Chambers was introduced to a Russian known to him merely as Herbert. Herbert questioned Chambers closely on his past disagreements with the Party then bluntly told him that he had been selected for underground work.

Chambers had no desire to leave the *New Masses*. That night, when he discussed it with his wife, she strongly opposed the move. In fact, she cried. For Esther was not, in the Party jargon, "thoroughly developed," and to her the contemplated step was highly distasteful. But as a Leninist, Chambers knew that he must accept the assignment. The father of Bolshevism had made it clear that the revolution could succeed only if the Party developed a core of professional revolutionists—not job-holding functionaries like the titular heads of the American party, but men from whom the Party could demand everything and expect all. These men, undemoralized by personal problems, had to be ready to leave their families for months or years, to go where they were sent and do what they were told. This is what Chambers had believed, what he had preached, and what he did.

Two days later, John introduced him to a short, wiry, monkey-faced veteran of the Russian civil war. His name was Ulrich and, not being a Party member or a strict Marxist, he was an anomaly in the underground. But he was an experienced revolutionary, and the Kremlin trusted him. Ulrich gave Chambers his first cover name—Bob—and his first assignment. So Whittaker Chambers the writer disappeared as completely as if he had dissolved into thin air. None of his Party friends knew what had become of him, nor was it their business to ask. He became a man of many names and of no name. He moved anonymously about the country, a "faceless man," his old identity lost in the musty files of the *New Masses* office. And, with each new underground assignment, he and his family assumed a new false identity as routine protection.

Before Whittaker Chambers was permitted to get too involved in underground work, however, Ulrich sent him to

Dr. Philip Rosenbleitt, a dentist whose office was in the Western Union Building on Broadway.

"I was sent there," Chambers testified many years later, "to have work done on my teeth. Rosenbleitt did a minimum of work on me but became very friendly and told me a number of interesting facts about underground work and Russian espionage . . . Actually I was sent to Rosenbleitt so he could make personal observations about me. It was my understanding that he was a kind of permanent agent and through his office passed a great many, if not most, of the Soviet agents in this country over a number of years.

"One operation Dr. Rosenbleitt told me about had to do with the mechanization of the Red Army. Representatives of the Irish Republican Army in London made a contact with the Soviet underground and worked out a deal whereby an officer of the General Staff in Washington—an Irish patriot—would turn over to Soviet agents here various information that he had access to. In return, the Russians would send two submarines with machine guns and other arms to the west coast of Ireland . . . At this end the deal was arranged by a sportsman and politician in Queens who knew the general on the staff.

"The general agreed to turn over to Soviet agents all the material relating to Christie tanks, and did so, which was why the foreign representatives were surprised to see those rather American-looking tanks that paraded during one of the celebrations in Red Square . . . The general was also a heavy-drinking man, and during Prohibition the Russian agents had to smuggle liquor into the country to keep him supplied." It was not a long-lasting arrangement because the submarines and the machine guns never showed up off the coast of Ireland.

During this early period in his secret work, Chambers was acting as the liaison man between the open Party—known as The Bank to Comintern operatives—and the underground.

Specifically, this meant that he was the go-between for Bedacht and Ulrich. But once the stamp of Rosenbleitt's approval had been placed upon him, Chambers became a full-fledged member of what he realized was an international organization in which he executed the orders of top Russian agents in this country. Dimly aware, during his open Party days, of the existence of undercover workers in the war against capitalism, he came to know intimately the degree and extent of their activities. It was not long before he became one of the top Americans in this Communist netherworld.

As an apprentice spy, his first work was as a courier. When a ship of the Hamburg-American line or the North German Lloyd docked in New York, the ring would spring into action. (After Hitler came into power, destroying Russian communications via Germany, the French Line was used.) Primary liaison men would quietly meet Communist stewards from the docked ship and receive from them innocent-looking typewritten letters or small, cheap mirrors. These "transmissions," which occurred about fortnightly, were delivered to Chambers who would carry them to one of three secret headquarters.

"The curious thing about it," Chambers told a Congressional subcommittee, "was the typed letter which was in German—they must have made about a hundred copies. It was always the same letter and the one phrase I remember out of it was, 'We live here as on a hot griddle.' " (The reference was to the rising depredations of the Nazi movement.) Between the triple-spacing, the real message would be written in colorless ink, which, when treated with potassium permanganate, would rise as a brownish script. These were the instructions for the underground.

The mirrors also bore secret messages. Describing their use, Chambers has said, "The back of the mirror was a malleable metal, covered with some kind of cheap fabric, and by taking a nail file it was very easy to lift one whole edge and remove the glass without denting the edge at all." Between the backing and the glass, strips of microfilm had been inserted.

The main headquarters, for processing these messages and for preparing microfilmed answers, was in Greenwich Village at 17 Gay Street, in a house owned by a Communist school teacher. A whole floor was occupied by the underground, and it was well stocked with photographic and chemical equipment. Another headquarters was the sumptuous apartment of Paula Levine, a fugitive spy wanted by the French police. A third was in Brooklyn, at the home of an assistant foreman of the *Daily Worker's* composing-room staff.

As Chambers rose quickly in the secret apparatus, he took on more important duties. One of these was to recruit new agents here. "A fairly common practice seems to have been to come to the United States to set up apparatuses in foreign countries, using this as a base," Chambers has testified, "partly for the recruiting of personnel and partly for money transactions through American banks." It was also his job to assist in the formation of these underground groups. In connection with this work, Chambers recalls a trip made to San Francisco. There he registered at the Golden Gate Y. M. C. A. under the name of Lloyd Cantwell (which he had borrowed from a good friend) and delivered to two Russian agents a money belt stuffed with $10,000. The money was earmarked for espionage and organizational work in the Pacific islands. As Chambers turned the money over, he must have wondered a little what fellow travelers who derided all talk of "Moscow gold" would have thought of the transaction.

(The connection between the open Party and the underground apparatus would also have shocked the liberal innocents. Chambers has recalled how one of the couriers from a German ship failed to make contact with the proper liaison man, "so he went to George Mink [later an NKVD operative], who was at the time a Communist organizer on the waterfront, and turned over to him the mirror and envelope. Mink gave [them] to J. Peters [head of the underground Party] who then gave them to me and they reached their final destination.")

Among the recruits sent to Chambers was Arvid Jacobson, a Finnish-American school teacher from Detroit. He was recommended by a Mrs. Morton, reputedly the wife of Otto Kuusinen, quisling Finn and a member of the Executive Committee of the Communist International. Chambers objected to Jacobson. The young man was too jittery, and he had a missing finger which would make him easy to spot. Despite Chambers' disapproval, however, the apparatus took in Jacobson. He was sent to Finland and was one of those arrested there in 1933 in a sensational round-up of Soviet agents.*

"Sometime in 1934, Dr. Rosenbleitt introduced me to a Soviet agent whom I knew as Bill," Chambers told a House Un-American Activities Committee group which met in secret session late in 1948. "Bill was a tall man with a rather lined face and a habit of squinting his eye—a Finn or an Estonian." The purpose of the meeting was more than casual. Bill proposed that Chambers go to work for the Soviet underground in London. "For that purpose, J. Peters, who knew of the meeting and knew of the purpose, introduced me to 'M,' † a literary agent, who was a member of the open Communist Party. 'M' was then shifted into the underground and separated from the open Party and attached to me more or less exclusively.

"The proposal was that the underground would finance an office for 'M' as a literary agent in London [as a cover for his illicit operations]. There was nothing hurried about it. It was a long-range plan and there was a great deal of discussion

---

* The story of Jacobson and of Paula Levine is told more fully in Chapter 9.

† Chambers gave the name of the agent, a man well known in the book trade, but for obvious reasons it cannot be printed here.

about it and very little done about it for some time." In the
spring of 1935, the plan had matured enough for Chambers
to grow a mustache as part of a disguise. To get him a false
passport, Party workers employed a routine and effective
technique. They dug through the files at the New York
Public Library till they had come across the death notice of
one David Breen who was born at approximately the same
time as Chambers.

A letter to the Board of Health was enough to secure a
duplicate of Breen's birth certificate. Armed with this,
"Breen" applied to the State Department for a passport which
was forthwith issued. Another Party member, employed by
the Atlantic City city clerk's office, planted a "birth certificate" in the municipal files there for "Ursula Breen" which
would cover for the Chamberses' little daughter.

At the last minute, however, the operation was abandoned.
Some time after, Chambers was again approached by Bill.
With him was John—the man who had helped bring Chambers into the underground. "John was to go to Tokyo to be the
head of a Soviet underground group and he wanted me to
organize for him the façade here which would make it possible for him to operate in Japan. I decided that since the
London project was put aside, the expedient thing was to use
'M' to front for the Tokyo operation.

"'M' and John got up what was called the American
Writers Feature Syndicate, whose purpose it was to secure
interesting material from abroad. As I understand it, 'M' went
among various feature syndicates and newspapers and tried
to get advance sales in this kind of stuff. John went to work
in 'M's' office, had a desk there and his name written on the
door. Deposits were made, I think in the Chemical Bank, in
the name of the syndicate. These deposits were to finance the
operation in Japan." At the same time, the false passport
routine was repeated for him, and John was transformed into
Charles Chase.

As Chase, he led an ultra-respectable existence in Tokyo.

Representing a supposedly bona fide literary agency, he lived
at the Y. M. C. A., took part in its activities, and even won its
handball championship. Behind this cover, he worked with a
Soviet spy ring which penetrated into the top Japanese government circles.* He might have remained there but for one
thing. A Moscow courier brought Chambers word that John
was not to be trusted. Within twenty-four hours, the "literary
agency" had been disbanded. Several days later, word arrived
in New York that it was all a mistake. Moscow had meant
someone else. But John was already on his way to the Soviet
capital for reassignment.

This, in rough outline, was Whittaker Chambers' underground work for the first three years of his activities. "I was
probably the busiest man in America at the time," he says
with some justice. For all this was but a part of his underground assignment. Concurrent with it was another assignment—one which required tact as well as devotion and one
which makes up the body of this book.

Moscow was preparing to forego its frontal assault on the
capitalist system. A new Party line was abrewing, the end of
the Party's Third Period and the beginning of that world-
wide seduction of liberals misnamed the Popular Front. To
begin unlocking the gates for the Trojan horse, Chambers had
been sent to get instructions from J. Peters,† whose innocuous appearance belied the powers he held in the legal and
extra-legal Communist parties. At a secret conference in
Washington, Peters had introduced Chambers to Harold
Ware. It was at this meeting that Whittaker Chambers first
heard the name of Alger Hiss. The year was 1934.

* So high did Soviet agents penetrate into the Japanese government that
one Communist operative was among the trusted officials who drafted the
papers which tied Japan to the other signatories of the Hitler-Mussolini Anti-
Comintern Pact.

† Shortly before the first Hiss trial, Peters (also known as Alexander
Stevens) fled the country to avoid deportation.

4

Of Alger Hiss

THE SPOTLIGHT SHIFTS NOW TO ANOTHER MAN, TO Alger Hiss who entered the Whittaker Chambers story as a minor character and became the catalyst of the most preposterous series of events in American contemporania. Alger Hiss enters this chronicle in 1934, but the roots of his participation began pushing upward many years before.

Alger Hiss was born on November 11, 1904, of a determinedly middle-class family in a determinedly middle-class section of Baltimore. His parents, Charles Alger and Mary Lavinia Hughes, merely perpetuated a grandparent's admiration for the rags-to-riches writer when they gave their fourth child his Christian name. But their choice was apt; from his very early days, Alger showed signs of an overweening desire to get ahead. As the child of a fairly well-to-do drygoods merchant, Alger's tribulations were not primarily economic. His problem was to rise from the inconspicuous respectability of his Baltimore environment and to earn a seat for himself in the world of great place.

But even in those early years, there were unsettling influences and events in the child's life which could only leave a mark, however hidden, in his character and outlook. When Alger was two and a half years old, his father slashed his own throat with a razor. This streak of tragic morbidity ran through other members of his family. Many years later, one of his sisters, Mary, committed suicide by drinking Lysol; his older brother, Bosley, died of Bright's disease, reportedly aggravated by drinking.

On the surface, however, Alger lived the life of a normal Baltimore boy, attending Public School 14 and supplementing his allowance by hauling spring water from Druid Hill Park to peddle in town. In later years, he made much of this enterprise and boasted that he had raised and sold squabs. His high school was the Baltimore City College, but before matriculating at Johns Hopkins University, he was sent to acquire the "finish" of Powder Point Academy, a military school in Duxbury, Massachusetts.

At Johns Hopkins, Alger's quiet good looks and indefatigable charm, as well as his unbusheled brilliance, made him a natural for Alpha Delta Phi, a fraternity which pledged only the wealthiest and socially most acceptable young men on the campus. And from the fraternity row point of view, he was a real find, establishing himself as a big-man-on-campus. Throughout his college years, Hiss "played it down the conventional alley," according to a good friend. He was a "smoothie"; there were "no rough edges" about him. Steering clear of the college cliques, he made it a point to be popular with both the students and the faculty. At college dances and Junior League affairs, he always appeared with one or another of Baltimore's debutantes. But he never boasted of his amorous exploits, nor did he share in the collegiate good fellowship which came out of a hip flask. He joined the proper clubs and ran for office successfully.

A campus myth soon developed about Alger Hiss. He was a sort of undergraduate superman; whatever he went after he got. His extracurricular record was extraordinary.

He signed up for R. O. T. C. and attained the highest rank there, that of colonel.

He went out for the dramatic society, the Barnstormers, a minor-league version of Princeton's Triangle Club, and became its president.

He joined the staff of the college daily, the *News Letter,* and ended up as editor in his senior year.

Of the eight Phi Beta Kappas in his graduating class—he won his key in his junior year—Alger was the only one active in college affairs.

When he ran for any office, however, he did not let merit and popularity speak for themselves. Like any good politician, he got out the vote. It soon became a standing joke that, at election time, Alger would rush to the library and comb the stacks, bringing out the bookworms en masse to vote for him. He had no trouble getting himself elected president of the student council.

He joined the Tudor and Stuart Club, an elite university group which attracted the literati, but he attended little more than its social functions. He also made it a point to join the Cane Club, a socially exclusive organization for collegiate drinkers. Once a year, the Cane Club would parade through the campus, half-drunk, wearing carnations, derbies, and spats. Hiss soberly took part in the parades, right down to the carnation, derby, and spats.

In bull sessions with other students, Alger Hiss would talk about going to Harvard Law and from there to a well-paying job with a big law firm. The possibility of entering the underpaid government service never entered his mind.

Alger suffered one big disappointment at Hopkins. He wanted desperately to win a Rhodes Scholarship and study in England for a while. Because part of the requirement was all-around competence, he went out for the track team—and Henry J. Turnbull, a classmate, recalls Alger's knobby legs flapping around the Hopkins cinder track. The scholarship seemed his, but it was awarded instead to the son of a general. It was politics, Hiss's friends still agree, but this did not make the disappointment any less keen. Nor did he win the Alexander Barton Cup award for the student who had done most for his classmates.

In 1926, the senior class at Hopkins voted Alger Hiss "the most popular," the "best all around," the "best handshaker," and the man who had done most for the university. The year-book, edited by Turnbull (now a prominent New York adver-tising executive who still remarks of his classmate, "What a brain"), summed Hiss up in this fashion: "Alger must be the most cultured and learned bozo in this neck of the woods. Many and various are the discussions that we have had with him. Many and various the topics—they range from soviet to style, from liberty to liquor, from Guelphs to Goodnow [then president of Hopkins]. And like Socrates, we admit our ignor-ance in the force of his irresistible logic and rhetoric." There was no significance to the "soviet" Turnbull says today. "I just needed an 's' to match 'style.' If anything, Alger was the most conservative guy on the campus."

From Johns Hopkins, Alger Hiss moved on to Harvard Law School. Cambridge was an eye-opener, as Morningside had been for Whittaker Chambers. The provincial *wunder-kind* of Baltimore was faced with real intellectual competi-tion for the first time, and he hardened under it. The easy affability which had propelled him at Hopkins was not enough here, so with the adaptability which was always one of his prime characteristics, he put it aside. The personal charm and boyish winsomeness remained, but they were tempered by a new seriousness.

Ambitious, keen, and hard-working, he stood out among the brilliant young men in his class. His teachers, men like Felix Frankfurter and Francis B. Sayre, had been deeply involved in the Sacco-Vanzetti controversy (Sayre defended the two anarchists in court), and Hiss absorbed their em-battled liberalism. Among his classmates were Leon (later Lee) Pressman and William Hastie—one destined to become a pro-Communist big wheel and the other the first Negro governor of the Virgin Islands—who affected a kind of Fabian socialism which Alger found attractive.

It was not long before Alger Hiss had hit his stride at

Harvard. A year after he got there he had won the $250 Herman Parker Scholarship. He was elected an editor of the *Law Review,* one of the school's highest honors, and even in this fast company he stood out. At monthly meetings of the staff, held at Gannett House, the editors would go over the material. Recent cases were assigned to the editors for analysis and discussion.

"Call it hero worship, or what you will, Alger was tops at these sessions," says Harold Rosenwald, who many years later joined the battery of lawyers defending Hiss against a Federal perjury charge. "I was goggle-eyed at his brilliance and often wondered if I would ever know as much as he knew."

Alger Hiss was chosen for another honor: he was invited to attend the highly exclusive seminar conducted by Professor Frankfurter. Meeting in a small room, Frankfurter's "little wienies," as anti-New Deal columnists later took to calling them, would drop into easy chairs while the Professor sat ramrod-straight in an armless wooden chair, putting his scholars through their paces. It was literally a meeting of minds, a give-and-take on legal principles and the philosophy of law. And for Hiss, a recent convert from straightway conservatism, it was a God-given opportunity to expand his horizons.

Graduating *cum laude,* Hiss stepped into one of the most coveted jobs open to a man leaving law school. He was made secretary to the great Supreme Court Justice Oliver Wendell Holmes on the recommendation of Frankfurter. For Hiss, this was recognition that so far as his old teacher was concerned, he had been top man in his class. He knew that other Frankfurter favorites—Francis Biddle, Irving S. Olds (chairman of United States Steel), George L. Harrison (president of New York Life), Tommy Corcoran, Dean Acheson—had risen to eminence in business and government. Putting aside vague plans to go into law practice with Lee Pressman, Alger packed his bags and went to Washington.

This was a tragic period in the great jurist's life. His wife,

for many years an invalid, had just died, and Holmes felt lost
without her ready companionship. He himself was ill, and he
had more need for a friend than for a secretary. So the tall,
young, brilliant, and ambitious young lawyer became both.
While the tired, white-haired man sat back, his eyes closed,
Hiss would read to him—philosophy, novels, even poetry.

Every night, Hiss would bring stories of the great man
home to the flat on Connecticut Avenue which he shared
with Charles H. Willard, a Harvard friend then with the
Wickersham committee, and Robert Cruise McManus, a
Time magazine writer. McManus recalls the night Hiss came
home, downed a highball, and announced that he had taken
Holmes to see a Marx Brothers film. "You should have seen
the old man," Hiss said. "He nearly fell off the seat laughing,
he thought they were so funny."

At this point in his life, Alger Hiss' future seemed cut out
for him. Once his year with Justice Holmes was over, he
would return to Boston to take up the practice of law, join a
distinguished Back Bay firm, and make a socially advanta-
geous marriage. He was already developing the slightly stuffy
manner which was to characterize him in his State Department days and seemed destined for a wealthy middle-class
success followed by slow fossilization among the bean and
the cod.

But the elements of fate which had led Whittaker Chambers into the Communist netherworld were operating to
change the course of young Hiss' life. The Eumenides, in
this case, took the unlikely form of Priscilla Fansler Hobson,
a primly attractive, headstrong girl—full of aggressions, snob-
bish ambitions, unformulated desires, and an acidulous wit.
She had spent her childhood among the Philadelphia Main
Line aristocracy, a background which she both rebelled
against and made her own. Her father, Lawrence Fansler, a
successful insurance man, originally from Evanston, Illinois,
was stern, religious, rigidly conventional—and Mrs. Fansler
shared all his attitudes.

Graduating from Bryn Mawr in 1924, Priscilla Fansler had gone to New York to work on the fledgling *Time*. After a year of this, she married Thayer Hobson and went with him on a seven-month jaunt in Europe. When they returned, Hobson took a position with a publishing house. But somehow, the two couldn't get along. She thought he was too "pragmatic," he that she was "fuzzy minded." Though they had a child—Timothy—they agreed to separate in 1927, and Priscilla went to Yale for postgraduate studies preparatory to teaching.

When Alger and Priscilla met at a Washington cocktail party after her divorce, they picked up a friendship which had developed briefly on an Atlantic crossing in 1924 and again in 1927 while she was at Yale and he at Harvard Law. A few months later, in December, 1929, they were married. Few of Alger's friends could understand the marriage. Priscilla was older than he, and her manner was more than slightly astringent. As a matter of fact, most of them cordially disliked her.

His one-year term as Justice Holmes' secretary completed, Alger Hiss and Priscilla returned to Boston, found a house in Cambridge, and settled down. Alger was perfectly satisfied with his law work in the firm of Choate, Hall, and Stewart. He liked being in Cambridge where he could spend frequent evenings at the Brattle Street home of Professor Frankfurter. But Priscilla grew restless. She felt that Alger was blundering into a comfortable dead end. In New York, she insisted, there were many opportunities for a bright young lawyer with good connections. Through her friends there, she was certain that he could quickly make a name for himself.

His ambitions stirred, Alger let himself be convinced. Without any difficulty, he was able to attach himself to the Wall Street firm of Cotton and Franklin. The Hisses took an apartment on Claremont Avenue, near Columbia University where Priscilla enrolled for some courses, including one in typing, and soon they were drawn into the intellectual ferment of the time and the environment. The depression had

hit New York hard. Apple vendors occupied the street corners and block-long breadlines crowded Times Square. It was
an era in which people looked for answers; and for many,
particularly among middle-class intellectuals and professionals, the answer was socialism. Norman Thomas spoke
with fire in those days of the need to end "poverty in the
midst of plenty" and hinted darkly of revolution.

To Priscilla, always a do-gooder, socialism had many
attractions. Together, she and Alger began attending lectures
at the Rand School, moving closer and closer to the socialists
on Morningside Heights. The proper Hisses, however, were
not particularly rare birds. Many students and professors
publicly advocated Marxism. In 1932, the captain of Columbia's baseball team and three members of the football team
joined the Socialist Party and made the fact public. After
what must have been a thorough soul-searching, Priscilla
Hiss decided to take the great step. On March 23, 1932, she
joined the Socialist Party's Morningside Branch—at that time
drifting rapidly into the Communist periphery.

And she really took it to heart. A friend who attended a
party given by the Hisses still remembers how he casually
greeted his hosts with, "It's a nice day, isn't it?"

"What's nice about it for the poor, exploited sharecropper?"
Priscilla answered him sepulchrally. It was a very solemn
occasion, the friend remembers; no drinks were served.

But perhaps a more important consequence of the move to
New York was the reestablishment of an old friendship. Lee
Pressman, who was now with the ultra-respectable Wall
Street firm of Chadbourne, Stanchfield, & Levy, picked up
his old ties with Alger Hiss. In this account, Lee Pressman
can be allowed but a relatively brief space, although in the
history of the New Deal he looms as a figure of great significance. In December, 1948, the columnist Tris Coffin, himself
a staunch New Dealer, wrote:

"The Big Brain of the radical wing of the New Deal was
Lee Pressman, brilliant, magnetic, domineering . . . One of

Pressman's associates in [the early AAA] days says of him:
'Lee attracted many of us to his wing because he knew all
the answers. He had a systematic day-to-day plan all mapped
out. He was absolutely sure of himself. He used people like
a machinist uses tools—when they are broken or worn out he
throws them away, coldly and impersonally.' To others who
didn't know him so well, Pressman was aloof and arrogant,
but respected for a mind that could make decisive, split-
second decisions."

What made Pressman run? He was a Brooklyn boy, born
of immigrant Russian parents in July, 1906, the product of
New York's teeming public schools and Stuyvesant High
School. At Cornell University, he began developing the
tweedy, pipe-smoking manner, going out for the swimming
and wrestling teams, but sticking close enough to his books
to make Phi Beta Kappa and win the scholarships which
helped pay his way through Harvard Law School. There, in
Alger Hiss' class, he was elected to *Law Review* as Note
Editor. When Hiss went to Washington as Justice Holmes'
secretary, Pressman became Jerome N. Frank's cub in the
plush partnership of Chadbourne, Stanchfield, & Levy. But
handling receiverships and dealing with the problems of big
corporations didn't interest him. The road to success here
was slow, dull, and, for a man of his gifts, unattractive. In
those days, Pressman claimed to be a League-for-Industrial-
Democracy Socialist, a follower of Norman Thomas.

Whether or not he became a Communist in the year 1933
is a matter for conjecture. The Socialist Party in the early
thirties was the object of an organized assault by the Communists who hoped to infiltrate it, capture its machinery, and
merge it with the tiny Communist Party. There were many
ambitious Socialists of that period who later boasted that
while they worked in the Socialist Party they held secret
membership in the Communist Party.

Socialist or Communist, Lee Pressman realized that the
place for him was in Washington. The nation's capital was

a boomtown for brilliant young men of leftist bent, and the universities were pouring their brightest products into the insatiable maw of the alphabetical New Deal agencies. The brain trust consisted of men like Raymond Moley and Rexford Guy Tugwell, both Columbia professors who had taken with them the pick of their ex-students. Harvard ran its employment agency through Felix Frankfurter and Tommy Corcoran. Through Corcoran, then running the Harvard Placement Bureau in New York, whole departments and commissions were loaded with Harvard *cum laudes,* and, parenthetically, it was this which created for him what was called the "greatest intelligence service in Washington."

While James A. Farley, nominally the chief source of patronage in the Democratic Party, fumed and fretted, the party hacks were pushed aside by a "new type of civil servant." When Jerome Frank went to Washington to become head of the Agricultural Adjustment Administration's legal division, he put it bluntly to Farley: "We've got to get young lawyers who are willing to fight for a cause. They will have to buck some of the biggest firms in the country and some of the ablest lawyers. And since we can't afford to pay them anything, we will have to get men who will work only for ideals."

Ideals is an elastic word, and in 1933 it could be stretched to include communism. One of the first acts of the Roosevelt administration had been to recognize the Soviet Union—and a leading New York newspaper, in a complacent editorial, ridiculed those who thought bolshevism was something to "frighten babes and grown-ups." Recognition of the world's most complete dictatorship had brought "a new security, a new influence toward peace." Vodka flowed like buttermilk and caviar was as plentiful as herring at Soviet Embassy parties. To question the motives of the Stalinists in those days was to court social ostracism.

Perhaps Pressman did not phrase it that way as he contemplated moving to Washington, but of such was the kingdom of heaven. He approached Jerome Frank, already with the AAA, for a job in that mixed-up agency. And Frank, knowing Pressman to be a terrific organizer, a glutton for work who got things done, and an excellent lawyer, readily agreed. Once with the AAA, Pressman proceeded to ingratiate himself with another power in that agency, Gardner Jackson—then head of its consumer council—by recalling with fervor and admiration the wealthy liberal's outstanding role in the Sacco-Vanzetti fight. Many years and many unpleasant experiences with Pressman were necessary to convince Jackson that he was being played for a sucker.

Solidly entrenched in the AAA, Pressman began to bring in his own friends. They were all clever young men, all absolutely loyal to Pressman. Among those he brought in were Nathan Witt, Charles Kramer, and John Abt. And, of course, his close friend Alger Hiss. Before leaving New York, Pressman had urged Alger to come to Washington with him. When Hiss decided to take the advice, it was Tommy Corcoran who sent him to Jerome Frank, but the ground had already been prepared by Pressman. This double recommendation, plus the prestige of Hiss' year with Justice Holmes, did the trick.

5

The Ware Cell

Going to Washington was perhaps the single most important move in the life of Alger Hiss. For it was in the feverish atmosphere of the early New Deal that he began to fulfill the promise of his college and law school days. And it was in Washington, too, that he fell further under the spell of Lee Pressman.

From the New Deal agencies—mostly the Agricultural Adjustment Administration—Pressman had drawn together a group of bright young lawyers and administrators, all politically ambitious and all loyal to him. This group, working together, was in a broad sense a cell even before it had begun moving in the direction of the Communist Party. In retrospect, it is fairly certain that Pressman was responsible for the indoctrination of these Washington careerists.

The doctrine he must have preached to them could be very attractive in those days. It offered an "inevitable" solution to the world's economic muddle, embodied in a movement which made a fetish of success, no matter how ruthlessly achieved. It also promised the backing of a small, disciplined Party and the vast, mysterious strength of the Soviet Union. Moreover, it gave its members the sort of superiority which allowed them a smug condescension in their dealings with the "muddle-headed liberals" of the New Deal—the Tugwells, Wallaces, Franks, and Jacksons.

Leninism was a hard, realistic philosophy for hard, realistic

men. It dealt with power struggles in crude terms and justified the natural impatience of the brilliant intellectual with
the slow, tentative, and wasteful motion of political democracy. To a "born bolshevik"—and this is how Whittaker
Chambers later described Alger Hiss—the flabby morality of
bourgeois democracy was fine for the herd, but something
for the "superior" man to cut across. Perhaps he believed in
a Leninist wave of the future.

The chances are that Hiss might have shucked off his
Leninism in time. What drew him from the Communist periphery into the Communist underworld was the timely arrival
of Harold Ware, a man of sharply perceptive mind, with an
unerring instinct about people, an uncanny soundness of
judgment, and a tutored devotion to the Soviet Union. In
other words, Hal Ware was a top-notch agent of the Communist International—the Comintern.

Ware's mother was Ella Reeve Bloor—today "Mother"
Bloor to all Communists—a fighting radical who bogged down
in the Soviet mire. His brothers and sisters had been weaned
on Marxism, and he himself was a charter member of the
Communist Party. As such, he had labored long and lovingly
for the cause. In 1920, he had driven across the country gathering information on American agriculture for Lenin. In the
early twenties, he had also organized the first Communist
front in the United States—the American Federated Russian
Famine Committee.

In 1921, on information supplied by a Federal agent who
had wormed his way into the councils of the underground
Communist Party, Justice Department officers raided Ware's
apartment on Bleecker Street in New York City to discover
that the humorous, breezy, and bespectacled Hal had in his
possession a full roster of all important Communists in the
country, as well as material on their activities. It was this
seized information which led, in part, to the Palmer raids.

Ware's main function, however, was that of a professional
American friend to the new Soviet state. As an agricultural

expert, he made repeated trips to Russia, helping train
Russian peasants in American agricultural methods. Through
Russian Reconstruction Farms, a front he had also organized,
Ware set up a model farm in the Urals, transporting both
farm machinery and farmers from the United States.

In 1925, Hal Ware met Jessica Smith in Moscow. Jessica
was beautiful and Hal was persuasive. Back in New York,
the two were married by Norman Thomas, then still a Pres-
byterian minister. But neither marriage nor agriculture could
sidetrack Hal Ware from his main duties as a Comintern
agent. In the late twenties, he attended the Lenin school in
Moscow, an institute of sabotage, revolutionary organization,
and espionage in which most Soviet agents get their training.
In the States, Jessica Smith had begun publication of the
slick *Soviet Russia Today,* an important propaganda organ
which still appears under her editorship.

In 1933, Harold Ware made his last trip to Russia. The
recognition of the Soviet Union by Franklin D. Roosevelt had
created vast opportunities for the undercover Comintern
agents, but it was necessary to determine exactly how to
operate. Maxim Litvinov, the first Soviet ambassador to this
country, had pledged that his country would not permit the
organization of any party or group "which has as an aim the
overthrow of, or the bringing about by force of, a change in
the political or social order of the whole or any part of the
United States." How seriously American Communists took
that promise was immediately made clear when the *Daily
Worker* editorialized:

"In this country, the Communist Party section of the Communist International basing itself on the principles of Lenin
and Stalin, will more determinedly than ever strive to win
the American workers to the revolutionary way out of the
crisis . . . for the final overthrow of the capitalist war-
mongers." But would this apply to the underground apparatus of the Comintern? This is what Ware was out to determine. And along with other Comintern agents, he was given

the order to begin the systematic creation of Communist cells wherever possible. Some of these agents were assigned to the colleges, some to the banks, some to industry. Ware, because of a seven-year tenure (1925–1932) as a dollar-a-year man for the Agriculture Department, was assigned to Washington to direct operations there. The idea was—at first—not espionage but infiltration. Edna Lonigan, in *Human Events* has skillfully described this process:

Each cell [was to divide] and breed others. Directors of the NKVD sat with their maps of the "terrain" of the Federal government, and moved their followers to one key position after another. Communists in government and the colleges were ordered to recommend their comrades for all desirable openings. They were told to locate the key jobs, to know when they would be vacant, and to pull the strings. Their people always had the "best" recommendations.

First the network placed its economists and lawyers . . . Then it moved its men into public relations. As the leaders learned more about the workings of the bureaucracy, they put their people into jobs as personnel directors. Assistant directors proved even better for the purpose. These officials were never in the headlines. But they saw the incoming applications; they could weed out those with anti-Communist records; or "expedite" those with key names and key experience to identify them . . .

The duty of the ablest Soviet agents [in those days] was not espionage. It was to win the confidence of those who directed policy. Their job was to attach themselves to higher officials or to the wives of these officials; to be friendly, charming, alert, intelligent, sympathetic; to be ready day or night to take on more responsibility.

So, each year, the network moved its men into higher and higher positions. When war came the veterans of eight years of conspiracy reached the highest policy levels. Always an invisible force was pushing the favored higher . . .

In this infiltration, the Soviet agents were unwittingly aided by some of the New Deal idealists—men who had been taken straight out of the academic cloisters and who, thrown into positions of power, nourished romantic illusions that they

were the new Machiavellis. Dr. William A. Wirt shocked
Washington when he testified that at a party for government
people given by Alice Barrows, his former secretary, he had
heard a newspaperman declaim:

"We believe we have Roosevelt in the middle of a swift
stream and that the current is so strong that he cannot turn
back or escape from it. We believe that we can keep Mr.
Roosevelt there until we are ready to supplant him with a
Stalin. We all think that Mr. Roosevelt is only the Kerensky
of this revolution. We are on the inside. We can control the
avenues of influence. We can make the President believe that
he is making decisions for himself."

Dr. Wirt was hounded out of service in the Office of Education—even though he was one of the country's leading edu-
cators—for this and other "premature" revelations of Communist infiltration in the government. Yet the statement was an
accurate summary of a viewpoint held by many.

It was Hal Ware's job to seek out the serviceable Party
material from this wilderness of confused liberalism and to
set up a master cell. According to information long buried in
American security files, he found this nucleus in the group
around Lee Pressman: Nathan Witt, John Abt (who married
Jessica Smith not long after Ware was killed in an automobile
crash in 1935), Henry Collins, Charles Kramer—and Alger
Hiss. These men, and others who came in later, were the
Washington cell No. 1. They usually met in a violin studio
at 1503 Connecticut Avenue, just off fashionable Dupont
Circle, the home of Hal's sister Helen Ware.

In setting up the master cell, Ware drifted in and out of
the Agriculture Department with such frequency that many
people took it for granted that he was employed there. His
"cover," however, was an organization known as Farm Research, Inc. But Ware's activities were not confined to this
department. Eventually he set up at least half a dozen other
cells, each one composed of from seven to ten carefully
selected comrades. Operating with complete immunity and

the support of unconscious dupes, they ranged from Triple A to other New Deal alphabetical agencies, and from there into the old line bureaus and departments—State, Treasury, War, Labor, Justice, Immigration—and even the White House retinue.

So well did Hal Ware do his work that when he died, Mother Bloor declared: "I find his boys and girls everywhere. It's my comfort."

It was Hal Ware who, according to Whittaker Chambers' later testimony, first realized the potentialities of Alger Hiss. With great astuteness, he permitted the young Baltimorean to remain a silent partner in the cell. And just so long as Hiss committed no atrociously overt acts, he was above suspicion. His Washington friends summed him up as a clever lawyer who was bound to go places, cautious and a little arrogant in personal relationship, highly aloof from the gadfly social life of the nation's capital. Very few of his friends, professional and otherwise, were ever invited to the Hiss home.

As in New York, Alger and Priscilla lived a closely private life, obviously devoted to each other, spending much of their leisure time together reading or going to concerts. They listened to music at home or took long walks along the Potomac to indulge Alger's hobby of bird-watching. Now and then, the couple would go on picnics to Rock Creek Park or on occasional boat trips.

During this period, Priscilla was busy too. For her, there was a spell of teaching at the Potomac School for Girls in Washington, a brief term with the Interior Department, and another with the Library of Congress. She was also winning a reputation as an intransigent reformer, always aching to help the oppressed. Other friends of the Hisses soon became aware that she was a domineering and ambitious woman. "She looks sweet and mild," said one friend, "but she isn't." Her marriage to Hobson had been a defeat; she was determined not only to make this marriage a success but to make Alger a success as well.

There was nothing particularly distinguished about Alger Hiss' work with the AAA. He wrote milk-marketing agreements and drafted many scores of opinions, regulations, and other legal matters which were sent to Jerome Frank's office for action. He worked hard and characteristically well. But he was just another of the one hundred and thirty-five legal assistants there, along with Adlai Stevenson, Telford Taylor, Mrs. Lenore Fuller (sister of James F. Byrnes), and John Lewin. He stood out only because of his association with the so-called left wing in the Agriculture Department and because of the close friendship he developed with Frank.

Early in 1934, Alger Hiss was marked for a job which would utilize his abilities to better advantage. The Senate Munitions Investigation under Senator Gerald P. Nye had just begun to get under weigh and its aims—to blast the "warmongering" producers of war goods—fitted in neatly with the then current Communist position. The Comintern and the Soviet Union were still at odds with the entire world, Popular Frontism was still to come, and the Treaty of Versailles still a favorite whipping boy. It was obviously to the Party's advantage to try to demonstrate that the World War I was an imperialistic squabble plotted by the munitions makers. As usual, the Communists felt no compunctions about perverting the fundamentally laudable purposes of the committee.

To Lee Pressman falls the dubious credit of getting for Hiss the Nye committee assignment. As the Party's Number One patronage controller in Washington, he knew that Gardner (Pat) Jackson was a good friend of Nye, as well as of Senators Homer T. Bone, James P. Pope, and Bennett Champ Clark who, with Arthur H. Vandenberg, made up the committee. Pressman also knew that Jackson had been responsible for getting Stephen Raushenbush the job of chief investigator for the Nye committee. So he went to see the "millionaire socialist."

"Pat," he said to Jackson. "I've got a young lawyer on the AAA staff who would be ideal for the Nye committee. I think you know him—Alger Hiss. Why don't you speak to the senators about getting him on the legal staff." Pressman had come to Jackson before with requests of this type. (One such had brought Charles Kramer, a New York economist, into the AAA's consumer council.) Jackson spoke to Nye, and a deal was consummated whereby Alger Hiss was "lent" to the Senate committee.

Looking back at the incident, Pat Jackson recalls: "Lee was young, incisive, clear-cut in his views, and apparently going in the same direction I was. One day he said to me, 'You speak to everyone. You move in and out of everyone's offices. You're blond and blue-eyed. I'm exactly the opposite of you. Let's work together. We'll make a good team.' I guess we did make a good team—for Pressman. He played me beautifully."

Hiss made his public debut with the Nye committee on September 10, 1934. The first witness he questioned was John S. Allard, president of the Curtiss-Wright Export Corporation, and from the start it was obvious that Hiss was going to cut quite a swathe with the committee and the public.

"Once we put Alger on the job, we had no worries," Stephen Raushenbush says. He was not only a good lawyer but an implacable cross-examiner. He went after witnesses stubbornly, humorlessly, and with a purpose. He prepared the evidence carefully in advance, and then nothing could stop him from getting it into the record. The St. Louis *Post-Dispatch* editorially labeled him "the man who digs out devastating facts," a "verbal battering ram" whose surname—"a sinister, sibilant monosyllable"—was "an echo from moist and somber Stygian darkness."

Grilling an Army officer, Hiss submitted exhibit after exhibit of Army mobilization plans into the record. Smiling, the officer said:

"Mr. Hiss, you have convinced me we should never go to war. It is too much trouble." There was laughter in the hearing room. Hiss went right on without cracking a smile, "I would like to mark as exhibits memoranda on the general subject of price control and excess profits . . ."

When the Du Ponts were called, Hiss charged them—falsely, as it later turned out—with having made a $2,000,000 profit on a $5,000 investment and later with the curious "crime" of having sold powder to the United States Army at half the price it had originally cost.

"It was then merely a fortuitous circumstance that the United States got its powder cheaper," said Hiss to Pierre du Pont.

"I don't understand that remark," Du Pont replied.

"Well," said Hiss. "Certainly patriotism played no part in this lower price." Du Pont fumed, but for the nation's press it was page one material. And Hiss continued to go after the "interests" hammer and tongs. So bitterly did he go after J. P. Morgan & Company—always a target of the Communists for its pro-British orientation—that Robert Cruise McManus, then a Washington newspaperman, was called in by one of its subsidiary companies.

"The Nye committee investigators are acting very peculiarly," McManus was told. "They're interested in laying their hands on everything they can, even data which can have no possible reference to the subject of the investigation. We'd like you to find out something about these men." Among those named by the Morgan people was Alger Hiss.

"Hiss is a friend of mine," McManus answered, exploding. "I'll do no such thing."

In the long-drawn-out hearings of the Nye committee, perhaps the most sensational aspect as far as liberals were concerned was the attempted crucifixion of Bernard Baruch, an adviser of presidents, whose personal morality had never been questioned even by his political enemies. But Alger Hiss, who was later to complain of the treatment he got from the House Un-American Activities Committee, seemed to be attempting deliberately to destroy the white-haired financier's reputation for integrity. And he had plenty of allies in this venture—from Father Coughlin to the Communist press. Even before Baruch testified he had been accused, by those playing the Soviet and fascist game, of having made millions out of wartime speculation.

The Senate committee's hearing room was packed as Hiss and Baruch faced each other. "To put an end to insinuations and innuendoes, the existence of which it would be childish to deny," Baruch opened the proceedings by submitting his income tax records. After long and tedious cross-examination, punctuated by occasional fireworks as the two men tangled, all that Hiss had achieved was to read reams of old World War I records into the testimony.

But so well was the committee's work done that Harry Elmer Barnes wrote in the February 14, 1935, issue of the New York *World-Telegram*, "The Communists must have uttered a resounding whoop . . . at the conclusion of the investigation of the Morgan firm by the Nye committee."

At this point, it is important to note that with the help of a few well-placed individuals, the committee became a dispersal center of Communist propaganda, its noble purpose perverted. Nye, hardly a radical, was seduced into appearing at *New Masses* forums, lending his name with ill-considered liberality to smear attacks on American motives.

When the party line changed from neutrality to collective security, Hiss had already left the committee. But before then, he met Whittaker Chambers.

6

The Underground Elite

LATE IN THE SUMMER OF 1934, FOUR MEN MET IN A Washington restaurant. They arrived separately, by prearrangement, and drifted casually to a secluded table well out of earshot of any other diner. To their waiter they must have seemed a strangely ill-assorted quartet. There were J. Peters, looking like a government clerk; Hal Ware, a remarkable combination of the professor and the race-track tout, with a manner that was curiously mobile even in repose; Alger Hiss, tall, thin, correctly dressed, the very model of a rising young government lawyer; and Whittaker Chambers—introduced to Hiss as Carl—a short, nondescript man, uncomfortable in the first white suit he had ever owned but very much the man of authority.

It was Peters who took the lead. The Party had new plans for some of its Washington members. A parallel apparatus was to be set up, consisting of Communists who seemed to be going places in the government. Alger Hiss was one such man, and he was not to be wasted in the routine business of Party membership, attending fraction meetings, and eventually destroying his usefulness by being identified as a Communist. A man with Hiss' prospects must be kept under

---

Obviously the story of Whittaker Chambers' relationship to Hiss could come only from Chambers. In retelling it, the authors have leaned heavily on Chambers' testimony, but they have checked and augmented his account with the results of other research.

wraps, nursed along, until he had risen in the government hierarchy to the point where he could be of real service to the Party. He accepted the new status, of course? Of course, said Hiss.

Good, said Peters. Now these were his instructions. He was to detach himself from Hal Ware's AAA cell immediately. Carl was to be his superior in the parallel apparatus. In line with Party discipline, he was to follow Carl's orders without question. Henceforth, he must be completely above suspicion, remaining aloof from anything that had the faintest tinge of left-wing activity. Only his comrades in the new apparatus were to know that he was anything but a rather conservative New Dealer. His home must be cleared of all Communist literature, all telltale books or pamphlets. And so the great step was taken.

It was, curiously enough, a great step for Whittaker Chambers, too. For all of his bolshevik training, he was a middle-class intellectual, and he liked people whose minds were agile enough to juggle abstract ideas. His years in the open Party and in the underground had therefore been lonely ones. Hiss was the first man he had met in the Party whom he could accept on his own terms. There was one other factor. Like most professionals in the underground, he had a great deal of scorn for the average "safe" Communist. Chambers saw in Hiss another bolshevik—one who had arrived at similar views on the revolutionary process by a different method, but an equally valid one. For where Chambers was emotion-motivated, Hiss was coldly calculating. Men thrown together by circumstance often become friends; Alger and Carl became very good friends.

At the start there was an obstacle to that friendship—Priscilla Hiss. The first time Carl visited the Hiss apartment on 28th Street, he sensed a certain antagonism on her part. She seemed not too happy about Carl, and though she was not openly hostile, he was a little puzzled and disturbed by her attitude. But the next time Carl and Hiss met, this was straightened out. Priscilla, said Alger, had pegged Carl for a foreigner and for this reason had been reluctant to accept a close relationship with him. But thinking it over, she had decided that Carl was a Russian, which not only made him acceptable but, in a Party context, appealed greatly to her sense of caste.

Amused and disconcerted, Chambers told J. Peters the story.

"Priscilla Hiss thinks I'm a Russian. What should I do?" The underground chief laughed.

"That's wonderful," he answered. "Let her think you're Russian. Let them all think you're Russian. It's as good a cover as any."

As a Russian, Carl was a great success, not only with the Hisses but with all his other contacts; it added glamor to the operation. That Chambers' English was strictly American made no difference at all. He was careful never to claim that he was Russian (though he never denied it either) but bolstered the theory in subtle ways—an occasional inversion in word order, mannerisms or phraseology that were slightly foreign. His general appearance and his neutral features which could easily be mistaken for Eastern European aided in the masquerade. Even so sophisticated an underground worker as Ludwig Lore, a former leader in the American Communist Party, was deceived. Meeting Chambers for the first time, he took him aside and said categorically:

"You're Colonel Dietrich of the NKVD. I've heard all about you and the work you did in Berlin."

Chambers looked at him blandly.

"I guess I shouldn't have said anything," Lore said quickly.

Aside from his one contretemps with Priscilla, Carl got along—in his own word—"swimmingly" with the Hisses. He saw them at least once a month, sometimes as often as once a week, and their apartment became a headquarters for him whenever he was in Washington. Carl and his wife "Lisa" discussed not only Party matters and Communist theory with

the Hisses but their common interests in literature and amateur ornithology. And as much as he could without revealing
his identity, Chambers talked about himself, his early years
in the Party, his adventures as an itinerant laborer when he
ran away from home as a boy, his experiences in Berlin.

The relationship among them was deep and warm. The
Chamberses shared the Hisses' intimate nicknames; there
were discussions of financial problems and their children's
schooling. Lisa painted a portrait of Timothy Hobson, Priscilla's son by her earlier marriage, and Priscilla occasionally
"sat" with Lisa's baby. "Is Carl staying overnight?" was
Timmy's standard question when Chambers visited them.
They took long drives into Maryland and Pennsylvania. But
they went to great lengths to prevent outsiders from knowing of the friendship between the two families. On the rare
occasions when this could not be avoided, a false name
would be invented for the Chamberses on the spot.

And on their part, the Hisses were proud of this close association with an important Party functionary. When Priscilla
chafed over the restraints of hidden Party membership, it
was to Carl that she took her complaints. He would explain
patiently to her that while open affiliation would permit her
to join committees, make speeches, and "do good" as she so
much wanted, such activities were minor compared to the
important work which the Party had assigned Alger.

In this general period, Chambers testified much later,
"J. Peters introduced me in New York to a Communist named
David Carpenter, who had also been working in an underground capacity in Washington. It was suggested that he
might be very useful in adding members to the special group
I was organizing. My special group eventually included
Alger Hiss, George Silverman, and [one other], and a special
relationship with Henry Collins and Lee Pressman. . . . In
addition to these men, I brought into the special apparatus
through Carpenter, Henry Julian Wadleigh [strangely
enough, never a Party member] . . . and Vincent Reno

[working then on the Norden bombsight and who was known as Lance Clark when he worked as a Party organizer in Montana]. Harry Dexter White, special monetary adviser to Secretary of the Treasury Henry Morgenthau, Jr., and father of the Morgenthau Plan for the pastoralization of Germany, was introduced to me by George Silverman."

(Pressman, still denying any Party affiliation, dropped out of the ring when he left the government in 1935 to become one of the most powerful figures in American labor circles. As general counsel of the CIO, he not only steered the policies of the union, but he controlled a vast amount of legal patronage. Through Nathan Witt and Ed Smith, he also exercised tremendous influence in the National Labor Relations Board, making it a kind of CIO adjunct. Young lawyers in Washington made it a point to know Pressman—and in certain circles he became known as Comrade Big.)

The importance of Carl's group was incalculable, even before it had worked up to espionage. It represented the vanguard of a small, tightly knit Party—there were less than 15,000 card-carrying Communists in 1935—devoted with a unique singleness of purpose to the creation of a Soviet America. Each man in high place, whether a member of an apparatus or merely under the influence of a member, became an entering wedge for the Communists as they began to filter into the once sacrosanct departments and bureaus. This not only gave the Party a magnificent patronage machinery which it used to lure others into its toils; it gave Moscow's bully boys a wonderful set of eyes and ears. When espionage became the order of the day, the Communists were all set.

During Alger Hiss' early Nye committee days, Carl's group had been involved in nothing more damning than infiltration and a concomitant effort to influence government policy. In the light of present events, this seems considerably more unpatriotic now than it did in the middle thirties. The political and moral atmosphere then was different. Franco's

Moors, aided by Nazi technicians and Italian troops, were crushing the Spanish Republic. Britain and France stood in seeming impotence or acquiescence before the onslaught of Hitler and Mussolini. To most observers, Europe was on the verge of open and cataclysmic warfare. And the United States sat idly by.

What force could stop the spread of fascism? For many Americans—even Americans who deplored a strict Marxist philosophy—there was only one answer: the Soviet Union. As the League of Nations wavered and bumbled, only the voice of Maxim Litvinov stormed and pleaded for "collective security," for a strong alignment among the anti-fascist powers which would block any further Nazi-Fascist aggression. Only the Russians seemed disposed to place Europe's largest standing army in the balance against the *Wehrmacht*. To question the motives of the Soviet Union then was to place one's self in the camp of the reactionaries. The warnings of the anti-Communist socialists and liberals—such as those who rallied about the small weekly paper, the *New Leader*—were brushed off as vicious or paranoid. They saw Communists under every bed.

Washington, New York, and Hollywood were full of agitating committees and organizations demanding a closer rapprochement with Russia or battling for a more belligerent American foreign policy—and in most of these groups there were Communists imposing the Party line on non-Communist innocents. Enthusiastic individuals in Beverly Hills, in Georgetown, and on Manhattan's Park Avenue opened their homes to friends and strangers, charging high prices for weak drinks and strong oratory, on behalf of a dozen causes.

This was the atmosphere in which the Communist Carls operated, this was their stock-in-trade, and it paid off handsomely. It drove decent men into the Party, helped them to submit to unpleasant Party disciplines and do the Party's bidding. Again by the dialectics of the situation, when the demands increased, the underground cells were promoted to more dangerous work. To influence policy or slip into the government had been a way station. The next step on the underground railroad was espionage.

Such is the nature of Communist indoctrination that the men selected for this hazardous enterprise accepted it without protest. If there were any objections, they were easily answered. It was all for the good of the Soviet Union and therefore for the betterment of humanity as a whole. The hoariest of moral heresies, that noble ends justify vile means, is a great convincer among people who have swallowed Lenin uncritically. In this case it helped make agents of Julian Wadleigh, Harry Dexter White, and many others. Alger Hiss, hard-headed, determined, and ambitious, needed no such moral blandishments. He could look his acts in the eye straight. "Hiss always knew perfectly well what he was doing," says Chambers. "He was a thoroughly developed Communist."

And Hiss was the first one in Carl's group to take the step. It came about this way. In 1929, the Comintern in Moscow had suddenly stopped subsidizing the American Communist Party, although it continued to finance its own direct undercover operations in the United States. Like a good bourgeois bureaucrat with designs on the budget, J. Peters as Comintern representative here cast about for ways and means to re-institute the subsidy. The best method, he decided, was to show the Politburo and the NKVD the potentialities of the American party. If certain fairly important State Department documents could be photographed and sent to Moscow, "as a token of possibilities" the Russians might be convinced that Comintern funds could be well spent here. So Peters directed Chambers to work on this project. As counsel and investigator for the Nye committee, Alger Hiss would be in a position to get these documents from the State Department. A little doubtfully, Chambers suggested the scheme to Hiss, the young lawyer readily agreed, and the papers were forthwith requested "by the Nye committee" from the office of Joseph C. Green. At Hiss' home, they were photographed by Chambers with a Leica.

The success of this operation, and Moscow's receptivity, encouraged Peters. By the end of 1935, Chambers was feeding Peters the cream of the Nye committee material, as well as turning over information and other intelligence from Wadleigh and Harry White to the Russian agent Bill.

But before the "elite" group really began to operate as a full-fledged espionage ring, several important shifts had to take place in Alger Hiss' official life. The first, early in 1935, was his return to the Department of Agriculture and the AAA, just in time for the big dust-up there. In the controversy which was coming to a head, Gardner Jackson, Jerome Frank, and the left group were on one side; Chester Davis and the right wing were ranged on the other.

The immediate cause of the break was the question of the sharecropper. Norman Thomas and H. L. Mitchell of the Southern Tenant Farmers Union had been pressing for a change in AAA benefit payments which were taking land out of production. Under the set-up devised by Secretary of Agriculture Henry Wallace, the farm owner profited—at the expense of the sharecropper who was being dispossessed throughout the South and the West. On the basis of a brief, written for Jerome Frank by Hiss, the battle was joined. Wallace, seemingly favoring the left wing, characteristically gave in to the side with the most power. In February, without once warning Frank, Jackson, and the others, Wallace suddenly announced that the entire left wing was fired. But there was one inexplicable exception. At the press conference at which Wallace made the purge public, Chester Davis said:

"There has been no suggestion of Mr. Hiss' resignation except in the press as far as I know. Mr. Frank, Mr. Pressman, Gardner Jackson, yes. These changes are desirable in my judgment, and I recommended them to Mr. Wallace. I think it is important to have in the key positions in the Triple A men who have some familiarity with farm problems and who have a farm background." This strange characterization of a Harvard-trained Baltimore boy fooled no one. It was obvious that Hiss had made some kind of a deal with the Wallace-Davis forces at the last minute in order to save his job. The "why" of it bothered the purgees considerably.

"Alger must have known at least a week before the purge that it was coming," Pat Jackson said in 1948. "If he had told us, we would have quickly resigned rather than give the ball to Davis. He undoubtedly told Pressman, and Lee told him what to do in order to remain in the Department as his pipeline."

This explanation, though it almost hit the nail on the head, missed the point on one important particular. It was Pressman, by all indications, who through his Party contacts learned of the coming explosion. And it was the Party which told Hiss to stay in the Department. To have him side with the "reactionaries" was in line with the new policy drafted by Peters-Ware-Chambers. On the surface, it cut Hiss off from the leftist elements in the government and created for him the conservative "cover" which the Party was anxious for him to have. From that time forth, Alger Hiss played the consummate, cautious career man.

The maneuver worked excellently. To this day, many of his AAA friends have not forgiven Hiss. When Hiss' lawyers approached a well-known jurist to ask him if he would appear as a character witness in the libel suit against Whittaker Chambers, he said tartly: "I have no way of knowing whether or not Mr. Hiss was ever a Communist. But as to his character—Mr. Hiss has no character."

But back in 1935, the consensus was that Alger Hiss had sold out to advance his career. A few days after the purge, Hiss himself seemed to corroborate this impression by asking Frank's advice; he had just been offered the position of general counsel to AAA, Frank's old job. What should he do? Frank looked him in the eye, told him he was delighted, but that there was a matter of principle involved. Hiss got the point and agreed to turn it down. But he was visibly crestfallen.

So bitter were the stories about Alger that he made a special trip to Cambridge to enlist the support of his old friend, Felix Frankfurter. The professor picked up his phone and called Jackson.

"Pat," he said, "Alger's been here with Priscilla complaining that you and Jerry Frank are going around Washington assassinating his character. Why don't you lay off?" Jackson tried to tell his side of the story, but Hiss had been so convincing that Frankfurter would have none of it.

Shortly after this, Hiss himself was out of the AAA. The New Deal was battling to save the agency, and Alger's services were requested by Solicitor General Stanley Reed. So Hiss went over to the Department of Justice where, with another lawyer, he worked night and day preparing the government's case and writing the brief which Justice lawyers were to plead unsuccessfully in the Supreme Court. Alger Hiss liked his work in the Solicitor General's office, even though he worked himself into a case of bronchial pneumonia. He was a lawyer, and as an assistant to Reed he could function as one.

In September of 1936, Assistant Secretary of State Francis Sayre, one of Hiss' Harvard Law professors, asked him to come over to the State Department as his assistant in the trade agreements division to work on the constitutional arguments involved in a test case of the Trade Agreement Act. Intending to turn down the bid, Hiss nevertheless told Whittaker Chambers about it. As his superior, Chambers told Hiss that he must accept, that he would be more valuable to the Party in the highly sensitive American foreign office. A disciplined Communist, Hiss gave up the job he preferred for a job he was ordered to take.

And now the great conspiracy began. There had been Communists in high places before. But never had the precincts of the striped-pants boys been infiltrated to this degree, and Whittaker Chambers and/or Carl was delighted. Hal Ware, a good judge of character, had picked a winner.

During this time, Chambers says, "I was involved in the English and Japanese business, I was in touch with the Washington people, and I was moving back and forth between Washington and New York. Then, perhaps in November of 1936, J. Peters introduced me in New York City to Colonel Boris Bykov, and my instructions were that I was to help him in whatever he wanted." Bykov, an important NKVD agent, was typical of Stalin's Russia, the embodiment of the post-Lenin dictatorship. A product of the Odessa slums, he had a keen, suspicious, rat-like outlook and the mind of a police inquisitor.

He was a small man with thin, red hair, reddish eyes, saturnine features, and a brutally sardonic manner which concealed his pathological cowardice. As a representative of the Soviet secret police, he had tremendous power over Communists—and like all cowards, he abused it. From their first meeting, Chambers hated Bykov and submitted to working with him only because of his rigid bolshevik self-discipline.

Chambers doubled as chief and courier of the Washington apparatus. It was his job to receive papers, notes, and documents from the various people in his ring and to transmit copies of them to Bykov. Two separate procedures were followed. Hiss' material was picked up by Chambers at weekly or ten-day intervals. Stopping off at the Hiss home, now in the more fashionable Georgetown and, ironically, opposite a police station, he would transfer the take to his own briefcase and rush down to Union Station and the Baltimore train.

At the Baltimore station, he turned them over to Felix Inslerman, a Johns Hopkins engineering student. Felix would microfilm the papers at his home, an apartment in a red-brick house on Callow Avenue and Lennox Street, and then meet Carl at a pre-arranged spot, returning the original documents and the microfilm. By midnight or 1 A.M., Carl would be back in Washington, and the following morning Alger Hiss would return the originals to the files. After a time, as the volume and the importance of Hiss' production increased, it was decided that removing the documents from the Hiss home might be too risky, and Priscilla was instructed to type out copies. This second procedure was suggested by Bykov.

(It was not until he testified before the House Un-American Activities Committee that former Under Secretary of State Sumner Welles recalled wonderingly that the trade agreements division of the department—in that period—had continually asked for secret material which had little relation to its own problems and work.)

In order not to put all the eggs in one basket, a usual espionage precaution, notes and classified material delivered by other members of the ring were microfilmed by David Carpenter at a studio near the Library of Congress. The Wadleigh material was usually delivered straight to Carpenter who merely turned over the microfilm to Carl. Both the Inslerman and the Carpenter microfilm were run to New York by Carl, the tiny rolls stuffed into a tobacco pouch.

As soon as Bykov arrived to take charge of the ring, he told Chambers he wanted to pay the boys in Washington. This was not sheer generosity on his part. By getting his agents to accept money, Bykov would be incriminating them even more fully. Psychologically, it was also a clever move since it degraded the whole operation and further destroyed the moral fiber of the people involved. When Chambers insisted that Hiss, White, and the others were "idealists" and would be offended and horrified by an offer of cash, Bykov smiled and said, "Very well, we will buy them some rugs and tell them they were made by the hands of Soviet workers."

In December, 1936, Chambers asked Meyer Schapiro, still a close friend, to buy four Bokhara rugs in New York and ship them to George Silverman. As the middle man in the deal, Silverman did the distribution. One he kept for himself, a second one he gave to Harry White, a third he passed on to Carpenter for Wadleigh. Getting the rug to Alger Hiss was more complicated. One night Silverman drove out to an isolated restaurant, The Yacht (a restaurant built in the form of a boat on the bank of the Potomac), pulling up a little beyond it and turning off his lights. Several minutes later, Chambers drove up with Hiss in Alger's Plymouth, parking ten yards beyond Silverman's car. Then Chambers picked up the rug and carried it to the Plymouth; the two cars drove off. But the payment, as far as Hiss was concerned, misfired. The Bokhara rug, a loud red with louder decorations, was a little too extreme for the Hiss taste, and it was put away.

On another occasion, Bykov decided that he must see Hiss personally in order to give him more specific instructions. All the way up from Washington to New York, Chambers tried to prepare Hiss for the meeting, fearful that Bykov's crudities would shock the correct young diplomat and destroy his romantic illusions about Soviet Russians. But to Chambers' surprise, when the three men sat down together at the Port Arthur Restaurant in Chinatown, Hiss showed immediately that he was utterly fascinated by the Stalinist Fouché. After an inauspicious beginning in which Bykov attempted to speak to Hiss in broken English, the interview switched to a corrupt German with Chambers interpreting, and everything went fine. Bykov, however, was not romantic about Hiss. From that day forth, he would ask Chambers mockingly, "How is *unser lieber advokat?*"

(Carl's group was only one apparatus functioning toward subversive and espionage ends in Washington. Chambers was aware that he was not operating alone in the government. But only by the sheerest accident did he collide with one of the other rings. Shortly after Hiss left the Nye committee, he told Carl that there was another man who was obviously "sympathetic" and "ripe for the picking." His name was Noel Field, and Hiss had sounded him out in the course of a long evening's discussion. The two men had come down to cases, and Hiss had put the question to Field point blank. "I'm already involved," Field had said cryptically.

(Some time later, Hiss met Hede Gumperz [later Massing], another chief of apparatus, at Noel Field's home. "I understand you are trying to get Noel Field away from my organization and into yours," she said. "So you're the famous girl who is trying to get Noel Field away from me? What *is* your apparatus anyway?" Hiss replied. Hede admonished him. "Now, Alger, you should know better than that. I wouldn't ask you that question." Hiss laughed. "Well, we'll see who's going to win," he answered. "Well, Mr. Hiss, I hope you realize you are competing with a woman," Hede Gumperz told him. Whereupon they agreed that, win or lose, they were both working for the same boss.

(As a routine matter, Mrs. Gumperz reported the conversation to her superior. Several days later, she was ordered with great finality to "forget Hiss . . . You've never seen him. You and I will also never speak of him." Chambers, too, reported the conversation between Hiss and Mrs. Gumperz, but to J. Peters. Had Hiss been indiscreet? Peters told him abruptly, "Forget about Noel Field!" And the matter was dropped. But Hiss did not forget. Two years later, when Francis Sayre was appointed High Commissioner of the Philippines, he asked Hiss to recommend a man as his legal adviser. Hiss wrote a glowing recommendation of Noel Field —who at that time was in Geneva busily assisting General Walter G. Krivitzky, head of Soviet Military Intelligence in Western Europe.)

For over a year, Chambers traveled back and forth between Washington and Baltimore, between Washington and New York, draining away some of America's most precious military and diplomatic secrets. Fifty-two times he made his trips, and he might have continued them until today but for one thing. He had walled-in his great Leninist faith against the assault of conscience and the attack of reason. He had lived within these walls safe from doubt.

But conscience and reason had continued their battle. And one day, like the walls of Jericho, his defenses crumpled. In short, early in 1938, Whittaker Chambers broke with the Communist Party, with the underground, and with his past.

7

Break and Run

LENINIST FAITH, LIKE TRUE LOVE, RUNS A SMOOTH
course only to a point. Then the Communist must come to
grips with the accumulated rationalizations, the doubts that
have been put aside but not quieted, the stifled questions.
What follows is in many ways a "dark night of the soul,"
feverish and disturbing in direct proportion to the Communist's emotional depth and intellectual insight. He emerges
from this struggle cynical and cold, his moral scruples atro-
phied, ready to accept anything and everything which the
godhead in Moscow sanctions. Or he experiences a complete
revulsion and disengages himself and his conscience from
the evil he once accepted.

In 1937, Whittaker Chambers reached that point of crisis.
He had closed his eyes to the sordid factional squabbles between functionaries. He had rationalized the liquidation of
the kulaks and the man-made Ukraine famine in which millions of peasants starved to death. These, he had told himself,
had been harsh means to good ends. He had pushed aside
his shock over the calculated degradation of Leon Trotsky.
He had submitted to working for Colonel Bykov though he
feared and hated him as a symbol of a betrayed revolution.
But until the Moscow purge trials in 1936, he had stubbornly
refused to admit to himself that the Soviet Union was a
police state.

The trials forced him into this admission. He did not need

to read the capitalist press to realize that the tragic mumbo-
jumbo of "confessions" was a hoax. The Old Bolsheviks who
took the stand—Bukharin, Zinoviev, Kamenev, Radek, etc.—
admitted to crimes so palpably concocted that their very confessions withered under casual scrutiny. If the fathers of the
Soviet state, almost without exception, had turned traitor,
something was wrong with Communism. If the trials were a
frame-up, then something was wrong with the Soviet state.
Either way, the great purge was something Chambers could
not dismiss from his mind. The impact of these conclusions
shook him.

Chambers' worst fears were confirmed when, at the home
of "M," he ran into John, just returned from Russia. In great
agitation, John dragged him out to the street where they
could talk freely.

"I've seen it," he said. "I've seen what the Soviet Union is
like. And I'm through. I won't work for those murderers one
hour longer."

Like many convinced Communists, John had expected to
see the beginnings of a great new society in Moscow. But he
had moved among the Communist expatriates there and discovered that they were all "perfectly wretched and trying to
get out of Russia." He had seen the secret police in action
and scrutinized the faces of the people who queued up for
food at the government shops. He had encountered fear
everywhere, and it had shattered his faith. Now he wanted to
get out of the underground. He still believed in communism,
but he could no longer work for the Russians and still live
with himself.

"Why do you tell me all this?" Chambers asked.

"Because I want you to break with me. I want you to get
out of the Party right away."

"Don't you realize that I must turn you in to Bykov immediately for what you've said?" Chambers asked, evading the
demand.

"I know," said John. "I know you must. But if you won't

break with me, do this one thing. Tell Bykov I want to make
a deal with the NKVD. I've got a thousand dollars I brought
back from Moscow. All I want is to keep this money and be
permitted to transfer back to the open Party. If they let me
do this, I'll never open my mouth."

Chambers passed the information along to Bykov. But
even as he spoke, he could see the plan forming in the police
spy's mind.

"Very well," Bykov told Chambers. "But tell him to come
to see me so we can negotiate." Both Chambers and John
knew what that meant. No one negotiates with the NKVD.

"I am going to California, and you have to give me one
day's jump on these people," John pleaded. "Hold them off
any way you can, but give me one day's jump on the train."
And Chambers agreed. Twenty-four hours later, he told
Bykov that John had taken off in a hurry for parts unknown
the day before. "Bykov was ready to kill me—as I expected
well he might," Chambers says. "Our relations were extremely bad, desperately bad, until John showed up in California and got in contact with the Communist Party." Then
Bykov quieted down. But he never quite forgave Chambers
for this breach of Party discipline. And his suspicious mind
began to play with the idea that Chambers was weakening.
His suspicious mind was right.

Chambers' first act against the Party was touching and significant; he read *I Speak for the Silent,* Tchernavin's account
of life in a Siberian slave labor camp. This was the first book
on the Party's proscribed list that he had ever read. In the
past, he had accepted as fact that these anti-Communist
books, written by the enemy, were all lies. So he approached
Tchernavin's autobiography "with the terror of a Catholic
contemplating mortal sin," Chambers says. "I was literally in
a fever when I began reading it. I read it straight through in
one sitting, and when I laid it down I was shattered."

"Experience and the record had finally convinced me that
communism is a form of totalitarianism, that its triumph

means slavery to men wherever they fall under its sway and spiritual night to the human mind and soul," he explains. "I resolved to break with the Communist Party at whatever risk to my life or other tragedy to myself or my family."

Once this decision had been made, Chambers began to work out the order of his going. Too deeply involved not to menace the entire apparatus, he knew it would be suicide just to tell Bykov, "I'm quitting." Since 1932, he had been completely cut off from his non-Communist friends. If he were to disappear, no one would be the wiser. His problem was therefore three-fold: he must safely hide himself and his family from the wrath of the NKVD; he must reestablish his identity in the world as Whittaker Chambers; and he must devise some form of "life insurance" to make his possible death more embarrassing to the Party than his continued existence.

He already had a pretty good hide-out. In 1936, driving through Maryland with Alger Hiss, they had come across a small farm—with house and barn—near Westminster, which had appealed to Chambers. Hiss had liked the place and put down a deposit but had later relinquished the property because Priscilla thought it was in a "nasty, narrow valley." Some time after this, Chambers secretly bought the farm. Here he now planned to hide with his family once he had shaken off any possible pursuers. But for his first refuge, he chose a two-room shack, on Old Court Road, about four miles out of Baltimore, perched on a hill which commanded all approaches. He decided on a place so near his scene of operations on the theory that his enemies would expect him to put as much distance as possible between himself and Baltimore.

To establish his identity, he went up to New York and, from the publishing firm of Longmans, Green, he got another book to translate—Gustave Regler's Spanish Civil War novel, *The Great Crusade,* eventually published with an introduction by Ernest Hemingway. Now if he disappeared, Longmans, Green would make inquiries. Then, to register his existence even further, he convinced J. Peters that he needed a government job as a cover for his activities. Through George Silverman, and within twenty-four hours of applying for it, he had a boondoggling job in the Natural Resources Planning Board of the WPA. He set himself down on the payroll as J. V. Chambers, holding this job until a few weeks before he broke. In November, 1937, he also borrowed $400 from the Hisses to buy a second-hand car—for his flight.

His best life insurance, he realized, would be evidence of the ring's existence. If, as he feared, the Russians should kidnap his wife or his children in order to get him to surrender to them, this evidence would be something with which to bargain for their safe release. If he himself were trapped, he could say, "The incriminating evidence which I collected is in safe hands and will be turned over to the police if I disappear." So, over a period of time, he did not destroy all the copies of documents which Felix Inslerman microfilmed. He saved them along with four short memos in Alger Hiss' handwriting and five long ones written by Harry Dexter White.*

During this period of preparation, Whittaker Chambers continued making his trips to Washington and New York, carrying those treachery-filled rolls of microfilm in his tobacco pouch. There was only one difference. When he saw Bykov, he now carried a knife, in case the Russian's small, reddish eyes ferreted out Chambers' secret resolve. He visited Alger Hiss and tentatively, very tentatively, voiced a few bashful doubts, but his hints were lost on the Hisses.

---

* The White memos, now in the hands of the Justice Department, were kept semi-secret until they were offered in evidence by the government during the second Hiss trial. They were not admitted on defense objections. Before then, several newspapermen, including the authors of this work, were permitted to see them. They are seriously incriminating, the FBI can prove that they are in White's handwriting, and the last sentence of the last memo reads, "The Secretary [Morgenthau] is reading *Red Star Over China* and seems to find it very interesting." After the second trial ended in conviction, Representative Nixon read the contents of these memos to the House of Representatives.

In April, 1938, Chambers felt that he was ready to take the step which would separate him forever from the Communist espionage apparatus. Making his final trip to the home of Alger Hiss, he picked up his last batch of State Department documents transcribed by Priscilla and took them to Felix in Baltimore for microfilming. Then, instead of going on to New York, he gathered up his family from their Baltimore apartment and brought them to the shack on the hill. But though he was free, he was far from safe. For an unarmed man, with a two-year-old boy and a five-year-old girl, there was no safety anywhere.

Keeping a twenty-four-hour vigil, the Chambers remained long enough in that house to make sure that they had not been followed. Whittaker left it once, to make a trip to New York in order to deliver the bulky package of documents, memos, and microfilm to his wife's nephew, Nathan Levine.

"Put this away in a safe place," Chambers told the young man. "If anything happens to me, give it to Esther."

"O.K., Whit," Levine answered. "But what if something happens to both of you?"

"In that case, open it yourself. You'll know what to do with it. You are an attorney." Nathan Levine stowed the manila envelope in the shaft of a blocked-up dumbwaiter in his mother's home in Brooklyn—and forgot all about it.

His "insurance policy" in order, Chambers returned to the Baltimore house, packed his family and their belongings into the car, and headed south. For three days and nights, they drove "as if the devil were perched on our tail-light." By the time they got to Daytona, Florida, he could drive no more, and the children were too sick to go any further. The best they could find in the way of shelter was one of a pair of houses in an isolated part of the town, backed by thick scrub which could furnish prowlers an excellent cover. But Chambers had no choice. He took it.

For a month, the Chamberses lived in that house. By day, Whittaker slept while Esther Chambers kept watch. At night,

Chambers remained on guard while he worked on the translation of the Regler book. Once his neighbor came to warn Chambers that strangers had been lurking about the place and hesitantly offered him a revolver. Gratefully, Chambers accepted it. But he had no cause to use it. The strangers turned out to be a gang of local petty thieves.

The month in Florida convinced Chambers that at least temporarily he had eluded the NKVD. The next step was to drive back to Maryland and the Westminster farm, stopping on the way to buy a shotgun. But he continued to live like a hunted man, "sleeping by day and watching through the night with gun or revolver within easy reach. That was what underground communism could do to one man in the peaceful United States in the year 1938." From time to time, he made quick trips to New York to see publishers or to pick up other translating assignments. In these months, too, his city-bred wife, Esther, was learning to run a farm, to milk cows, to be what a friend later called "honest to the land."

Just before Christmas of that year, Whittaker Chambers faced another problem: what to do about the friends who still remained in the underground. "It always seemed proper that they should have an opportunity to break away themselves," he said much later. There was considerable risk involved for him, but he felt conscience-bound to come out of hiding and to make the effort. And he tried to convince three of his former accomplices—Harry White, George Silverman, and Alger Hiss. With the first two, his effort was little more than perfunctory.

He called Harry White and asked to meet him at the Schulte's at 15th and F. To his surprise, he saw immediately that the Treasury official had not been warned against him. "Come to inspect the posts?" White asked jovially. As they walked the streets of down-town Washington, Chambers tried to get White to break away from the apparatus, but it was useless. When they said good-bye, Chambers the conspirator did White one last service. He noticed a street

photographer poised to take their picture together, but he
was able to whirl White around in time, for which White
thanked him profusely. Chambers' efforts with Silverman
were just as hopeless. But there was still Alger Hiss, the
"closest friend I ever had in the Communist Party."

Chambers arrived at the Hiss home on Volta Place just
before dusk. "I went to the door, I suppose about seven
o'clock. I was afraid of an ambush, but when I got there,
only a maid was at home. I waited nearby, and very shortly
Mrs. Hiss drove up, and we went into the house together
. . . Mrs. Hiss attempted to make a call while I was there
which I can only presume was to other Communists, but I
quickly went to the telephone and she hung up. Hiss came in
shortly after and we talked. I tried to break him away from
the Party."

Of all the members of the apparatus, Hiss alone seemed to
have been tipped off about Chambers' defection. And he was
prepared with a lure to use on the "renegade." "Too bad you
broke," he told Whittaker. "You know, I understand you
were in line for a new and more important job in the Party.
Why don't you come back with us?" Chambers told him why
he could not return to the Party's fold and why it was im-
perative for the Hisses to leave it. All through dinner they
discussed this, as Chambers relived for them the thinking,
weighing, and agonizing he had done before he came to the
conclusion that Russia was a police state. He told them about
the brutalization of the communist ideal by the Stalinist
bureaucracy, about the moral error of Leninism, and of his
religious experience in arriving at his present anti-Communism. Several times during the course of that evening,
young Timothy asked, "Is Carl going to spend the night with
us?" Finally Priscilla could no longer ignore the child's question. "No," she said violently. "Carl is *not* spending the night
with us."

The irony was fine and Dostoievskian when the two men
parted. There was Alger Hiss, clinging to his treasonous

activities but secure and respected in his pleasant Georgetown home. And there was Whittaker Chambers, by the act
of rejecting the underground an outcast and a harried man.
As they stood at the door, this irony must have struck Hiss.

"What kind of Christmas will you have?" he asked, less the
self-righteous commissar and more the human being.

"Not too good, I'm afraid," said Chambers.

"Wait a minute," Hiss said, leaving him but returning a
few minutes later to hand over a miniature rolling pin. "For
your little girl," he said.

Chambers thrust it in his pocket, too shocked by the mean-
ness of the gift to say a word. Good enough for a renegade's
daughter? he thought.

"You won't break with the Party, then?"

"No," said Hiss, but there were tears in his eyes. "Good-
bye."

"Good-bye," said Chambers walking out of his friend's
house for the last time. At home he pulled the little toy out of
his pocket and looked at it. Then he threw it into the furnace.

Early in 1939, Whittaker Chambers went to see his old
friend Robert Cantwell, an editor on *Time* magazine. Almost
a year had passed since he broke with the Party. Now he felt
that he could rejoin the community of free men with reasonable safety. Through Cantwell, he was hired as a writer, picking up the career he had dropped in 1932. But he was not
yet through with the communizers. When he had been on the
magazine for a short time, one of the staffers stopped him in
the hall. "I'm glad you came to do books for us," she said
with a meaningful look. "We thought they'd hire that Trot-
skyite Philip Rahv." Chambers suspected then that though
his reputation as a *New Masses* writer had preceded him,
news of his break had not spread. When another staffer,
known to Chambers as a fellow-traveler, asked him to join
Time's Newspaper Guild unit, Chambers was certain of
this.

"We know you're a Communist," the man told him reassuringly.

"I think not," Chambers answered. Before long Whittaker Chambers found himself surrounded by a cold circle of hostility as the *Time* Communist cell began spreading false rumors about his private life, his character, and his politics. But he had expected this and it did not disturb him too much. He was involved now in a metaphysical search, impelled by the conviction that it was "the absence of God which made communism a failure." In this search, his first step was to submit to the urging of a friend and return to the Episcopal Church. He was confirmed by Bishop Manning at St. John the Divine's on Morningside Heights in New York.

But there were great events in the making—events which would lead him to tell his story to many people and which, again by the dialectics of the situation, led inevitably to the historic disclosures which shook the country in the summer of 1948.

8

The Slow Unfolding

"I HAD BEEN SO LONG IN THE CATACOMBS OF THE underground movement that I was entirely lost in everyday American life," Whittaker Chambers says of his early days out of the Communist Party. And in many respects, during those first months on *Time*, he was not really out of the catacombs. He still moved about like a hunted man. The old conspiratorial habits were not easily downed, and he lived in the continual fear that his old associates would yet strike at him or at his family. He made no appointments with strangers and, on several occasions when he was to meet people he wasn't quite sure of, he took his wife's nephew, Nathan Levine, along as a bodyguard.

In point of fact, Chambers had two definite indications that the underground had not forgotten him. The first came from a publisher, a man who seemed light-years away from the Communist netherworld. It was a shock to Chambers when this acme of respectability, this trusted friend, told him one day, "Ulrich wants to see you."

"Ulrich?" Chambers fenced. "Who's Ulrich?"

"You know Ulrich. From Berlin," the publisher reminded him. Chambers needed no further reminding. Ulrich had been one of his first associates in the underground.

"How do you know Ulrich?" Chambers asked in alarm.

"Don't worry," the publisher answered. "I admire you for having broken. I wish I had the courage to do the same thing.

I got involved when I was a young man, a Third Secretary at the British Embassy in Berlin. I've never been able to cut loose." Chambers left the publisher's office hurriedly and never returned.

The second incident was more to the point. Grace Hutchins, the Party functionary who had been a witness at the Chambers' wedding, telephoned Reuben Shemitz, Mrs. Chambers' brother, very shortly after the big break. As a result of the call, Grace Hutchins paid a visit to Shemitz's law office. "She said she wanted to see Whit on a matter of life or death," Shemitz still remembers. "She assured me that no harm would come to my sister or her children if Whit would get in touch with someone known as Steve." Chambers ignored the summons, but its thinly disguised threat was sufficient to deepen his very justified suspicion of strangers.

His problem, moreover, was not merely one of psychological rehabilitation. He was faced with a moral imponderable—one which every ex-Communist must solve for himself: "Should I be an informer?" To reject the Communist ideology and to realize that the movement is an enemy which must be crushed is a personal value judgment. To fight communism "by act and written word" and to "live an industrious and God-fearing life" require no inner struggle. But to expose men who have once been friends, even comrades, requires high justification. Even the realization that patriotic duty demands it makes the struggle no easier.

Early in May, 1939, seeking to lay before the American people an account of the espionage ring which was plundering the government (and still unwilling to destroy the individuals who made up that ring), Chambers hesitantly made contact with Isaac Don Levine. To Levine, then collaborating with General Walter G. Krivitzky on the latter's sensational revelations of Soviet espionage in Europe and the United States, Chambers brought a manuscript describing his elite group vaguely but completely lacking in the kind of concrete detail which would make it publishable.

"Without names, dates, and places, no one will believe your story," Levine told Chambers. The ex-Communist was not yet ready to go that far. But the meeting between the veteran anti-Communist journalist and Chambers was not unfruitful. "Little by little Chambers gained confidence in me," Don Levine has written in *Plain Talk* magazine. And though, adds Levine, he still refused to write in detail of his experiences, "he finally agreed to my proposal to bring him together with Krivitzky.* By now I was aware from my conversations with each that tying the two men together were many threads of the international Soviet network."

When the two former Soviet agents, both hunted men, faced each other for the first time, it was in an atmosphere of mutual suspicion. Sitting at opposite ends of the sofa in Levine's sitting room, each looked straight ahead, not uttering a word. Finally Krivitzky broke the silence.

"Is Russia a fascist state?" he asked.

Chambers was not yet ready to make that equation. But there was something about the naiveté of the question which disarmed him completely. The tension suddenly relaxed and the two men began talking eagerly to each other.

"There we were," Chambers muses, "like two men out of the Pleistocene age who suddenly confront each other in Times Square." It was, in a sense, a homecoming for each of them. Hour after hour, the two men exchanged anecdotes, impressions, discovered they had dealt with the same men on numerous occasions—till Levine left them alone and went to bed. At eight o'clock the following morning they were still talking, and when they parted that evening, neither Krivitzky nor Chambers had talked himself out.

Although the impact of this twenty-hour talkfest was not immediately apparent, it shook Chambers. Now he was no longer completely certain that he should keep quiet. But the clincher was the Hitler-Stalin pact on August 26, 1939. To all

---

* Who was later to be found mysteriously shot in a Washington hotel room.

well-informed people, that one great treachery of the Soviets meant that war between Germany and the Western powers was inevitable. To those who were aware that Stalin's hand reached deep into the American government, the pact was a double shock. They knew that henceforth the Gestapo would have at its disposal all the information which Communist spies gathered in this country and relayed to Moscow.

Several days after the signing of the pact, Whittaker Chambers decided that he could no longer remain silent. But knowing the set-up in the State Department, he realized that to carry his story there would be to notify the Communist apparatus of his intentions and probably to put his head in a noose. Seeking Levine out, Chambers agreed to make a full revelation, but only to the one man with full power to take the necessary drastic steps. That man, of course, was President Roosevelt. And Levine readily offered to try to arrange an audience with the President.

His first port of call was the office of Marvin H. McIntyre, secretary to FDR. But though McIntyre was friendly, he felt that this was not something he could take up directly with Roosevelt. He suggested instead that Levine first speak to Assistant Secretary of State Adolf A. Berle, one of the President's confidential advisers who was then in charge of State Department security. No formalities were necessary here; Berle and Levine knew each other fairly well. And at Berle's suggestion, it was decided that Chambers have dinner with the Berles on September 2nd.

History, like time, marched on. Hitler invaded Poland on Friday, September 1st. The following afternoon, Chambers flew down to a jittery Washington, tensely waiting for Britain and France to declare war on Germany. It was in this atmosphere of uncertainty and apprehension that Levine, Chambers, and Mr. and Mrs. Berle sat down for dinner at Woodley House, the Henry L. Stimson estate which the Berles were occupying. There are three accounts of what went on that evening: Isaac Don Levine's, Whittaker Chambers,' and Adolf Berle's. Because Levine and Chambers seriously contradict Berle and to a minor extent each other—and because all three accounts were at one time or another told under oath—it is best to let the three protagonists of the meeting speak for themselves.

After dinner, when Mrs. Berle had retired [Levine wrote in the October, 1948, issue of his magazine, *Plain Talk*], the three of us took up for the first time the subject of the conference. It was a very warm evening. The scene of the conversation and startling autobiographical story unfolded by Chambers was the study, then the lawn under a magnificent old tree, and then the study again when Berle began making notes.

It was my understanding that this information would be conveyed by Berle direct to the President and that [for Chambers there would be] no ill consequences from his revelations . . .

The general picture drawn by Chambers that night was of two Soviet undercover centers or rings which, to his first-hand knowledge, had operated in Washington for years. One concerned itself with the control of labor and with patronage for Communists in the Federal Service; the other with political and military affairs. Both groups were gathering and supplying confidential data to Moscow.

We learned that the business of filching from State Department and other secret government files had been well organized by the Communist apparatus, that most of the important papers would be microfilmed and replaced before they had been missed, and that the material would be delivered to Soviet couriers, operating under aliases, for transmission to Russia.

It was clear that Chambers knew his way about official Washington like a veteran in the Federal employ, and he showed unusual familiarity with the inside of the State Department. He named six officials as having knowingly furnished confidential data to Soviet undercover agents. Mr. Berle and I were shocked by the list, which included the Hiss brothers,* then in inconspicuous positions . . .

When Chambers cited . . . the case of a deputy to a Cabinet officer, a certain assistant secretary of an important department

---

* Donald Hiss, who categorically denied knowing Chambers and swore he had never been a Communist, was accused only of membership in a Party cell—never of espionage.

[Harry Dexter White, of the Treasury] who was collaborating with Soviet agencies and sharing with them confidential matters of national policy, Mr. Berle exclaimed:

"But I know him very well, and I can't believe it!"

. . . Chambers tried to impress upon us the nature of totalitarian espionage, that Moscow would prize information about pending government policies and decisions more highly than routine military blueprints . . .

Upon my return after midnight to the Hay-Adams House, I jotted down on a sheet of hotel stationery most of the names that had been revealed during the evening. I could not recall, for example, the first name of Donald Hiss, and in my list of State Department officials the Hiss brothers are recorded as follows: "—— Hiss. Alger Hiss." Similarly, the name of Lauchlin Currie, with which I was not familiar then, was written down by me as "Lockwood Curry."

The name of Nathan Gregory Silvermaster [later to figure in the Elizabeth Bentley spy ring] was also unfamiliar to me. My memorandum includes these notes: "Nathan Silbermeister, alias Gregory Masters, Greg. Silvermaster, Nathan Silvermaster—personal statistician to President in Agr. Dept."

Parenthetically, several days after this meeting, Don Levine was lunching in a secluded Arlington, Virginia, restaurant and spotted Harry D. White in close conversation with Lawrence Todd, a Tass Soviet news agency (read: NKVD) correspondent.

Whittaker Chambers' recollection of that interview differed in some particulars from Levine's. Before the House Un-American Activities Committee, Chambers mentioned few details and listed only names.

Representative Richard Nixon. When you saw Mr. Berle then did you discuss generally the people that were in government, or did you name specific names?

Chambers. I named specific names, Mr. Hiss among others.

Nixon. Did you name Mr. Witt?

Chambers. I certainly did.

Nixon. Mr. Pressman?

Chambers. Mr. Pressman.

Nixon. Mr. Perlo?

Chambers. I think so.

Nixon. Mr. Kramer?

Chambers. Probably.

Nixon. Mr. Abt?

Chambers. Certainly.

Nixon. Mr. Ware?

Chambers. Yes.

Nixon. Mr. Collins?

Chambers. Yes, I think so.

Nixon. Mr. White?

Chambers. No; because at that time I thought that I had broken Mr. White away, and it was about four years later that I first told the FBI about Mr. White.

Nixon. You told the FBI four years later when you had become convinced you had not broken him away?

Chambers. Yes.

Representative Karl Mundt. Mr. Collins was also in the State Department?

Chambers. Yes; I think he went in during the war.

Mundt. He belonged to the Alger Hiss cell in the State Department?

Chambers. He did . . .

Nixon. Mr. Chambers, were you informed of any action that was taken as a result of your report to the Government at that time?

Chambers. No, I was not. I assumed that action would be taken right away, which was, of course, rather naive of me; and it wasn't until a great deal later that I discovered apparently nothing had been done.

Then, on various occasions subsequent to this testimony, Whittaker Chambers amplified this statement—at least one time under oath. He told Berle, said Chambers, all about Colonel Bykov and about the head of a United States Steel Corporation research laboratory, who reported regularly to Bykov on experimental developments in the industry. And he stated further that he gave Berle the active address of an underground "communications center" between local Communist agents and Moscow. This center was a drugstore on upper 14th Street, N. W., in Washington, owned by Hyman

Kolodny, an NKVD agent.* "By no possibility, it seems to me, could Mr. Berle have supposed I was describing the workings of a Marxist study group," he insisted.

Greatly agitated by what Chambers had told him, Berle said, according to Chambers' recollection, "We may be in the war within forty-eight hours; and we cannot fight a war unless we have a clean government." Then, even before Levine and Chambers were out of the room, he had picked up the telephone, apparently to call the White House. Chambers returned to New York, expecting action. Later on he was told that Berle had gone to Roosevelt and had been told "to go jump in the lake, only in coarser language." This particular incident was given wide currency by sources close to Berle when the case broke in the summer of 1948.

In startling contradiction was Adolf Berle's own testimony before the Un-American Activities Committee. That it came just before the presidential election, when his candidate Harry S. Truman was deprecating the whole affair as a "red herring," might have led Berle to play down the espionage angle. But it could not explain why Berle, a declared anti-Communist, seemed to be doing his utmost to discredit Whittaker Chambers and to minimize the importance of the whole conspiracy.

"Mr. Chambers related to me [Berle told the Committee] that he had been a member of the undercover Communist group from 1934 to the end of 1937 . . . He said that in addition to the New York core, the Party policy, the Communist Party policy, had been to try to develop a group of sympathizers who might be of use to them later in the United States Government.

"This was not, as he put it, any question of espionage. There was no espionage involved in it. He stated that their hope merely was to get some people who would be sym-

* Curiously enough, Kolodny's drugstore was next door to the cleaning and dyeing shop of William Rosen, a Communist Party member who was deeply involved in the complicated business of Alger Hiss' old Ford. Cf. Chapter 14.

pathetic to their point of view. With that in mind apparently
a study group of some sort had been formed of men who
were interested in knowing something about Russia and Russian policy and the general Communist theory of life and so
on . . . He mentioned Alger Hiss, Donald Hiss, Nathan
Witt, and Pressman . . . He said that these men, it was
hoped, would go on, as they called it, underground; that is to
say, they would not appear as part of the well-known or open
Communist group, but they would simply be there and be
sympathetic . . . He did not make any direct statement that
any of these men were members of the Communist Party
[but] men who were sympathetic . . . and to whom they
might have access . . . in case anybody brought a request
there . . ."

   Robert Stripling. Did you subsequently do anything officially or
unofficially about this information?
   Berle. Yes, I did a great deal. I was disturbed a good deal, but
not so much at the three or four men named . . . The idea that
the two Hiss boys and Nat Witt were going to take over the United
States Government didn't strike me as any immediate danger . . .
I checked on the two Hiss boys. Specifically I checked with Dean
Acheson . . . Acheson said he had known the family and these
two boys since childhood and he could vouch for them absolutely.
I further checked and found that Mr. Justice Frankfurter would
give them an exactly similar endorsement . . . Schematically,
however, I believed that Chambers was telling the truth as he saw
it, so I caused the Department to establish very close relations
with the FBI . . .
   Stripling. Were you at any time every suspicious of Mr. Hiss?
   Berle. A better way of saying it is: I was worried . . . At that
time Mr. Hiss did take what we would call the pro-Russian point
of view. Now, that was a reason for worry. It is not necessarily a
reason to draw the conclusion that he was a disloyal man . . .
There was one other thing that worried me, too. At that time we
were all trying not to tell anything that ought not be told, and
there were pretty consistent leaks whenever anything went
through [Hiss'] office.

After more general questioning, in which Berle was complimented for his "forthrightness," the former Assistant Secretary of State added gratuitously:

"I have had some experience with men who have been in [the Communist apparatus] and then got out of it. They sometimes tend to exaggerate a little the depths of the experience they have had. They have obviously been through a violent emotional experience . . . [The Communist movement] is a most damned infernal nuisance, and in time of war could be dangerous. I should question whether their actual importance at any time, except in a few limited areas in Washington, was as grave as they like to make out . . . I am by no means clear that Hiss would have been taken into the Communist Party . . . People make contributions without being members of the Communist Party. We all of us know boys that have chipped in on this, that, and the other campaigns, or made donations or what not at one time or another without ever being allowed in the fold." *

It is futile at this time to speculate as to the relative accuracy of these three accounts. The important fact is that Whittaker Chambers did tell Adolf Berle enough to shake the usually self-assured Assistant Secretary. When Chambers returned to New York after the interview, he was certain that within a matter of days he would be arrested for espionage along with the whole kit and kaboodle of still-loyal-to-Moscow Communist agents. He waited in vain.

But Don Levine was not so patient a man. When he realized that Berle did not—or could not—effect a housecleaning in the State Department, Levine felt that he was duty-bound to press the matter where and as he could. The record of his futile efforts, even during the period of the Hitler-Stalin pact

* Adolf Berle's testimony was on the 30th of August, 1948. During the second trial of Alger Hiss, people who remembered his words wondered how they could jibe with his notes, produced in court, of the 1939 conversation. Filling four typewritten pages, they were headed "Underground Espionage Agent." Alger Hiss was last on the list.

when friendship for the Soviet Union was at fairly low ebb, is an indication of the powerful forces within the government which blocked a full investigation of the Chambers charges.

Levine spoke to Loy Henderson, then chief of the Russian section of the State Department and a staunch anti-Communist who had served at the American Embassy in Moscow. To Henderson, Levine divulged a sizable portion of the story which had been told to Berle. Of course, Henderson was powerless to act and loth to sign his political death warrant by single-handedly making a public issue of what can only be described as a conspiracy of silence.

Early in 1940, Don Levine went to a friend, Senator Warren Austin—later chief United States representative at the United Nations—with a "fairly comprehensive account" of the Soviet underworld in Washington. For some reason, Austin did not feel that it was up to him to carry the explosive information to the American people. In March of the same year, Levine furnished sufficient evidence to Martin Dies,* chairman of the House Un-American Activities Committee, to warrant a full-scale investigation. But though the scatter-brained Texan issued a public statement that he would soon hear testimony from the "head of the OGPU" in America, he seemed much more interested in pursuing hapless liberals and belaboring fellow-travelers than in busting open the spy ring.

When William C. Bullitt, former Ambassador to Russia and a one-time Soviet partisan, heard what both Chambers and General Walter Krivitzky had revealed to Levine of Soviet espionage infiltration in the government, he went straight to the White House with this startling intelligence. But though Bullitt was on a first-name basis with Roosevelt—a confidant and friend of the President—he was not able to achieve his purpose. FDR laughed and told him not to worry. State

---

* Robert Stripling, then a committee investigator, was also present, but the name of Chambers never registered with him either.

Department officials to whom Bullitt repeated his warning reacted with a similar lack of concern.

Levine was still trying to get action in March, 1941. Calling on Walter Winchell at the Roney Plaza Hotel in Miami, he laid before him much of the Chambers disclosures, telling the columnist about the six Soviet agents then operating freely in the government. Winchell, who for some time had been using his powerful and widely syndicated column as a stick to belabor anti-American forces, both Communist and fascist, held a reserve commission in Naval Intelligence and was a frequent guest at the White House. Aghast, he too agreed to take the matter straight to the President. Like Bullitt, he got nowhere.

Finally, during the 1944 presidential campaign, Governor Thomas E. Dewey was made privy to the much-repeated story. "I urged upon Dewey the vital need of informing the American people during the campaign of the shocking state of affairs inside Washington," says Levine. Dewey promised to raise the question in a speech—and then he attacked A. A. Berle as a fellow-traveler. This same stumbling inability to cope with the problem was exhibited, ironically enough, by the man who would have been Dewey's Secretary of State had the New York governor won the presidency in 1948. He was John Foster Dulles, who, despite frequent warnings, was one of those responsible for Alger Hiss' election in 1946 as head of the Carnegie Endowment for Peace.

But Isaac Don Levine was not the only man anxious to tell the Chambers story. In the early months of 1940, Will Allen, then labor editor for the Washington *Daily News,* was sprung from his regular beat and given a special assignment.

"There's been lots of talk about Communist infiltration in the government," his boss told Allen. "We've published plenty of fragmentary stories on the subject. But no one has ever followed all the leads and tied them together in a neat bundle. If you could do that, it would be one hell of a good yarn."

So Will Allen began digging in the vast bureaucracy of New Deal Washington. His first big strike was the office of Nathan Gregory Silvermaster in the Department of Agriculture. Allen had long experience in covering Communist activities; he knew a great many of Washington's Communists and fellow-travelers by name and by sight. When he walked into Silvermaster's office, he was struck by the fact that at nearly every desk there was a card-holder or Party-liner busy doing the government's work. He knew he had hit upon something.

By investigating Silvermaster, his friends, and his associates, both in public and private life, Allen began getting the material he had been seeking. But as he probed further, he discovered that all his significant information seemed to be leading in one direction—to New York. Allen followed his story there. Taking a room at the Barbizon Plaza, he hit all the tried-and-true sources of information on Communist shenanigans. But he got nowhere; he had hit a blank wall. Then, one day, an anti-Communist friend told him:

"You know, there's a guy in New York—I don't know his name—who was a big shot among the Washington Communists. I don't know where he lives or what he does, but he's broken with the Party and I understand he's got a hair-raising story to tell. If anyone can give you the story you're looking for, this man can."

Most people would have shrugged off this wafer-thin lead. But Will Allen, a good newspaperman, knew that all it takes to track down even the most tenuous fact is brains, persistence, good contacts, and lots of leg work. By combining all four, he finally got what he wanted: a phone number he could call. When he had called this number, all he could do was leave a message that he was stopping at the Barbizon Plaza, that he was anxious to discuss the Communist Party with someone who knew its inner workings, and that he would wait for a return call.

Then, for three days, Will Allen sat in his room, having his meals sent up and waiting for a call he was not sure would ever come. On the third day, Whittaker Chambers—highly suspicious but curious as to his mission—telephoned him. After a long conversation in which Allen painstakingly established his *bona fides* and explained what he was after, Chambers agreed to meet him in the lobby of the Barbizon the next evening.

Even then, it took considerable coaxing on Allen's part to get Chambers to come up to the room. Once there, Allen shucked off his coat and prepared to get down to cases. But Whittaker Chambers refused to remove his own heavy overcoat, though the room was hot. Sitting stiffly, he continued to act wary, talking little and listening poker-faced to Allen's pleas for information.

"What's the good of telling you what I know?" Chambers finally asked. "You won't be able to do anything with it."

"Just try me," said Allen. "You know what my paper feels about the Commies. They've spent a lot of their money and my time on this story. Why should you doubt us?"

After some discussion, Chambers was still unconvinced.

"Just try me out," Allen urged.

"All right," Chambers said finally. "I'll try you out. If you give me your word that you won't reveal your source, I'll give you the names of four NKVD men now operating in Washington. That's enough for a story. If you use that, I'll tell you more. But, you'll see, your paper won't touch it." Years later, Will Allen had forgotten three of those names. The one that he remembered, however, was significant—Kolodny, the man who ran the drugstore and letter-drop near William Rosen's tailor shop.

Delighted, Allen packed his bags and returned to Washington. Looking for infiltration, he had hit upon espionage. But he was smart enough to realize that the story he had dug up was a little too big for a newspaper—even a newspaper chain—to handle. "Why don't we make a deal with the FBI," he told his boss. "We'll give them the tip, they can track

down these boys, and we'll get an exclusive in return." On
this basis, he passed the names of the four Russian secret
police operatives to the Bureau. To his surprise, the FBI was
dubious.

"You'll have to clear this with the State Department," he
was told. So Allen tramped over to the big gingerbread building on Pennsylvania Avenue and marched into the office of a
friend who handled security matters there.

"Look," he told the friend. "What I'm going to tell you is
off the record. But before I tell you, I want you to know that
I'm not at liberty to reveal the source. Now, this is it. I've got
the names of four NKVD men operating here in Washington.
And the FBI won't move in until it gets clearance from the
State Department."

The friend smiled. "I see you've been talking to Whittaker
Chambers," he said.

"Look," Will answered him. "You've probably got three or
four names of people who might have given me the information. And you'll toss them at me, one by one, hoping that I'll
give it away. I just can't tell you the name of my source."

Again the friend smiled. "You're wrong. There are several
who have that information. But only one of those has broken
with the apparatus, and that's Whittaker Chambers. You
might as well forget about the whole thing, Will. The Department doesn't want those men arrested. Knock them out of the
picture and the Russians will send four more. Maybe we
won't know who those are—and that'll be really dangerous."

Will Allen's big search ended there. But in retrospect, the
questions remain: Where did the Department get those
names? Was it through its own intelligence service? And, if
the Department was aware of Chambers' NKVD activities,
why did high Administration officials attempt so strenuously
to belittle his testimony before the Un-American Activities
Committee until the revelation of the pumpkin papers?

9

Rings within Rings

ONE DAY IN APRIL, 1934, THE NEW YORK "TIMES" PUB-
lished a short dispatch from Helsinki. Tucked away on an
inside page, it was a sidebar to the more sensational account
of the arrest in Finland of twenty-eight Soviet spies.

UNITED STATES SAID TO HARBOR BIG SPY RING, SURPASSING THE FINNISH OR FRENCH BANDS

This correspondent learned tonight from well-informed persons, whose identity he is forbidden to disclose, that in the United
States there exists beyond doubt an espionage organization perhaps surpassing in magnitude both the Finnish and Mme. Lydia
Stahl's group arrested in France.

It is understood strong evidence has been gathered to support
this assertion apart from statements made by the American, Arvid
W. Jacobson, who was convicted here yesterday, and by Robert
Gordon Switz, American, who is under arrest in Paris.

Secret connections between the United States and Europe have
been developed on an extensive scale by a group of clever agents
. . . Certain clues also lead to Canada,* but the activities in the
United States of subversive bodies forming part of an international network were far more extensive.

The story went unnoticed, lost in the upsurge of fellow-
travelerism which had hit the United States. Most Americans

---

* In 1945, when Igor Gouzenko escaped from the Russian Embassy in
Ottawa, he brought with him ample and startling proof of the existence of
the Canadian ring.

could not be bothered with nonsense about Soviet spies. Russia was our friend. But the *Times* correspondent had hit upon something. It would take fourteen years before such a story would make a dent on the public consciousness—and before tangible evidence of the Soviet spy ring operating in America would come to light. For the "international network" truly existed, tying together Whittaker Chambers, J. Peters, and a host of others to the subversive adventures of the Comintern.

The story of Jacobson and of Switz bears telling if only because in many ways it is a precursor of the infinitely more dramatic Hiss-Chambers episode. It is significant and interesting to note how the *dramatis personae* of this tale are linked with the earlier one.

In the early thirties, the Communist Party attracted many people—some bitter, some desperate—whose native intelligence and advanced education made even deeper their rejection of a social order which failed to use their talents properly. Many were unemployed. Still others were stagnating in ill-paying jobs. Convinced that their cause was the only solution to depression and war, they eagerly accepted Comintern assignments and eventually slipped into the employ of the Fourth Section of the Red Army, Soviet Military Intelligence. As American citizens, with American passports, they could operate in respectable circumstances wherever they were assigned.

Typical of these disaffected Americans were Arvid Werner Jacobson and Robert Gordon Switz. That there were many such people recruited for the Kremlin's espionage services we know from the testimony of Whittaker Chambers, General Walter G. Krivitzky, and others.

Arvid Jacobson was born in 1905 in Watton, Michigan, the son of poor Finnish immigrants who were nevertheless able to give him a good American education. At the University of Michigan, from which he graduated with honors in 1928, he majored in mathematics. In those days, he was socially conscious in a mild way, joining the Fabian socialist Student League for Industrial Democracy. But this gentle phase was of brief duration. Several years later—while a teacher in a Detroit high school—he startled the school board by announcing that he had joined the Communist Party.

"Marxism-Leninism logically poses the issue of overthrowing the system which makes depressions possible," he told Wellington Roberts, a board member.

As he became prominent in the Detroit Communist Party, Jacobson came to the attention of the Red Squad and was questioned several times by the Detroit police. He made fiery speeches frequently, and the dossier on him grew bulky.

But reconciling the daytime role of teacher who must choose his words carefully with his nighttime activity as a militant Communist became increasingly difficult. One day a comrade from New York showed up at Jacobson's Northville home. They talked for an hour. In a few weeks, the comrade returned. The next day Jacobson notified the school board that he was going to New York to do research at Columbia University and would not return to his teaching job that fall of 1932. But Jacobson did not register at Columbia when he and his wife reached New York. Instead he took the first step into the underground; he reported to J. Peters—the same J. Peters who worked so closely with Whittaker Chambers—on the ninth floor of the old loft building at 35 East 12th Street, headquarters of the Communist Party USA.

Espionage was a crowded calling after World War I, as one nation coveted the military secrets of all the others. Riga, the capital of the Latvian Republic, was a thriving center where spies of all lands operated almost without hindrance. It was neutral territory where newspaper correspondents tried to buy "inside" information on Soviet Russia, the great unknown.

Strategically situated as a barmaid in one of the better hotels was a quick-minded and ambitious Latvian peasant girl, Mary Emma Schul. Though lacking formal education, she learned to speak several languages, including English, and before long she was peddling information to the highest bidder. In the late twenties she went on the Soviet payroll and thereafter flew regularly to Moscow. She called herself Mrs. Louise Martin and lived according to her concept of the wife of an American millionaire, the role she affected to explain her heavy spending. She traveled widely and had important duties.

It was to Mrs. Martin, in her suite at the Adlon Hotel in Berlin, that Arvid Jacobson was sent. Mrs. Martin directed Jacobson to enter the University of Helsinki as a graduate student, a cover for his espionage activities, and to find a home near the university campus from which he could operate as her liaison with members of the Soviet ring in Helsinki.

Jacobson found a modern cottage on a tree-lined street near the campus and played the role of an affluent American student. The Jacobsons would invite fellow students to their home where there was always plenty to eat and drink. To divert suspicions from his real activities, Jacobson would voice anti-Soviet and pro-fascist opinions to his new friends.

In September, 1933, Helsinki rocked with the news that the official photographer of the Finnish General Staff, a Lieutenant Vilho Pentikainen, had fled to Russia after stripping staff headquarters of its top secret documents. Pentikainen had last been seen traveling in a car at high speed from Helsinki, toward the Soviet frontier. A staff investigation, conducted in secrecy, established that the lieutenant had been on the payroll of a mysterious Mrs. Martin. He had also been seen entering the Jacobson home.

Soon after the Pentikainen incident, the manager of Finland's largest munitions plant, Lieutenant Colonel Walter Asplund, died under mysterious circumstances. In the best of health, he keeled over after a hearty dinner. An autopsy showed that he had been poisoned; an investigation, that the

model of a new German Army rifle on which his company
had been working had disappeared.

On October 27, 1933, Mrs. Martin gave a party in her
luxurious Helsinki apartment for Mr. and Mrs. Jacobson, as
well as for many Finnish society figures, politicians, intellectuals, and film and stage stars. But while the party was
going on, the Jacobson home was being searched by secret
police. Military documents from general staff headquarters
were discovered there, hidden in a clothes closet.

Two hours later, the police broke in on Mrs. Martin's party,
arresting Mrs. Martin, the Jacobsons, and six other guests.
Simultaneously, nineteen other arrests were taking place all
over the Finnish capital. They included Jenny Antilla, a maid
in Colonel Asplund's household who was later convicted of
poisoning him. Her husband, Aksel, was also arrested, but he
managed to escape with the aid of the local Communists. In
1940, he reappeared as Minister of Defense in the quisling
Finnish government set up by the Soviet Union during its
invasion of the tiny republic.

Although Mrs. Martin protested her innocence to the last,
most of the other conspirators, including Jacobson, admitted
their guilt. (Only Mrs. Jacobson, as an unwilling accomplice
of her husband, was released.) Mrs. Martin was sentenced to
eight years of hard labor by a Finnish high court, Jacobson to
five. The high crimes charged against them consisted of stealing vast numbers of official documents and of plotting the
deaths of several Finnish officials and technicians.

The arrest and conviction of Mrs. Martin's Finnish ring,
however, was but one result of the raid on Jacobson's home.
Among the papers police found there, was a postcard with a
series of hieroglyphics drawn on its back. The card, postmarked Paris, was from a Mme. Lydia Tcheckalov Stahl.
The hieroglyphics were undecipherable, but the name of
Mme. Stahl rang bells. She was listed in the secret files of
every police force in Europe.

Middle-aged and hardly beautiful, Mme. Stahl had great

personal magnetism. From the early twenties, she had worked diligently for the Soviets, usually acting as a courier in her travels about Europe and the United States. In 1932, on a trip to New York, she worked closely with the underground group that included Whittaker Chambers and Robert Gordon Switz. On her return to Paris, the counter-espionage agents of the Deuxième Bureau, France's political police, put her under routine surveillance, following her to several rendezvous with Mrs. Martin. But with little concrete evidence to go on, nothing was done.

The arrest of the Martin ring and the postcard linking Jacobson to Mme. Stahl gave the French police the handle they had been looking for. Then things began to move rapidly. A week before Christmas, in 1933, less than two months after the Finnish ring was broken up, the French police rounded up twenty-two suspected spies. One of them was Robert Gordon Switz.

Switz, whose story parallels Jacobson's in many respects, was at this time a full-fledged operative who had already performed a successful mission in the Panama Canal Zone. He had been approached in 1931 by a Russian friend of one of his brothers. The two men had discussed everything from Switz's interest in aviation to Soviet Russia. And in Switz's words, "Before I knew it I had become immensely interested in the Russian experiment from a humanitarian point of view. At that time, I really became a Communist."

Shortly after this encounter with the Russian, Switz was on his way to Moscow in the guise of an aviation instructor. There, instead of instructing, he was himself instructed—in the arts of espionage and sabotage. Returning to New York, he made contact with the underground apparatus and received his first assignment. On May 21, 1932, he sailed aboard the S.S. *Santa Clara* for Panama.

In October, 1932, a clerk in the Canal Zone's dead-letter

office opened a bulky envelope, mailed to Herman Meyers, 1859 East Ninth Street, Brooklyn, which had been returned stamped "Addressee Unknown." The letter had been mailed by a James J. McCarthy. There was no such person in the Zone. Inside the envelope, the clerk discovered diagrams of Canal defenses, documents, and a map of Fort Sherman.

"These look like secret military documents," he told post office inspector S. C. Russell excitedly.

They were. One was a memorandum detailing anti-aircraft artillery installations in the Zone. Another was the text of a plan, described by the sender as a "complete plan for the subjugation of Panama in case of revolution."

Army officials did not try to hide their alarm. A year earlier, the arrest of a Russian named Ivan Krassin had led to the discovery that, through a Communist employed at the RCA All America Cables office, Moscow had access to all telegrams coming into or leaving the Zone.

While typewriter experts worked on the "dead" letter— now very much alive—the commanding officer of Fort Sherman, Colonel C. G. Bunker, discovered that confidential papers had been systematically rifled from his own files. The experts finally traced the typewriter on which the incriminating letter had been typed. In the spring of 1933, Corporal Robert Osman of Colonel Bunker's staff was arrested.

Osman, a tall young man with a dark, intelligent face, had joined the regular Army in 1931 to relieve his laborer father of a financial burden. At the time of his arrest, he had passed an examination which might have led to a lieutenant's commission.

At his court martial, Osman admitted that he had been a Communist sympathizer in New York. He testified that he had received money from a Communist named Harry Duryea whom he had met at a Young Communist League dance. He said their correspondence was carried on through a third party because Duryea was the son of a rich man who objected to his politics. Duryea had visited him twice in Panama, Osman testified. But who was Duryea? He could be traced neither in New York nor in Panama.

Osman was sentenced to twenty years at hard labor and dishonorably discharged from the Army. But the case was not over. A few months later, his parents visited Louis Waldman, the New York labor lawyer, and asked him to appeal their son's case. They said he was not a Communist. Waldman, then and now a staunch anti-Communist, warned them that he would take the case only if he were convinced that Osman was a naive victim of the Communists. After extensive inquiries, he took the case without fee.

On his way to Panama in May, 1934, to plead Osman's case, Waldman was thumbing through a copy of *Time* magazine when his eye was caught by the picture of a "long narrow head of a young man with a small, ungenerous, dissipated mouth, cynical, pulled up to one side almost to the point of distortion; the nose was long and thin with a slight malformation at the bridge; and even in the black and white photograph the shading of the full and wavy hair suggested that it might be blond." [*]

Waldman played a hunch. He cut out the photograph so that only the face, head, and shoulders remained. A few days later, he met Osman for the first time. They had a long, private chat in the anteroom of the military detention barracks. Suddenly, Waldman pulled out the *Time* photo. Watching Osman closely, he said: "Robert, tell me the truth. Do you know this man?"

Without hesitation Osman declared: "Sure I do. That's my friend, Harry Duryea." It was, in fact, Robert Gordon Switz, on trial in Paris for espionage.

On the basis of this, authorities established that Switz had registered under his own name at a Panama hotel after arriving on the *Santa Clara* on May 26, 1932, and again on March

[*] From *Labor Lawyer* by Louis Waldman, E. P. Dutton & Company, Inc., 1944.

27, 1933, after arriving by plane from Miami. On his first arrival, Switz had told immigration authorities that he came as the guest of Major General Preston Brown, commanding the Canal Zone garrison. Brown's son, Dorrance, had been a classmate of Switz's brother, Paul, at Yale, and the spy had actually been the general's dinner guest. This connection had given Switz entrée into the Zone's military installations. He had used his own name throughout, except in his dealings with Osman. After a tough legal battle, and the personal intervention of President Roosevelt, Waldman won a reversal of conviction for his client.

The loss of Osman, to some degree the innocent dupe of a Comintern agent, made very little difference to the world-wide underground. But his connection with Robert Gordon Switz and with the activities of international Russian spies might never have been revealed had not the Finnish and French authorities succeeded in breaking up important rings in those countries.

Switz's Panama operation had firmly established him in the New York underground as a courageous and effective agent. One day Switz appeared at the office of Robert V. Scott, manager of the Roosevelt Aviation School. To Scott, the young man seemed to be "very smart" and knowledge-able in "whatever subject someone might bring up in conversation." When Switz said he wanted to represent some American business firm in Europe, Scott introduced him to J. N. A. Van Den Bouwhuysen, an aviation company official. On Van Den Bouwhuysen's recommendation, Switz was commissioned to represent the company in Europe.

In Paris, Switz made straight for Mme. Stahl whom he had known in New York. On orders from Louise Martin, she introduced him to Merkowitz Reschezki. The meeting took place in the aquarium of the Trocadero, a favorite rendezvous spot for members of the Paris ring. Reschezki, aware that he was under suspicion by the French police, looked about to see if they were being observed. "Only the fish don't have ears," he said nervously. Then he explained the methods of the ring's operations to Switz.

Each spy was known to the others only by a number, he said. The identity of each spy was known only to him. And he was transferring this knowledge to Switz. "624" was a retired Army officer who was editing an important military publication. "653" was a French engineer in Army Ordnance. "312" was a Rumanian woman dentist who kept a radio transmitter in her office. At his suggestion, Switz was to be known as The Aviator.

Reschezki also told Switz how much he was to pay each agent—a matter of prime importance. Few of its members were working strictly for the cause. Many of them were not above selling their wares to the Germans. Reschezki explained that it was Switz's job to keep the various operations running smoothly and to transmit the "output" regularly. Here Mrs. Switz was to assist him. It was her duty to handle the photographing of all documents and to mail them to a letter-drop in Switzerland.

But almost from the start, Switz was marked as a subversive. Despite the respectability of his cover job as an American salesman and his membership in the American University Union (he claimed to be a Yale man), Switz had aroused the suspicions of the police by a "chance" meeting with Reschezki near the Eiffel Tower. From that moment the Switzes were under twenty-four-hour surveillance. Police suspicion was further aroused by the fact that the Switzes rarely went out together. When either one left their room in a small hotel on the Rue d'Antin, the other remained. Probing further, the Deuxième Bureau discovered that, for a man registered as a salesman, Switz paid remarkably little attention to business.

The Finnish spy case in November put the Switz ring on the alert. Orders went out to members to lie low until the heat had been turned off. The Switzes kept to their room. Unaware that Jacobson's postcard had given the French authorities the link they needed, Switz felt certain that in time he would be able to resume operations.

What protected him, however, was not lack of evidence in the hands of the Bureau, but the international political situation. For eight months, three hundred agents of the Deuxième Bureau, the police, and the Sûreté Générale had been on the track of several spy rings which reached into top Army circles. But no arrests had been made. The French government was then trying to negotiate a treaty with the Russians, and it was feared that any round-up of Soviet spies would wreck the whole project. Finally, after high-level discussions, the government decided to give the Bureau a green light.

On December 19, 1933, Paris police forced their way into Mme. Stahl's apartment. They found her dressed in Mandarin costume, sitting cross-legged on the floor reading a Chinese book. Protesting that she was being insulted and her Chinese studies disturbed, she was rushed off to headquarters. Several hours later the telephone in Switz's hotel room rang. Listening in on the tapped wire, police heard an unidentified voice warn, "They have arrested Mme. Stahl and some others. And you have been discovered. Leave as soon as possible."

The telephone clicked, and a badly frightened Switz told his wife that they must pack and leave immediately for the hideaway they had prepared at Fontainebleau for just such an eventuality. Switz telephoned the hotel desk clerk that they were checking out. But when he opened his room door, he discovered that the "flics" were waiting for him. To the accompaniment of indignant protests that "I'm being framed," his room was searched and incriminating papers found.

Under questioning, Switz insisted that he was a lover of France, that the papers found in his room were planted. Asked to account for the 19,000 francs found on his person, he conveniently forgot where he had got them. The police were not impressed by his protestations. In their sweep that day, they had arrested ten spies, uncovered the secret radio transmitter in the woman dentist's office, turned up films of French fortifications and copies of military documents, and sent one American woman fleeing the country.

The missing American was Mrs. Paula Levine, a thirty-two-year-old New Yorker, who had worked closely with Marjorie Switz. Not long after her flight, Mrs. Levine reappeared in New York. Her apartment off Fifth Avenue was used as a secret headquarters for the Whittaker Chambers underground.

The Moscow press bitterly denounced both the Finnish and French governments. Commenting on the Paris arrests, *Izvestia* declared: "The rightist press of Paris and the White Guards [sic] are giving their readers canards about Soviet espionage to detract attention from . . . the Stavisky banking frauds. The Soviet government has nothing in common with these vile, low affairs."

The left-wing press of France is no different from its counterpart in the United States. Assailing "spyitis," the Socialist *Le Populaire* described it as a "disease with which the police inculcate the public every so often." The Communist *L'Humanité* snarled that the entire affair was cooked up by the French steel trust in order to destroy good relations between the Soviet Union and France.

The rest of the French press was much more interested in the Switzes. There was nothing romantic about their plight. Mrs. Switz's cell in the ancient Petite Roquette prison was cold, the food was poor, and she was separated from her husband. Switz was not happy either. He began to lose weight and to show signs of the strain he was under. But neither he nor his wife would crack. Obviously the weakest links in the spy chain, the Switzes still held out, month after month.

Magistrate André Renon, before whom the Switzes were brought periodically, did not despair. By putting off the date of the actual trial, he hoped to wear down either Marjorie or

Robert. Now and then, the two were permitted a tantalizing glimpse of each other. When their trunks were sealed in their hotel room, they were allowed to kiss and say a few words to each other. In court they were permitted to hold hands briefly. At every appearance before Renon, Switz—now gaunt and heavily bearded—refused to admit his complicity. But the government's patience was rewarded—although in a totally unexpected way.

In Geneva, a Swiss citizen walked into the French Embassy with a package under his arm. He had smuggled it in from France for a fee, he said. Reading of the arrests convinced him that there might be some connection between the spy ring and his package. When Embassy officials opened it, they found a roll of films of French fortifications. And on the films was a beautiful set of Switz's fingerprints. A single blonde hair in the package, compared under a microscope with Marjorie Switz's hair, was identical with hers.

Confronted with the new evidence, the Switzes broke down completely. For seven hours, under the close questioning of Renon, the two young Americans told their story. Two stenographers, working in relays, took it all down. On the basis of this confession, twenty-two new indictments were handed down. The most sensational development was the arrest of Lieutenant Colonel Octave du Moulin, a highly respected retired Army officer and member of the *Légion d'honneur*. Du Moulin, who wrote under the pen name of "Charras," edited a military journal called *Army and Democracy*. Bitter because he had not risen in the Army, Du Moulin had been easily persuaded to turn over reports of secret sessions of the École Supérieure de Guerre, France's War College. The 5,000 francs he received monthly from Switz were also an important element in Du Moulin's treason.

After a long trial, Mme. Stahl, Du Moulin, and seventeen others were sent to jail. Paula Levine was sentenced to five years *in absentia*. The Switzes were freed under a clause permitting leniency for those whose confessions implicated others. As Switz was being released, a police official told him: "Go pick out a nice desert island and stay there for many years. Moscow's arm is long, and Moscow won't forget."

In April, 1935, Switz disappeared from view. It took Arvid Jacobson two years and four appeals to the Finnish President before he won his pardon. Then he, too, disappeared from sight.

10

New Lives

THE PUBLIC AND PRIVATE LIVES OF ALGER HISS AND Whittaker Chambers, once they had taken separate ways, were similar in two respects alone. Each man rose to great heights in his chosen profession. And each man hugged a secret. It was this secret, held in common, which eventually destroyed their two brilliant careers.

In 1939, when Assistant Secretary of State Francis B. Sayre left the Department to become High Commissioner of the Philippines, Alger Hiss was already definitely on the rise. He had acquired the correct and stuffy striped-pants manner of the diplomatic corps and was marked as a man with a big future. Hiss' next job in the Department was as assistant to Stanley Hornbeck, head of the highly important Far Eastern Division. Hornbeck, a former Harvard professor, was regarded as an extreme conservative by Washington New Dealers. But as time went by, the key decisions which came out of Hornbeck's division took on an increasingly pink hue. Its personnel—and its policies which favored the Chinese Communists—became more and more suspect. Whether Hiss played a role in this change is a matter for conjecture.

In 1941, Dean Acheson came into the State Department as an assistant secretary. Though an outsider, and as such handicapped in his main job of liaison between the Department and Congress, he had behind him all the prestige of a social, wealthy, and decorous background. Shortly after Acheson

105

took over his duties and requested Donald Hiss as his aide,
A. A. Berle paid him a visit to warn him about the Hiss
brothers. Repeating the current rumors of Alger's and Donald's Communist sympathies, Berle typically added, "I must
emphasize that [this] information is unconfirmed. But I did
think you ought to know about it." Acheson called in Donald
and asked him whether he had ever had any Communist
associations. Donald denied any such thing, and Acheson
told him he considered that "the matter was closed." That
same year, the FBI undertook a routine check of Alger Hiss.
But this Hatch Act investigation proved nothing except that
Alger was a very circumspect government official. Though
rumors of his leftist proclivities persisted, the investigators
turned up not the slightest trace of a connection with even
the mildest Communist front.

By 1942, the year when Hiss became special assistant to the
adviser on political relations for the Department, there was
no longer any need to be touchy of the Communist question.
Uncritical acceptance of Russia after Hitler broke the Nazi-
Soviet pact became, in the words of Arthur Krock, "so much
the fashion that even to point out [flaws in Soviet-American
relations] was to bring down the charge of sympathy with
'fascism.'" So ridiculous did this terror of offending Russia
become that at the request of the State Department the publishers of Leon Trotsky's biography of Stalin suppressed the
book and recalled reviewers' copies which had been sent out.

During the period of this love feast, Berle was in disrepute
for his "antagonistic" views. Yet he kept his eye on Alger Hiss.
His testimony before the House Un-American Activities
Committee is contradictory and puzzling. But in private conversation, Berle has since asserted that material which Hiss
handled had a tendency to reach the Russians. When this
material was taken out of Hiss' territory, the leaks seemed
to stop. Yet neither Berle nor any of the Department's security
officers seemed to hinder Alger Hiss, and he continued to
make his mark. His capacity for work and his ability, as one

of his superiors once said, "to pick the brains of his colleagues in an off-hand way and use the material as though it had originated with him," propelled him rapidly into the Department's higher levels. When the Office of Special Political Affairs was created in 1944, with Leo Pasvolsky as director, it was another steppingstone for Hiss. Within seven months, he was the OSPA's deputy director—a sensitive and key position.

In August of 1944, Hiss attended the Dumbarton Oaks conference as executive secretary. When he returned, all matters pertaining to the proposed security organization came under his direct supervision. With Harry Hopkins, Cordell Hull, and others, Hiss worked on the first drafts of the United Nations charter. His relations with the pro-Soviet Hopkins were cordial, but there was much friction between Hiss and the aged Hull as the younger man "excoriated" the Secretary for his lack of faith in the then Soviet-approved Charles de Gaulle.

(In 1944, a reporter obtained a copy of an FBI report which linked Hiss, Nathan Gregory Silvermaster—a notorious Communist despite his immunity in the government—and twenty others. The reporter learned that this information had been submitted to the State Department in 1943 but that it had been ignored.)

When Edward Stettinius, one of Roosevelt's less felicitous choices, succeeded Hull, he found Hiss' quick, retentive mind and invaluable experience in the Department a veritable godsend. Thanks to this good opinion, Alger was appointed a Presidential adviser. In that capacity, he attended the Yalta Conference. Early in 1945, the Yalta-bound Stettinius plane put down in Marrakech, Morocco. Stettinius, Hiss, and H. Freeman Mathews spent the week-end adding the finishing touches to various proposals which were to be presented to President Roosevelt. Among these was the disastrous policy of setting up "unity" governments in Poland and Eastern Europe—the very policy which delivered large sections of Europe to the Communists. The next day, Stettinius and Hiss conferred with British representatives in the hope of convincing them that the Chinese Communists should be thrust down the throat of Chiang Kai-shek.

How important was Hiss' role at Yalta? He himself testified that "I think it is an accurate and not an immodest statement to say that I [helped formulate the Yalta Agreement] to some extent." There is also the mute testimony of the phone directory published for the American delegation in the Crimea. At a meeting so star-studded with the biggest figures in our political, military, and diplomatic worlds—figures such as General Marshall, Admiral King, Stettinius, Hopkins—protocol was important. President Roosevelt's phone number was "1." Alger Hiss' was "4." Yet in the monumental *Roosevelt and Hopkins,* Robert E. Sherwood gives not one single mention to Hiss.

Stettinius weaves the name of Hiss repeatedly into his account of the Yalta Conference. As Stettinius' aide, Hiss moved in and out of negotiations, holding strategically important positions. When Roosevelt asked Stettinius "to get a lawyer to consult with him over the wording of the Polish boundary statement, I called Alger Hiss," the Secretary wrote.*

At one point during the bitter fight over Russia's demand for sixteen votes in the United Nations, Roosevelt, Hiss, Stalin, and a Russian interpreter were left alone in a conference room. The rest of the high brass cooled their heels outside. When Roosevelt, then a dying man, came out of the room with Alger, he announced to his advisers that an "agreement" had been reached which would give Russia three votes against America's one. To the protests of the American delegation, Roosevelt wearily answered:

"I know I shouldn't have done it. But I was so tired when they got hold of me. Besides, it won't make much difference." Who were "they"? Stalin and the interpreter? Or Stalin and

* From *Roosevelt and the Russians at Yalta* by Edward Stettinius. Doubleday & Company, New York, 1949.

Hiss? Years later, under questioning by the House Un-American Activities Committee, Hiss hinted at the answer. Asked about Yalta, he said, "I still think it was a very valuable agreement for the United States."

It is known that he led several discussions on United Nations problems and that after one of them General Marshall remarked, "That young man, Hiss, did a remarkable job in his presentation." At any rate, when the conference adjourned, Alger Hiss was a happy man; he was twelfth of the thirteen signatories to the Yalta Agreement; and he had been approved by Stalin, Churchill, and Roosevelt as general secretary of the upcoming San Francisco Conference.

At the San Francisco Conference, in the spring of 1945, Hiss proved that he was an organizational wonder. As general secretary, it was his duty to see that the wheels went round—and they literally spun. And again he proved a godsend to Stettinius, flanking him at press conferences and helping him over the rough spots. "As far as most of the Conference delegates, consultants, advisers, and the general public are concerned," wrote one reporter, "Mr. Hiss is a cross between Sitting Bull and Mr. Shakespeare's Patience on a Monument."

But even here, in full view of the American public, there were certain aspects of his activities which puzzled people. For one thing, Hiss had a totalitarian view of the press. He went so far as to tell William O. Player of the New York *Post* that persons in responsible positions must determine what the people should know about the historic deliberations. "All you pressmen are interested in, it seems to me, is developing controversies," he snapped one day. "Why don't you report the good things, the areas of agreement we have reached?"

The American Federation of Labor was bitter against Hiss for favoring the then Communist-tolerating CIO. The AFL charged that the United Nations offices were being used to promote a new labor body. And true enough, the Soviet-dominated World Federation was conceived at San Francisco. International labor leaders who attended had a way of turning out to be Communist or pro-Communist, it was noted. There were press reports that Alger Hiss was responsible for the appointment of Dalton Trumbo, a high-priced screen writer,* as a ghost writer for Stettinius at the conference. There were rumors that Hiss was responsible for the employment, in the State Department and at the conference, of David Zablodowsky, proscribed from government service by the Civil Service Commission. So pressing were these rumors that Stettinius called together some members of the American delegation to report, as Senator Arthur H. Vandenberg recalls, "that he had heard such rumors, had checked them, and found them without substantiation."

Back in Washington, the continued rumors of Alger Hiss' Communist affiliations continued to leave his superiors untroubled. As the white-haired boy of the State Department, he was named director of the Office of Special Political Affairs to succeed the brilliant Leo Pasvolsky. Pasvolsky's retirement from government service gave Washington's Party-liners considerable pleasure; one more anti-Soviet antagonist had been removed from a section which was, according to the *Christian Science Monitor,* "a major voice in department affairs and a vital factor in formulating foreign policy."

On November 25, 1945, following the sensational findings of the Royal Commission investigating Soviet espionage in Canada, a fifty-one-page report was circulated by American security officers for the use of sensitive government departments. A copy of this report was placed on President Truman's desk. One paragraph of this still-secret document bears quoting:

Igor Gouzenko, former code clerk in the office of Col. Nicholi Zabotin, Soviet military attache, Ottawa, Canada, [who escaped from the Soviet Embassy with enough espionage records to put the Canadian Communist spy ring behind bars and to point to the

---

* When he testified before the HUAC in 1947, Trumbo was confronted with two party cards, Nos. 47187 and 39300, but refused to admit or deny that they were his.

existence of four other such spy rings operating in that country
and in the United States] when interviewed by a representative of
[the FBI] and officers of the Canadian Royal Mounted Police,
stated that he had been informed by Lt. Kulakov in the office of
the Soviet military attaché that the Soviets had an agent in the
United States in May 1945 who was an assistant to the Secretary
of State, Edward R. Stettinius.

Alger Hiss had been Stettinius' assistant at Yalta in February of 1945. He had given aid and advice to the Secretary
then and afterward. He was the only assistant to Stettinius
who had ever been accused of membership in a Communist
underground ring. Even the most casual investigation would
have turned up A. A. Berle's notes, then on file with the FBI—
as well as State Department security reports—implicating
Hiss. Inexplicably, no investigation was made. Neither Truman nor the State Department took any action.

In January, 1946, Hiss boarded the *Queen Elizabeth* to
attend the London session of the United Nations General
Assembly. He went as principal adviser to the American
delegation and in this capacity was thrown into frequent
contact with John Foster Dulles, a leading Republican spokesman on foreign policy and a member of that delegation. By
coincidence, the Endowment was then looking for a successor
to Nicholas Murray Butler who had retired as president of
the Carnegie Endowment for Peace, a $20,000-a-year position.
In an informal get-together with newsmen aboard the ship,
Dulles asked for a few suggestions.

"Alger Hiss," Bert Andrews, chief of the New York *Herald
Tribune*'s Washington bureau, said promptly. James Reston
of the New York *Times* agreed that it was a good nomination.
But he had one reservation: to take Hiss out of the Department would rob it of a brilliant talent at a time when the best
men were leaving for private jobs.

Dulles seemed impressed by the recommendations of the
two top Washington correspondents. While still in London,
he asked Hiss if there was any chance that he might leave

government service. And Hiss indicated that he had wanted to leave his ill-paying job for some time. But he mentioned to Dulles that Stettinius wanted him to stay on for a while. On his return to Washington, Hiss spoke to Under Secretary Acheson, indicating that he would like to leave the State Department. And Acheson made it clear that though the Department would regret losing him, he did not feel he could stand in the way of Hiss' advancement.

But before Hiss had left the Department, there was one more flare-up of the Communist accusation against him. Congress at the time was restive. Bit by bit, the story of the Yalta secret concessions was leaking out, and indignant senators and representatives, who had not been consulted, wanted to know who had engineered the "great betrayal" in the Crimea. The veto power in the United Nations, the admission of the Ukraine and White Russia which gave Russia three votes in the General Assembly, the division of German reparations, the cession of Sakhalin and the Kuriles to the Soviet Union, and the agreement to turn over to the NKVD refugees who had escaped the Russian terror—these were some of the points which had worried Congress.

Early in March, 1946, some of Secretary of State James F. Byrnes' former senatorial colleagues warned him that attacks were being prepared which would name Hiss a Communist. The new Secretary of State called Alger in and asked him pointblank, "Are you a Communist, Mr. Hiss?" Hiss looked Byrnes in the eye and denied the charge. Byrnes reluctantly accepted Hiss' words. But he had one suggestion to make.

"This is a very serious matter," he said. "I think all the stories center from the FBI. I think they are the people who have obtained whatever information has been obtained. I think you would be well advised to go directly to the FBI and offer yourself for a full inquiry and investigation."

"If there is any embarrassment to the Department about this," Hiss told Byrnes before he saw the FBI, "I will of course be prepared to resign. I don't like to resign under fire or in a fight."

The interview between Hiss and Daniel M. Ladd of the Bureau neither settled matters nor brought them to a head. Asked to make a statement, the State Department official denied that he had ever been associated with any individuals or organizations which "might lend credence to such a charge." That this was patently untrue, the FBI knew. They asked him about Lee Pressman, about Henry Collins, and about his membership in the International Juridical Association, an organization he had worked with in 1932. (Its head at the time was Mrs. Carol Weiss King, lawyer for Gerhart Eisler and other Communist leaders.) He sloughed it all off casually.

Parenthetically, it can be pointed out that Hiss never once mentioned the International Juridical Association when testifying before the House Un-American Activities Committee and, in fact, disclaimed membership in any Communist fronts. When he was on the stand in his first trial for perjury, he made a great show of not quite knowing how to pronounce "Juridical" and made it sound like "Juridicature." He also called it an "editorial" group dealing with "labor" problems, whereas it was, and is, a sort of legal seminar for the Communist Party's lawyers' holding company, the International Labor Defense.

At a meeting of the Carnegie Endowment trustees, Hiss was proposed and elected in fifteen minutes; and on December 13, 1946, a public announcement was made. That same day, Dean Acheson, then Acting Secretary of State, issued his regrets to the press, characterizing Hiss as one of the Department's "very best men" and lauding his "outstanding devotion and ability." Byrnes, who had been growing increasingly suspicious of Hiss, was pressured by Acheson into signing an already-prepared letter of recommendation. During the Hiss trials, Byrnes was dissuaded from testifying against Hiss only because it was felt this very letter would nullify his testimony.

But before Hiss had assumed his new office, Dulles received what should have been a disturbing letter from Larry S. Davidow,* a Detroit lawyer who had served with the Republican policy-maker at ecclesiastical conferences.

"The information we have would indicate that Mr. Hiss has a provable Communist record," Davidow wrote. "If you are interested in becoming more familiar with this situation [reliable individuals in Washington] will disclose it to you in full confidence . . ."

Dulles answered, in a letter dated December 26, 1946: "I have heard of the reports which you refer to, but I am confident that there is no reason to doubt Mr. Hiss' complete loyalty to our American institutions . . . I feel a little skeptical about information which seems inconsistent with all that I personally know . . ."

Much later, people who saw copies of the correspondence wondered how Dulles could have so easily dismissed the evidence against Hiss *even before he had learned what it was.* In fairness to Dulles, however, it is important to note that he did get in touch with Hiss over the telephone and that Hiss contrived to put Dulles' mind at rest by simply lying to him. He told Dulles that there had been some reports about him but that he had "particularly" and "specifically checked" with Secretary Byrnes and had been told by Byrnes that they had been "laid to rest." Hiss had not checked with Byrnes at all.

More significant was Hiss' careful avoidance of any mention that for many years he had been under investigation by the FBI, that he had been the subject of quiet Congressional scrutiny, and that Byrnes himself had been alarmed by these reports. Nor did he add that so loud were the voices against him that on his withdrawal from the State Department, the

---

* Other strong warnings were also given Dulles by Alfred Kohlberg, now publisher of *Plain Talk.*

Christian Science Monitor could state, "More than one Congressman, whenever the subject of leftist activity in the State Department is mentioned, pulled out a list of suspects that was invariably headed by Mr. Hiss."

On February 1, 1947, Alger Hiss became the president of the Carnegie Endowment, a corporation with an annual budget of $400,000. Immediately, that proclivity to join everything in sight, so outstanding during his college days, again came to the fore. In fairly short order, he was: a director and member of the executive committee of the Association for the United Nations; chairman of the executive committee of the Citizens Committee for Reciprocal World Trade; member of the council of the American Geographical Society; a director of the Woodrow Wilson Foundation; a member of the board of trustees of the World Peace Foundation.

As president of the Carnegie Endowment, he was also constantly in demand as a speaker and as a writer. At Johns Hopkins, he was awarded an honorary degree. He delivered addresses at Haverford College and at Northwestern University, popped in and out of United Nations deliberations, and wrote for such differing publications as the Quaker organ, *The Friend,* and the New York *Times.* Nowhere in his speeches or his writings, however, was there as much as a single word of criticism of the Soviet Union. Even the most tolerant non-Communist, dealing in the field of international affairs, lost patience with Russia now and then. Not so Alger Hiss.

At a time when Soviet intransigence was increasing, he praised the Russians for "having made progress toward agreement with other peoples in recent sessions of the United Nations." The United Nations, he said on another occasion, had been "one of the best means of dissolving the so-called [sic] Iron Curtain." On atomic energy—a field in which the Soviet United Nations delegation had exacerbated the entire body—Hiss found that the "Russians have come a long way toward meeting with other nations." He favored the Marshall Plan but took the fellow-traveling position that it should be another UNRRA, administered by the UN bureaucracy.

But this was surface dressing. Alger Hiss must have known that something was brewing. He had been investigated in 1941 under the Hatch Act. He had gone to the FBI himself in 1946. Now, in May, 1947, the FBI visited him again to ask him if he was a Communist, if he had taken part in Communist activities while in the government, and if he knew Whittaker Chambers. (Later on he was to testify that he had never heard that name until Chambers took the stand in Washington on August 3, 1948.)

Then, in February, 1948, the noose tightened. Dulles felt he could no longer ignore the stories about Hiss. He "searchingly questioned" Hiss. Along with his denials, Hiss was forced to admit that he had been subpoenaed and questioned by the Federal grand jury probing espionage. But he "reassured" Dulles that it was a "routine" appearance.*

Again Dulles was willing to accept these reassurances, plus those of a State Department official whom he has never named, and to let the matter ride.

On the night of August 2, 1948, Alger Hiss' phone rang.

"This is the New York *Star*, Mr. Hiss," said James Parlatore, a reporter.

"Yes?" answered Hiss.

"Do you know a Whittaker Chambers?" Hiss was silent, then he replied slowly, "No, why?"

"Well," the *Star* reporter told him, "he's supposed to be an editor of *Time* and he's going to appear before the House Un-American Committee and he's going to name you as a Communist."

"Ridiculous," Hiss snapped.

Two days later, after Chambers had testified, the *Star*

---

* Shortly after this, Attorney General Tom Clark, for reasons which can only be hazarded, called in the top members of the Washington press corps to inform them off-the-record that Hiss and the other people called by the grand jury had been cleared.

called Hiss again. What the accused man had to say was more revealing than he perhaps realized.

"I'm not a politician, but it just struck me that five of the eight persons mentioned—myself, Pressman, Witt, Kramer, and Abt—were employed by the Department of Agriculture while Wallace was there. I don't know, but this might be an indirect attack at Henry Wallace." Unwittingly, he had again called attention to his link with the early and notorious Washington cell.

The rise of Whittaker Chambers in the *Time-Life* organization was, in its own way, as phenomenal as Hiss' had been in government service. It was the more phenomenal because Chambers started out from scratch—and because he lacked Hiss' propensity for seeking out propitious friendships. From his first day at *Time*, moreover, Chambers was surrounded by hostility. The large Communist cell which flourished in the Luce empire during the early forties was determined to see him ousted, by any and all means.

In those early days, when Chambers was the most vulnerable, the cell did everything within its power to bedevil him. Party-liners thwarted his efforts at every turn. When he was assigned to a story, his research material would disappear. Other research material, necessary to verify points he had made in a story, would also disappear just before deadline. This was direct sabotage. At his every mention of communism, the claque would attempt to drown him out. Insidious little stories would spread about him, starting nowhere and going far.

His warnings against the Communists on *Time* were taken as eccentricities or as the fulminations of a vicious man. And they hurt him in his day-to-day life. Ralph Ingersoll, later to edit *PM*, was diddling with the idea of Marxism then. There were others in the seats of the mighty who had gone considerably beyond Ingersoll. Chambers was a thorn in their side. In an attempt to undercut him, they had him shifted from department to department. But try as they might, they could not minimize his outstanding abilities as a writer and editor. Slowly but perceptibly, he rose in *Time's* shifting hierarchy. Even in so stylized a magazine, his writings stood out for their sharp insight and broad scope.

Movie reviews, book reviews, foreign news—all these passed through his hands. He worked with a boundless persistence. As the Monday night deadline approached, he would work the clock around and around—often forty-eight hours at a stretch. Now and then at office parties, he would unbutton enough to tell friends something of the netherworld from which he had emerged. (Henry Luce was eventually given many of the salient details by Chambers himself.) Or he would attempt to explain the nature of communism to some of the shaky souls who seemed to be succumbing. He made few friendships, but those he did make were deep and lasting. When he found hidden talent, he nurtured it. It was Chambers who spotted Henry Grunwald, trained him as a writer, and set him on the road from office boy to associate editor.

Chambers' underground past caught up with him only casually. In 1943, two FBI agents visited him. Before talking to them, Chambers checked with Berle on the advisability of speaking his piece. When Berle assented, Chambers told them part, though far from all, of his story. It was a long rambling interview, almost pointless. When the questioning was ended, one of the agents told an amused and astounded Chambers, "You interest me greatly." Not until 1945 was there any further sign of that interest. Then, the Bureau sent another man with a photo of J. Peters for Chambers to identify. Chambers was asked for a long statement. From that point on, the FBI bothered him only when it wanted particular information on a specific person in the Party.

In those first *Time* years, Chambers was moving gradually toward Quaker faith. He had felt when he broke with the Party that the absence of God made communism a failure.

His break itself had been a deep religious experience, but it had remained unresolved. There was a great void in his life which the Episcopalianism he had accepted in 1939 did not fill. In his memorable cover story on the Protestant philosopher Reinhold Niebuhr, Chambers was to write many years later, "To this unending effort to know God, man is driven by the noblest of his intuitions—the sense of his moral incompleteness—and by hard experience."

He had gained that hard experience in the desperate days of his break when he was a rootless, directionless man reaching out of the darkness. The shoddy materialism of Communist ideology had blunted his intuition. But it had come to sensitivity again when Chambers emerged into the light. He knew once more what his boyhood confusions had vaguely uttered—that "as twentieth-century civilization reaches a climax, its own paradoxes grow catastrophic." This had led him before to communism and to the service of Lucifer, the fallen angel. Where he had once chosen between hell and purgatory, however, he now faced two other alternatives. "Man stands at the juncture of nature and spirit," he wrote in the Niebuhr story. In choosing the spirit, he chose God; and in choosing God, he turned to the mystical exegesis of the Quakers.

This was no sudden conversion on the road to Damascus. There was a thin continuity which led him to it, a sentimental awareness that his grandmother had been a Friend and a sharp recollection of long conversations in which Priscilla Hiss had harked back to childhood days in Quaker meeting houses. Characteristically, he read George Fox, the fountainhead, in preparation. Before taking the step, he attended meetings of the Society of Friends in New York and in the country, not far from his Westminster farm. In 1941, Whittaker Chambers became a Quaker.

"Whit Chambers was always ready to illuminate reality," his *Time-Life* friend and colleague John Chamberlain wrote for the October 15, 1949, *New Leader*. "Pudgy in appearance, he was hard and disciplined underneath his misleading exterior. He had a good deal of gaiety, he was extremely interested in religious subjects, he would work like a truck horse to deliver on an assignment, and he would go off to the country to work equally hard at getting in the hay. During the years in which I knew him he was becoming more and more enamored of country life. He took pride in the fact that he was one ex-Communist who refused to make a living out of being an 'ex.'

"He often boasted that his son and daughter were having a good birthright; they were growing up in the country, in a sober American community. They would have a pride of place, a stability, that his own generation had never known. His daughter Ellen often repeated a Quaker prayer before meals that went:

> God made the sun
> And God made the tree.
> God made the mountain
> And God made me.
>
> I thank thee, O Lord,
> For the sun and the tree,
> For making the mountain
> And for making me.

"Whittaker wanted his children to be religious in the sense of that prayer, which breathed a glad acceptance of the sacredness of human life . . ."

The acceptance by Chambers of a Quaker philosophy is crucial in this narrative. For it not only brought him into the community of God-fearing men; it raised specific questions in his mind and led him to commit his perjuries before the House Un-American Activities Committee and the Federal grand jury. As an uncompromising enemy of communism, it was his duty to fight it "in word and act." But as a Quaker, he was also bound to respect the human element. Fully aware that at some time or other he would be called upon to bear witness against Hiss, Harry Dexter White, and the others, he decided deliberately to withhold evidence of espionage. Years later, as he sat in the witness chair during the second Hiss trial, Chambers explained his motivation.

"My purpose had been to destroy and paralyze the Communist conspiracy in the government," he said quietly. "At the same time I wished to do as little injury as possible to the human beings involved . . . In my own case, I had been given time to work out a new life. In breaking with the Communist Party, time is a most essential factor. I wanted to give these people the same opportunity I had . . .

"There was a distinction in my mind between disclosing the ultimate perfidy of espionage and the mere fact of communism. In general, I think there are two kinds of men. One kind believes that God is a God of justice. The other believes that God is a God of mercy. I am so constituted that I will always range myself on the side of mercy."

So Chambers initiated no further move to expose Alger Hiss. And as time went by, the underground period of his life must have seemed remote indeed. Once he resurrected it symbolically in a piece for *Life* written at the request of Henry Luce. Titled "The Devil," it was a morality sketch, an allegory on evil in which Lucifer was the head of an underground elite subverting God—ironically, an elite to which some of society's best people belonged. It anatomized the Reason which does not understand and the Scientism which explains nothing.

But for the most part, Chambers' work in the Luce organization moved along a different road. He wrote the measured and knowledgeful pieces on the Renaissance and the Reformation which appeared in *Life*. He wrote a long essay on the Pope. His cover story on Niebuhr was hardly in keeping with the tone of a popular magazine, but in the more rarefied religious circles it caused much comment. His review of Toynbee's *History of Civilization* again was recognized as outstanding. Rich in aphorisms, it was wracked with man's ordeal, with the realization of our time's plague.

There were other stories he wrote, lyric and moving and alive, such as his cover story on Marian Anderson, the Negro singer. Because he felt that "the theme of the greatest music is always the birth of the soul," he wrote the story for *Time's* Religion Section and not for Music. But he did not devote himself solely to the life and art of a warmly religious woman. He carried his exposition further, into a gleaming description of the Negro spiritual.

"It was the religious voice of a whole religious people— probably the most God-obsessed (and man-despised) since the ancient Hebrews," he wrote. "One simple fact is clear— [the spirituals] were created in direct answer to the Psalmist's question, 'How shall we sing the Lord's song in a strange land?' . . . Grief, like a tuning fork, gave the tone, and the Sorrow Songs were uttered."

"There was no gainsaying the predictive accuracy of Whit Chambers' journalism," Chamberlain says. "He was always ahead of his colleagues, for he knew how totalitarians could be expected to behave in any given instance. He wasn't fooled by Teheran, Yalta, or Potsdam, and he would have been a better adviser to Jimmy Byrnes than anyone on Jimmy Byrnes' State Department payroll.

"Journalism that is more than a step ahead of mob attitudes isn't very popular. At the very height of the American-Russian love feast, Whittaker Chambers wrote a brilliant fantasy called 'The Ghosts on the Roof.' In this fantasy Tsar Nicholas returned to earth to announce his conversion to Stalinism. Why had the last of the Romanovs chosen to go over to his executioners? For one compelling reason. Stalin was in process of gaining all the ends in foreign policy for which the Romanovs had worked unsuccessfully throughout the centuries. Printed in *Time*, which is manifestly a news weekly, the fantasy may have puzzled many. But if truth is a matter of accurate illumination of reality, then 'The Ghosts on the Roof' was the truest sort of news."

But time was running out for the senior editor of *Time*. His resolve to speak out against the "evil thing" had yet to be put to the test. One day, newspaper headlines blazoned the story of Elizabeth Bentley's confession. The clock struck coldly for Whittaker Chambers. The eleventh hour had come.

11

The Bentley Story

THE COMMUNIST ESPIONAGE APPARATUS IS LIKE A flowing river, ever changing yet always the same. From year to year, its leaders and its personnel drop out or are replaced. But their successors, however different they may be individually, still function in the same way. If time brought any change, it was this: the Washington spy ring operating in the late thirties under Whittaker Chambers had been a well-behaved river, carrying its modest goods to Moscow. By the time the United States was busily engaged in defeating the Axis powers, the river had overflowed its banks. An eddy of this espionage torrent is the Bentley story.

Elizabeth Bentley, Communist, was an anomaly to the New England town in which she spent the first seven years of her life. Born in New Milford in 1908, she was descended, through her school-teacher mother, from the old settlers of Connecticut and could claim kinship with many families in the district. Her father, originally from Morristown, New Jersey, was a solid middle-class citizen—a Republican, a Prohibitionist, and a leading member of the Congregational Church.

But New England, for all its traditional conservatism, was also a cradle of American idealism. The philosophical dreams that briefly came to life at Walden Pond and Brook Farm filled the mind of "bookish, brainy" Elizabeth. As her father's

124

business took the Bentleys from city to city, this idealism was further confirmed, particularly in the expanding industrial towns where Betty saw at first hand the economic misery and social inequality of capitalism at its crudest.

The depression was at its worst when Betty Bentley graduated from Vassar College in 1930. But the full extent of her undergraduate protest had been a half-hearted membership in the League for Industrial Democracy. For two years, Betty taught languages at Foxcroft, a finishing school in Virginia. Then she went back to school, to study Italian at Columbia University in New York. It was at Columbia that she fell in with that large and active group of campus Communists which followed the leadership of James A. Wechsler, then editor of the Columbia *Spectator*.

Her Italian studies took her to the University of Florence in a Fascist Italy where, she recalls, "almost everyone sneaked around corners and whispered in everybody else's ears." When she returned to Columbia in the fall of 1934, to get her master's degree, she was "in violent revulsion against fascism" and "looking for something to do to fight against it." As it had been for many other young people, communism seemed to be the answer. Her first step in the direction of the Party was the American League Against War and Fascism, the organization which launched the "popular front" in this country, to which she could give the benefits of her first-hand observations. Gradually, the Party indoctrinated her. The big argument was: "If you feel like a liberal, and if you feel that conditions are bad, then you should ally yourself with the group that will be strong and disciplined and intelligent and that can really do something." In those days, the argument seemed to make sense.

It took Betty Bentley until March, 1935, to become a card-carrying member of Harlem Unit No. 1 at Columbia University, under the Party name of Mary. For three years, as she drifted in and out of the WPA Writer's Project, her activities were those of the average Communist. She marched in picket lines, sold *Daily Workers*, paraded on May Day, and seriously studied Party literature.

In 1938, Elizabeth Bentley took a job in the Italian Library of Information. There she was struck by two things: that the Library was a part of the Italian government's Propaganda Ministry and that it was a distribution center for Fascist propaganda. Like a good anti-Fascist, she carried this knowledge to Communist headquarters on East 12th Street, eager to make the best possible use of her position in the enemy camp. This act, certainly not a reprehensible one, lifted the trap door to the Communist underworld for Betty.

The Party welcomed Elizabeth Bentley's offer. She was told to destroy her Party card immediately, end her attendance at unit meetings, and dissociate herself from her Communist friends. From that moment on she was to be a member at large whose only connection with the Party would be through a contact she knew at first only as John. In the Communist Party, "you take orders and don't ask questions." Betty did as she was told.

For about a year, during which she seriously believed that she was fighting Fascism, Mary collected evidence of Italian and Spanish Falangist connivance in this country. She kept lists of visitors to the Library of Information and made a record of Fascist propaganda literature being disseminated in this country. All these things she turned over to John at prearranged meetings in restaurants and on street corners. For a long time she was unaware that John was really Jacob Golos, president of World Tourists, Inc., or that this "respectable travel agency" was a front for Soviet espionage operations.

It was an even longer time before she knew that World Tourists transmitted stolen information concealed in food and clothing packages for the Soviet Union or that it was a kind of underground "consulate" which supplied transportation and credentials to Comintern agents. But World Tour-

ists, headed by Communist functionaries such as Alexander
Trachtenberg * and Robert William Wiener, served exactly
that purpose. When Gerhart Eisler went to the Soviet
Union in 1935, it was World Tourists which arranged for a
fake passport issued under the name of Samuel Liptzen.

Much of Elizabeth Bentley's early work for Golos was
pretty innocuous. She did detailed research on such people
as Herbert Hoover, Thomas E. Dewey, members of the
Roosevelt Cabinet. During the Finnish-Russian war, she supplied data on members of the Finnish Relief Committee.
Part of this information went to Russia; part was used in
smear attacks published by the Communist press. And somehow, the thirty-year-old woman fell under the spell of Golos
—an unattractive little man, middle-aged, and even then
seriously ill of heart disease.

When Golos felt that Betty was trustworthy, he informed
her that she was to receive mail for him; in other words, she
was to be his "letter-drop." This mail would be addressed to
her, but any letters bearing a Canadian or Mexican postmark
were to be passed on to Golos unopened. Later, Elizabeth
Bentley was to testify that "All of that ended at the time that
Trotsky's chauffeur was shot in Mexico . . . because one of
the people writing letters was one of the men who shot him."
The Canadian mail, she suspected, came from Fred Rose, a
Canadian Communist leader who was caught in a round-up
of atomic spies in the famous Canadian spy case.

In 1940, a friendly taxi driver whose stand was near the
World Tourists office told Betty Bentley that the FBI had
been around, asking questions about her and Golos. Put on
the alert, Betty realized that she was being followed. As a
result of this knowledge, she and Golos were put on ice by
the apparatus. But the FBI had done its work well. With
the aid of a State Department official, it had gathered enough

---

* Trachtenberg was the commissar at the "Cultural Conference" held at
the Waldorf-Astoria in the spring of 1949 which, under the guise of urging
world peace, was in reality a sounding board against the United States and
the Western democracies.

evidence to send Golos to jail for a variety of crimes against the United States, including passport fraud. But by one of the inexplicable circumstances which in those years seemed to operate in favor of Communist subversives, Golos was picked up on a relatively minor charge. And even this was not pressed. Indicted under the Voorhis Act for failure to register as the agent of a foreign government, he pleaded guilty and received a suspended sentence. A fine of $1,500 was also imposed on him.

The most important consequence of Golos' arrest was that it destroyed the usefulness of World Tourists as a cover. Golos therefore set about creating a new front to handle his business, the United States Service and Shipping Corp. The nominal head was to be "an impeccable businessman," a "sympathizer," but "not a known Communist." Betty Bentley was made the vice president and secretary, but actually she ran the whole organization at a salary ranging from $200 to $800 a month. A severe heart attack at this time limited Golos' direct participation.

This illness, and his close personal relationship with Betty, led Golos to turn more and more of his directly subversive work over to her. And so, almost by indirection, the idealistic New Englander became a courier for part of the great network of spies operating in Washington. As a collateral "descendant" of Whittaker Chambers, she plunged into the great river of espionage.

"It started in 1941," she testified before the Ferguson subcommittee investigating the Loyalty program, "at about the start of the Russian-German war, when Golos told me that he had received from Earl Browder the name of N. Gregory Silvermaster who was working for the government, who was interested in helping get information to Russia, and who could organize a group of other government employees to help in this work. Silvermaster was with the Farm Security Administration [and] was probably an agent of the NKVD . . .

"Since I was the only person that Golos completely trusted, he began to turn over to me some of the work that he was doing—the gathering of information from Communist Party members and sympathizers, the great bulk of them employed by the United States Government . . . Little by little, I took on one group and another. It was a gradual process . . . It started out modestly by being political and as time went on we started taking on military [information] too . . .

"Silvermaster came to New York to see Golos at the behest of Earl . . . and arrangements were made for me to go to the Silvermaster house [in Washington] and make the acquaintance of Mrs. Helen Silvermaster . . . I was told to say that I was Helen and that her husband had arranged for me to come down."

A regular routine was worked out whereby Elizabeth Bentley (alias Mary, alias Helen) visited the Silvermaster home every two weeks and carried back with her to New York material gathered by the Silvermaster ring. Those who supplied Silvermaster were, like the members of Chambers' elite group, mostly people who posed as non-Communists and who kept their connection with the underground extremely secret. Much later, Betty began picking up information from another group led by Victor Perlo, a Chambers alumnus, and made up of open Party members who had been ordered to drop out of Party affairs in order to work more inconspicuously.

From a total of about thirty people in the two groups and about twenty more individual contacts, employed in every sensitive government department or bureau with the exception of the Navy and the FBI, came detailed, classified information on:

Phases of American policy toward China and the Balkans;

Figures on aircraft production and plane allocation to various theaters of operations;

Descriptive material on the then-secret B-29 Superfortress.

Once she brought a formula for making synthetic rubber

out of garbage.* On another occasion, the Russians were "very excited" when she informed them that our intelligence was on the verge of breaking the Russian code. So accurate was her information on D-day, she recalls, that the member of her group who supplied the information won an office pool on the invasion date.

The material grew so voluminous that Betty Bentley had to carry it in a shopping bag. To handle the widening scope of the ring's operations, a home-made microfilm apparatus was brought into use. "In the basement of the Silvermaster home they had a Contax camera and the set-up all ready for putting documents in and holding [them] in place. When [William Ludwig] Ullman [who lived in the Silvermaster house] was available, he did it because he made himself into an expert photographer.† When he was away, or if it was too much for him to handle, Mrs. Silvermaster pitched in."

Early in 1941, Elizabeth Bentley was introduced to Mary Watkins Price, then secretary to Walter Lippmann. This was an invaluable contact. Lippmann's highly influential syndicated column gave him a kind of semi-official status with the State Department. Through his high-level sources, he was often in possession of information which was definitely not for publication or dissemination. In his locked files, he kept copious notes of conversations with top figures in diplomatic circles. "From the first time we met, until she left Mr. Lippmann's employ," Betty testified, "[she furnished me with whatever] she was able to get from her boss' files. He had a great deal of information on our relations with Britain [which] was very interesting to Mr. Golos."

Betty also had a more delicate assignment. There were a number of people, "misguided idealists" in her estimation, who were either too highly placed or too wary to risk meeting her openly. With these people, she made appointments

---

* Actually, potato peels.

† Ullman denied that he had ever photographed government documents but refused to say whether or not he had ever furnished Silvermaster with a camera for that purpose.

to meet in the park or on a street corner. Occasionally they met in an out-of-the-way restaurant. From them she rarely got documents; their information was usually verbal. And for all of her Party sources, she served the utilitarian purpose of collecting dues and supplying them with the Party litera-ture which tells a Communist what and how to think.

As Elizabeth Bentley grew more and more adept, she took pride in her skill as an operative. "I always allowed myself a good half hour before an appointment to go running in and out of department stores, places with two entrances, and into deserted streets where you can see what is going on, to be sure there was no one behind me . . . When you took a taxi-cab you got off a block or two before your destination, waited until the taxicab turned around, and then proceeded on foot." Once, when an FBI agent was on her trail, she ducked into the ladies' room of a department store, knowing he could not follow her, and calmly left by a second exit.

All this time, though she was betraying her country to the Russians, she "didn't think about it."

On Thanksgiving Day in 1943, Golos had a sudden stroke and died in Elizabeth Bentley's apartment. Elizabeth called Grace Hutchins, a functionary of the International Workers Order, the Communist burying society, who quietly secured a death certificate from a Party doctor and took charge of the funeral arrangements. Aware that death might come unex-pectedly, Golos had made preliminary arrangements for Betty to continue the work without him. A few days after the funeral, she was approached by Catherine who intro-duced her to Bill. For about a year, these two people served as liaison between Betty and the NKVD agents who took the Washington rings' haul out of the country.

But though Betty continued her job as courier, and even took on the further responsibility of heading the two Wash-ington spy rings, the death of Golos had aroused her to an awareness of what she was doing. "The effect of Golos was wearing off" is the way she put it. And the analysis was sound. It was Golos, more than any ideological conviction, that had brought her into the underground work. It was her relationship with him which had kept her there. When he was no longer with her, she realized the enormity of her actions.

"Having worked with Mr. Golos, whom I took to be a great idealist, I had been terrifically shielded from the realities behind this thing, and when he died I was thrown into direct contact with the Russians." As it had been to Chambers, this was a chilling experience. Even the Communist mind found it hard to rationalize the police-state mentality. "The Russians thought I knew what was going on," she said. "They made no bones of their contempt for American Communists . . . and of the fact that they were using the American Communist Party as a recruitment center for espionage. They behaved like gangsters."

There was another jolt in store for her—the bureaucracy of the American Party. "I was thrown in contact with Browder," she recalled, "and it was quite a shock to find that high functionaries of the Communist Party were just cheap little men pulled by strings from Moscow." Browder's luxurious life, his country home, and his limousine and chauffeur didn't sit with her very well either.

Sensing her growing cynicism, the Russians tried heavy-handedly to buy the devotion she once bestowed freely; they offered her a fur coat, an air-conditioner for her apartment, and a fat salary. Already fed up, the manner of their offering further repelled her, and she refused to accept the gifts or salary. When this tack failed, they tried another—flattery. In mid-November, 1944, she was instructed to meet Al in front of the Edison Theater on Broadway and 103rd Street in New York. Al was a Russian whom she later identified from photographs as Anatol Gromov, the First Secretary of the Russian Embassy.

As Betty and Al walked along Riverside Drive, he delivered a long speech "to the effect that the Supreme Presidium of the U.S.S.R. had awarded me the Order of the Red Star for my extremely valuable services to the Soviet Union." Typically, all he had to show was a picture of the medal, torn from an American magazine. Two months later, Gromov showed her the medal and a presentation certificate, but he never gave either of them to her.

Then the element of fear was introduced. A suggestion was made to her that she might "go to Russia under cover and receive a course of training over there . . . It frightened me considerably." And when the subject of leaving was mentioned, she was told: "Nobody ever leaves this. Nobody ever leaves the service."

At this point, the Russians played directly into her hands. Leery of her trustworthiness, they put her on ice under the pretext that there were leaks which made her too "hot." In December, 1944, she was ordered to turn over her remaining contacts to a successor, and though she remained in touch with the apparatus, she was no longer a part of its activities. But her obsession, to get herself out of the whole business "without endangering myself," continued. "I realized I was one person fighting a vast machine," she testified. "I could either walk out and forget it had happened or I could go to the FBI. It took me a year to get to the point."

Late in August of 1945, Elizabeth Bentley went to the FBI. But like all people who have been in the underground, she had the idea that government bureaus were full of Communist spies. Instead of going to the Washington or New York FBI offices, where she feared she might be recognized as she walked in, she traveled up to a field headquarters in New Haven. Once there, she lost her courage, merely disclosing that she was an ex-Communist and that she was afraid her life was in danger. The New Haven FBI reported her conversation to New York and arranged an appointment there for her.

It took some doing before she talked freely. To FBI officials, the outline of her story was not news. But the names she earnestly mentioned staggered them. Among those she accused were a White House adviser, a Treasury official, a State Department employee, and a host of other strategically placed government employees. Even to men whose work was counter-espionage, her story was unbelievable. Wary that she might be a plant, or worse a double agent, they refused to take her seriously.

For months she lived through that cliff-hanging frustration and suspense which are the stock-in-trade of Hitchcock thrillers. She had the facts, but no one seemed to believe her. Finally, the FBI was sufficiently convinced to put her to the test. Return to the espionage network, she was told, and bring us the kind of concrete evidence which will prove your story. Simultaneously, the FBI would continue its own investigation. Reluctantly, Betty Bentley agreed.

In October, she informed the FBI that she had an appointment with Gromov. Obviously, it was his job to determine if she was trustworthy after her period of inactivity. As they walked along the deserted Hudson River waterfront late at night, Gromov's speech and manner were ominous. "He told me something was wrong with me because I would not accept the money that was piling up in Moscow for me. He kept pressing me and told me that unless I accepted the money he had in his pocket, he would consider me a traitor and I knew what that meant. Finally, I got him away from the dock region, and he gave me the money."

Gromov, of course, did not know that this transaction was witnessed by FBI agents or that the envelope, containing $2,000 in $20 bills, was to land in an FBI safe.

But Gromov was shrewd enough to realize that something had happened to Elizabeth Bentley. Though she was permitted to hold her job with the United States Service and Shipping Corp. until it was liquidated in 1947, she was no longer given the sort of espionage assignment which would have clinched the case for the FBI. She still made trips to Washington, but all her contacts seemed to have been warned to be careful with her. Trailed at all times by government agents, she could prove merely that the people she had named really knew her.

But she had demonstrated enough to convince the Department of Justice that a grand jury investigation of Communist espionage was long overdue. Still without concrete evidence, but with the approval of President Truman, the government moved ahead. Thomas J. Donegan, an ex-FBI man practicing law, was appointed special assistant Attorney General by Tom Clark. On March 22, 1947, a Federal grand jury was impaneled in New York City to hear Elizabeth Bentley's story and to question the people she named. If one of these principals could be made to crack on the witness stand, Donegan reasoned, the case would break wide open.

12

The First Break

Looking back over the course of the Bentley
story, it is hard to understand why Mr. Truman sanctioned
the grand jury investigation in 1947—fully aware of the import of Elizabeth Bentley's charges—and then did his best to
nullify her testimony in 1948. Was truth confounded when
uttered by his political enemies? Or had the President been
unaware that the Bentley disclosures would put squarely on
the record the inadequacies of the Roosevelt-Truman security policy? Or as some have suggested, had he believed that
by burying the story in secret grand jury proceedings he
could still the rumors once and for all?

At any rate, Mr. Truman did call the grand jury into session. And a badly frightened Elizabeth Bentley began the
piecemeal recital of her activities in Washington. At first,
attempts were made to keep her identity secret, even from
the jury. She was called to the stand as Mary and the particulars of her personal life veiled. Eventually, however, as she
gained confidence, she agreed to forego these precautions.

On the basis of her testimony, the jury, which was meeting
for a few hours every week, issued dozens of subpoenas to
the people she named and others on FBI suspect lists. But
any attempts to make the witnesses go beyond a routine
description of their government jobs were met by evasions
and refusals based on the constitutional ground that to
answer might tend to incriminate or degrade. The focus of

the investigation was the "house in Washington"—the Silvermaster home whose photographic studio had been used to microfilm papers and documents.

Witnesses who could be linked circumstantially with the Silvermasters claimed that their visits to the house were purely social. Others produced photos of themselves to prove the innocence of their errands. Simultaneously, the mills of political influence began to grind. One prominent senator, indirectly implicated by the activities of a subordinate, reportedly went as high as the White House. What followed there made good gossip at the National Press Club bar, but for obvious reasons it never got into print.

Veiled stories began to appear in the Washington and New York press, referring to the grand jury hearings. There were rumors that witnesses had cracked, that the case reached so high into the government that the Administration planned a whitewash. There were rumors that, in a presidential election year, no indictments would be drawn up. And from government sources came staunch denials. It was not political expediency but lack of concrete evidence that was the cause of the deadlock in the grand jury room. Whatever the reason, the hearings continued for over a year, producing nothing beyond public and private conjecture.*

Quite suddenly, in April, 1948, Federal Attorney John F. X. McGohey was called in to work with Tom Donegan; the Justice Department had decided to shift emphasis. From this point on, the espionage angle was forgotten and McGohey began to wade through the voluminous FBI files on the Communists to prepare an indictment under the Smith Act. His job was now to convince the grand jury that the Communist Party was conspiring to teach the overthrow of the government by force and violence.

This change-over was an open secret among newspapermen. The more cynical of them took it as a face-saving device

---

* It is interesting—and puzzling—to note that Alger Hiss was called and Whittaker Chambers studiously ignored.

—or worse, tacit admission of an Administration whitewash. For Betty Bentley, the Justice Department's new tack came as a shock. Motivated by her sense of revulsion toward communism, she had gone to the FBI expecting quick results. Now, after a year of strain as an almost constant witness, the government had left her high and dry. In this state of mind, she thought of Frederick Woltman, the New York *World Telegram's* Pulitzer Prize-winning expert on communism, whose first wife she had known as a student at Vassar.

She saw Woltman, and told him on an off-the-record basis not only the story of her activities as a spy-courier, but also explained her predicament. What would be the best way to get some action? she asked him.

"Congressional committees will certainly open the story to the public, no matter what the grand jury does," he reassured her. But as long as she was under grand jury subpoena, there was little that she could do. Once she was free of that, he would be able to act, he promised her. When he alerted his editors, preparations were made for publishing this "exclusive" at the proper time.

Meanwhile, McGohey was moving ahead with the conspiracy case. It took him three months to build up his presentation. In the process, he drew on FBI dossiers, the testimony of FBI "confidential informants," and a library of standard Party literature: the "Communist Manifesto," the writings of Lenin and Stalin, texts of public and private utterances by Communist leaders, and Party "textbooks" such as J. Peters' "Manual of Organization." The date of the conspiracy was set at 1945 when the Communists, on instructions from the "dissolved" Communist International, expelled Earl Browder, discarded his line of moderation, and returned to the old precepts of violent revolution and forceful capture of the state machinery.

Sixteen months after it convened to hear espionage testimony, on July 20, 1948, the grand jury handed down indictments against the dozen members of the Communist Party's national board, the American "Politburo." Except for the American press, the Bentley story would have been dead and forgotten.

But once the indictment had been handed down by the grand jury, the *World Telegram* felt free to publish the Bentley disclosures. For some time, Nelson Frank, a reporter, had been interviewing Betty Bentley. When the time came to get into print, rewrite man Norton Mockridge was assigned to take Frank's notes and whip them into shape. Under their joint by-line, a series of stories appeared which hit New York and the country very hard indeed. Without mentioning names—Elizabeth Bentley was Mary and the other principals were described as a "high Treasury official," a "Presidential adviser," etc.—the two newspapermen told a basically sound, if rather enthusiastic, version of the facts.

The long-dormant Un-American Activities Committee leaped to secure the testimony of the witness, now released from Federal subpoena. For weeks, they had been itching to do so. But the Ferguson subcommittee, engaged in investigating the Loyalty program for the Senate, moved even more quickly. Working through Nelson Frank, who had elected himself Miss Bentley's spokesman, Senator Ferguson got first licks. From Betty Bentley he and his subcommittee heard a veiled version of her involvement with the espionage network, the nature of the information she procured, and her experiences with the FBI. The only name she mentioned was that of William Remington, a young government official then under the Senate's scrutiny.[*]

The Thomas committee, on July 31, the following day, got all the names and the lion's share of the headlines. It was, for a while, a Roman holiday for both the committee and the public, a cloak and dagger orgy. As name followed name, in seemingly endless profusion, the American public heard for the first time what a small group of anti-Communist experts had long known—that the ramifications of Stalin's tree

---

[*] Remington was later cleared by a Loyalty Board.

of treason were multitudinous. In a few months, most of this was forgotten as public attention became focussed on the tragic struggle of Whittaker Chambers and Alger Hiss. But, particularly in Washington, during the summer of 1948 Betty Bentley's casual utterances and accusations created an incredible tension.

First on the Bentley list was Nathan Gregory Silvermaster, a wiry, sharp-faced little man with upswept grey hair and a wispy mustache—a ferret-like version of Charlie Chaplin. But there was nothing funny about his record or his testimony. Beyond calling Miss Bentley a "neurotic liar" and branding her charges "false and fantastic," Silvermaster retired behind a barrage of "I refuse to answer on the grounds that any answer I may give may tend to be self-incriminatory." It was a statement which the committee would hear with monotonous regularity from the assorted Communists and crypto-Communists testifying on succeeding days.

But in the case of Silvermaster, there was no need to rely on his reluctant testimony. The committee had to hand a voluminous Civil Service Commission report on the witness which made it difficult to understand how any official could have hired him.

Born in Russia in 1898, Silvermaster entered this country from China where he had attended school. He received a B.A. from the University of Washington in Seattle and a Ph.D. from the University of California. In 1927, he became a naturalized citizen of the United States, though, according to the Civil Service report, he was already a member of the Communist Party.

"There is considerable testimony indicating that about 1920 [he] was an underground agent for the Communist Party . . . He has been everything from a fellow-traveler to an agent for the OGPU. He has been known and listed in the files of the Seattle Police Department, the Thirteenth Naval District, the San Francisco Police Department . . . and the FBI as a member and leader of the Communist Party."

"[He] was closely associated with Sam Darcy and Harry Bridges"—two functionaries of the Party—"He was agitation propagandist of the Fillmore subsection in the San Francisco 13th District Communist Party," the Commission reported in 1942. "The overwhelming amount of testimony indicates beyond reasonable doubt that Nathan Gregory Silvermaster is now, and has for years been a member and leader of the Communist Party, and very probably a secret agent of the OGPU."

From August, 1935, to November, 1938, Silvermaster worked for the Farm Security Administration. From November, 1938, to July, 1940, he was on the Maritime Labor Board. From July, 1940, to December, 1944, he was in the Agriculture Department. On July 16, 1942, the Civil Service Commission recommended, "Cancel eligibilities . . . and bar him for the duration of the National Emergency." Instead, Silvermaster moved over to an $8,000-a-year-job as a Treasury Department economist where he stayed until 1945. He transferred then to the War Assets Administration with a raise to $10,000. When he resigned from government service in March, 1946, it was simply because, in the postwar cutbacks, he refused "to accept an arbitrary demotion in status."

How was Silvermaster able to remain in government service? The answer was very simple. He had a friend in Lauchlin Currie, a Presidential adviser. Currie had interceded for Silvermaster and got some big names in the government to vouch for him. Silvermaster was never transferred from one job to another, a process which would have given the Civil Service Commission a chance to refuse him clearance, but was "loaned" instead.

Going into great and convincing detail, Elizabeth Bentley described Silvermaster's role as spymaster, his influence in placing Communists in government jobs, and told how documents were photographed in the basement of his house. From that point on, the names came thick and fast.

William Ludwig Ullman of the Treasury Department,

later in the Air Corps; Victor Perlo * of WPB; Charles
Kramer,* an aide first to Senator Kilgore and later to the
on-again-off-again pinko Senator Claude Pepper; Robert
Miller of the Office of the Coordinator of Inter-American
Affairs; George Silverman,* who went from the Railroad
Retirement Board to an Air Force civilian post; William Gold
and his wife Sonia; John Abt;* and a score of others.

All of these people she named both as Communists and
members of the Silvermaster ring. There were two eminent
men she named but did not accuse of Party membership.
About Harry Dexter White, Assistant Secretary of the Treasury, author of the Morgenthau Plan, and appointer of Communists to sensitive German occupation posts, she said: "I
don't know whether Mr. White was a card-carrying Communist or not . . . He gave information to Mr. Silvermaster
which was relayed to me . . . From what they said, Mr.
White knew where it was going but preferred not to mention the fact." Of Lauchlin Currie, she said: "He was not a
Communist, but he did give information on this government's attitude toward China, [and] toward other governments . . . Mr. Currie came dashing into Mr. Silverman's
house, sort of out of breath, and told him that the Americans
were on the verge of breaking the Soviet code . . ." Some
of the people who gave her information, she testified, "may
have thought it was going to the Communist Party headquarters for the use of Earl Browder, or others may have just
guessed the truth. It was just not discussed."

Elizabeth Bentley's testimony was followed, three days
later, by Whittaker Chambers'. But though his subsequent
duel with Alger Hiss gradually crowded out the Bentley testimony, many of the succeeding days were spent in long futile
hearings in which the Thomas committee sought wearily to
get some sort of adequate rebuttal from the people Betty
Bentley had named.

The pattern of these hearings was quickly established. A

* Named by Chambers in his testimony a few days later.

witness would be sworn, he would make a denunciation of the committee, read a statement flatly denying the over-all charges, and on point-by-point questioning retire behind the protection of the Constitution. "I refuse to answer on the grounds of self-incrimination" became a shibboleth. Witnesses refused to say whether they knew one another, whether they were Communists, whether they had visited the Silvermaster home. One witness even claimed that to admit he had ever been in Washington's Union Station would be self-incriminatory. Another refused to confirm or deny membership in the American Legion.

A few of the witnesses—Robert Miller, one-time chief of publications in the State Department, was among them—admitted that they knew Elizabeth Bentley under various names. But they denied that they had given her classified material and went to some pains to discredit her personal character. She was "neurotic," "unhealthy and unnatural," a "nuisance." They had tolerated her to a point and then refused to have anything more to do with her.

But, in a sense, these witnesses were the small fry. Much bigger fish were Lauchlin Currie and Harry Dexter White. And being bigger, they ran away with the hook. Currie admitted that he had known both Silvermaster and Silverman— as well as others among the accused. But he denied that he had ever interfered to save N. Gregory Silvermaster from being discharged as a security risk. He had merely requested the Undersecretary of War, Robert P. Patterson,* to investigate the charges, and Silvermaster had subsequently been cleared by G-2.

Though he had never been accused of membership in the Communist Party, he emphatically denied any such affiliation. "I have never been affiliated with any organization or group sympathetic with the doctrines of Communism or engaged in furthering that cause," Currie added. "I have never had any reason to believe that any friends of mine or even

* Patterson performed a similar role in the Hiss case.

acquaintances or associates were Communists." In this, he
went along with most of the witnesses. Washington was full
of Communists and fellow-travelers—many of whom made
no bones of it—but witness after witness stated in seriousness
that he knew no Communists.

Curiously, the committee made only one feeble stab at
probing this statement. Yet in its own records, there were
scores of pages dealing with Currie's activities in behalf of
the Washington Committee to Aid China, a Communist
front so blatant that Mrs. Eleanor Roosevelt had withdrawn
her support.

This same uncoordinated behavior was demonstrated by
the committee when it questioned Harry Dexter White. The
charges against him were serious; he had been named by
both Elizabeth Bentley and Whittaker Chambers as a Communist or a collaborator. In 1942, he had been casually listed
in a Civil Service Commission report as a "known Communist." And his name had been mentioned on the floor of Congress as a Party member in 1945. Of the people named as
Communists and/or spies by Chambers and Bentley, almost
half were either friends of White or people he had employed
in the government. He was, moreover, author of the Morgenthau Plan for the pastoralization of Germany—a plan which
had the wholehearted support of American Communists and
the Soviet Union.

Had the committee bothered to investigate, it would have
learned, too, that White's appointees—men who worked for
the Treasury Department in Germany—were with few excep-
tions Communists or fellow-travelers. What anti-Communists
drifted into the Treasury unit investigating cartels were
quickly transferred or returned to the United States.

Yet the committee permitted White to lecture it on Ameri-
canism, to talk of "star-chamber proceedings" with a glibness
which fooled everyone except those who knew what the
term means, and to act as if the hearings were a musical
comedy routine. Like Currie, White didn't know any Com-

munists. He professed to be shocked by the behavior on the stand of some of his friends and ex-colleagues. But he would never admit that anything short of a Party card would convince him of a man's communism. And, he indicated, even the Party card would not really clinch it.

The committee could repeat, *ad infinitum*, that someone was lying, that somewhere there were grounds for a perjury indictment. But it was frustrated and stymied by its own limitations and by the refusal of the Truman Administration to open its intelligence records to committee investigators. It might have remained at that but for the persistence of Alger Hiss, the foresight of Whittaker Chambers, and the memory of a Washington reporter.

Ed Nellor, then of the New York *Sun's* Washington Bureau, recalled having heard a version of the story Chambers had tried to tell in 1939. He suggested to the committee that it call Chambers. Perhaps he might be able to break the deadlock. On August 2nd, Whittaker Chambers learned that a subpoena had been issued summoning him to appear before the Un-American Activities Committee. Seeking out his good friend, John Chamberlain, Chambers agitatedly expressed a complete repugnance to the whole idea.

"I always feared I'd have to cross this bridge," he told Chamberlain, "but I hoped not to." Says Chamberlain: "The popular picture of Chambers rushing to Washington to 'get' Alger Hiss just doesn't square with his behavior around the *Time* office on the day he got news of his subpoena . . . He kept repeating that he had never made a business of telling about his Communist past." But there was no turning back. As an avowed enemy of communism, fighting it "in word and act," he could not back down now. Fully aware that he was jeopardizing his career, Chambers sat down that night to write the statement which was to lift the curtain on the first act of the high drama.

13

High Drama in a Hearing Room
I

THE BENTLEY STORY HAD SHOCKED THE COUNTRY. But for many reasons it was merely the curtain-raiser for the tragic drama that was to unfold in the hearing room of the House Un-American Activities Committee. For one thing, Elizabeth Bentley was a small figure in a great conspiracy. Both her part and her own character were small compared with the tremendous conflict which engulfed her. For another, her story had been vitiated by the "blonde spy queen" tag which the newspapers saw fit to tie on her.

In comparison, Whittaker Chambers' tight-lipped, quiet, but emotion-charged testimony hit the committee and the country with an impact little known in a nation as politically superficial as ours. On August 3, 1948, at 11 A.M., Chambers was sworn in by Representative Karl E. Mundt in a hearing room of the New House Office Building. Speaking in a voice keyed so low that newspapermen at the press table had difficulty in hearing him, Chambers had gone through the preliminaries of testimony. But as he progressed in this story, the resonance had come into his voice, giving it an impressive and sincere ring. As a senior editor on *Time*, he could speak with considerable authority. As a man superbly equipped to express himself, he was able to broadcast this authority. But it was the inner conviction which made his words stand as truth.

"Almost nine years ago," said Chambers, "I went to Washington and reported to the authorities what I knew about the infiltration of the United States Government by Communists. For years international communism, of which the United States Communist Party is an integral part, had been in a state of undeclared war with this Republic. With the Hitler-Stalin Pact, that war reached a new stage. I regarded my action in going to the government as a simple act of war, like the shooting of an armed enemy in combat.

"At that moment in history, I was one of the few men on this side of the battle who could perform this service."

Then, briefly, Chambers described his reasons for joining the Communist Party in 1925 and his reasons for breaking when he did.

"Yet, so strong is the hold which the insidious evil of communism secures on its disciples," he added, "that I could still say to someone at the time: I know that I am leaving the winning side for the losing side, but it is better to die on the losing side than to live under communism."

". . . I had sound reason for supposing that the Communists might try to kill me. For a number of years I had myself served in the underground, chiefly in Washington, D. C. . . . I knew at its top level, a group of seven or so men, from whom in later years certain members of Miss Bentley's organization were apparently recruited. The head of the underground at the time I knew it was Nathan Witt, an attorney for the National Labor Relations Board. Later, John Abt became the leader. Lee Pressman was also a member of this group, as was Alger Hiss . . . The purpose of this group at that time was not primarily espionage. Its original purpose was the Communist infiltration of the American Government. But espionage was certainly one of its eventual objectives . . . Disloyalty is a matter of principle with every member of the Communist Party. The Communist Party exists for the specific purpose of overthrowing the government, at the opportune time, by any and all means; and each of its members, by the fact that he is a member, is dedicated to this purpose."

Under the scattered, often disorganized, questioning of the committee, Whittaker Chambers pieced out other parts of his voluminous past in the Communist underground. He consciously and carefully made it a point to avoid the charge that the people in his elite group had been engaged in espionage. He said then that the primary aim of his Communist group was infiltration and the influencing of public policy, although its eventual purpose was espionage. Only the astute and long-time student of the Communist netherworld could realize, by Chambers' insistence that his life had been in danger, that the stocky, greying *Time* editor was touching on matters far more grievous to the national interest than subversive penetration. What implications there were of espionage were often obscured by Representative John Rankin's ceaseless attempts to drag into the hearing every one of his pet hates in and out of the New Deal and to twist Chambers' words into anti-Semitic utterances. That the committee did its best to ignore Rankin's outbursts was very much to its credit.

When the name of Harry Dexter White was brought up, Representative F. Edward Hébert asked:

Hébert. White was being used as an unwitting dupe?
Chambers. I would scarcely say "unwitting." He was, as nearly as I know, perfectly willing to be used.

So far, Alger Hiss was still a minor character in the drama. His name had been mentioned several times in passing. At one time Representative Karl E. Mundt singled him out for rather extended reference, but that was all:

"Mr. Chambers," said Mundt, "I am very much interested in trying to check the career of Alger Hiss . . . As a member of the Foreign Affairs Committee, the personnel committee, I have had some occasion to check the activities of Alger Hiss while he was in the State Department. There is reason to

believe that he organized within the Department one of the
Communist cells which endeavored to influence our Chinese
policy and bring about the condemnation of Chiang Kai-shek,
which put [Carl Aldo] Marzani * in an important position
there, and I think it is important to know what happened to
these people after they left the government . . ."

But that was all. From there on, Chambers continued to
describe his activities and to explain patiently to the committee the nature of a Communist cell. When he had finished
his testimony, Mundt, acting chairman of the committee
in the absence of J. Parnell Thomas, thanked Chambers
warmly.

"The Chair would like to say, Mr. Chambers, in conclusion,
that we sincerely appreciate the testimony you have given
here today. It is a tremendously difficult job to prove the
thinking of the American Communist mind, and it is from
men like you . . . who have been through the valley of the
shadow and seen the error of their Communist philosophy
and had the courage and good patriotism to renounce communism openly and to make available to the law enforce-
ment and investigating agencies of the government your information . . . that slowly and surely we are piecing together
this pattern of the Communist conspiracy and helping to
educate a rather gullible America."

This was on Tuesday. By Wednesday, the hue and cry
against Chambers for mentioning Alger Hiss and Harry
White had begun. Both men had powerful friends in the
government and in the press. Here started the fiction that a
vindictive Chambers had thrust himself into the limelight by
irresponsibly hurling charges at prominent persons. Elmer
Davis, in his nightly broadcasts for the American Broadcast-
ing Company, unqualifiedly denied that the charges against
his friend White had any basis of fact. With equal vehe-
mence, he came to the defense of Alger Hiss. It was, he inti-

---

* A State Department officer who was jailed for falsely swearing in a
government application that he was not a Communist.

mated, a plot to smear the New Deal. When, shortly after his appearance before the House committee, White died of a heart attack, there were loud shouts that he had been "murdered."

The staid New York *Times*, usually staunchly against sin, reflected that "we have a precious heritage in this country of protection of the innocent against false accusation, of a fair trial even for the guilty. What price a few headlines if those rights are compromised . . ." The Washington *Star* published a cartoon depicting an open sewer manhole labelled "The House Un-American Activities Committee."

On August 5th, Alger Hiss, a slim, smiling man of forty-three, dressed in a neat grey suit, took the stand in a crowded congressional hearing room. As newsreel and television cameras ground, klieg lights glared, and flash bulbs popped, Hiss suddenly assumed the role of top counter-protagonist in a drama which with the inevitability of a Greek tragedy unrolled to an almost predictable conclusion. With the exception of Harry White, Hiss was the only top-flight witness in a long series of hearings who did not withdraw behind the skirts of his constitutional privilege by pleading self-incrimination. Instead, he went on the offensive, denying everything that had been said against him.

"I am here at my own request," Hiss told the committee in his opening statement, "at my own request to deny unqualifiedly various statements about me which were made before this committee by one Whittaker Chambers the day before yesterday. I appreciate the committee's having promptly granted my request. I welcome the opportunity to answer to the best of my ability any inquiries the members of this committee may wish to ask me.

"I am not and have never been a member of the Communist Party. I do not and have never adhered to the tenets of the Communist Party. I am not and have never been a member of any Communist front organization. I have never followed the Communist Party line, directly or indirectly. To the best of my knowledge, none of my friends is a Communist . . .

"To the best of my knowledge, I have never heard of Whittaker Chambers until in 1947, when two members of the Federal Bureau of Investigation asked me if I knew him . . . So far as I know, I have never laid eyes on him, and I should like to do so . . . I have known Henry Collins since we were boys in camp together . . . Lee Pressman was in my class at the Harvard Law School . . . Witt and Abt were both members of the legal staff of the Agricultural Adjustment Administration . . . Kramer was in another office of the AAA, and I met him in that connection. I have seen none of these last three men I have mentioned except most infrequently since I left the Department of Agriculture. I don't believe I ever knew Victor Perlo.

"Except as I have indicated, the statements made about me by Mr. Chambers are complete fabrications. I think my record in the government speaks for itself."

This point-blank denial as well as his complete failure to identify Chambers from photos shook most of the committee. After discussing Hiss' position and the various jobs he had held in the government, the committee floundered for an opening. Mr. Rankin asked what the witness's present employment was.

Hiss. I am president of the Carnegie Endowment for International Peace.
Hébert. Do you know Mr. John Foster Dulles?
Hiss. I do. He is chairman of my board of trustees.
Hébert. Did he assist you in any way in getting your present position?
Hiss. He urged me to take my present position.

But this line of questioning was pointless. Hébert, the presidential election in mind, had dragged in Dulles' name simply to belabor the Republican candidate, Thomas E. Dewey. Hopelessly, Mundt let Hébert's questions peter out, then remarked:

"I want to say for one member of the committee that it is extremely puzzling that a man who is senior editor of *Time* magazine, by name of Whittaker Chambers, whom I had never seen . . ."

Hiss. As far as I know, I have never seen him.

Mundt. . . . should come before this committee and discuss the Communist apparatus working in Washington, which he says is transmitting secrets to the Russian government, and he lists seven people—Nathan Witt, Lee Pressman, Victor Perlo, Charles Kramer, John Abt, Harold Ware, Alger Hiss, and Donald Hiss—

Hiss. That is eight.

Mundt. There seems to be no question about the subversive connections of the six other than the Hiss brothers, and I wonder what possible motive a man who edits *Time* magazine would have for mentioning Donald Hiss and Alger Hiss in connection with those other six.

Hiss. So do I, Mr. Chairman . . .

Mundt. You can appreciate the position of this committee when the name bobs up with those connections . . . All we are trying to do is find the facts.

Hiss. I wish I could have seen Mr. Chambers before he testified.

At this point, Rankin came up with one of his inimitable remarks, turning on Chambers, whom he had so easily praised just two days previously. "After all the smear attacks against this committee and individual members of this committee in *Time* magazine," said Rankin, getting a big laugh, "I am not surprised at anything that comes out of anybody connected with it."

By the time the hearing had ended, all the committee members with the exception of Richard Nixon were busy making amends to Hiss for the inconvenience they had caused him. Of the people who attended, either press or spectators, the thumping majority believed that Hiss was telling the truth and Chambers, for some obscure private motive, lying. It was as complete a reversal of position as the committee had ever seen.

Immediately after the hearing was concluded, the committee went into executive session. Consternation is the only word which describes the feeling of the members. Mundt, speaking for the others—again with the exception of Nixon— stated categorically that it was quite apparent the committee had been taken in by Chambers. Unless a collateral issue were developed, he said almost in panic, an issue which would take the public mind off the Hiss fiasco, the committee would suffer a great deal of damage. Hébert's view was a little different. He felt that the best way to handle the case was for the committee to wash its hands of both Hiss and Chambers and to send the file of the August 3rd and August 5th testimony to the Attorney General. Tom Clark could then determine who was lying, who telling the truth.

To all this, Richard Nixon objected strenuously. He had listened to Hiss and watched him on the stand with a great deal of attention.

"I felt," he confided afterwards, "that Hiss was much too careful a witness in his testimony for one who purported to be telling the whole truth without qualification. I noted that throughout his testimony, he never once said, 'I have never known Whittaker Chambers.' He always insisted on using the qualifying phrasing, 'I have never known a man by the name of Whittaker Chambers.' Could Hiss have known Chambers under another name?

"I felt also that Hiss seemed to put on a 'show' when he was shown a picture of Chambers. His statement that 'this might look like you, Mr. Chairman,' and his elaborate ex- planation all combined to make me think that he actually did recognize the picture and was attempting to give a dis- arming statement concerning it.

"All in all, I felt that Hiss was a very smooth witness, but between him and Chambers, Chambers had been the more convincing witness. But I could only offer this as a personal suspicion on my part."

So Nixon made his own proposal to the befuddled com- mittee. It was this proposal which, in effect, led to the great climax of the case. Nixon urged that although the committee could not as yet determine who was lying on the question of Hiss' affiliation with the Communists, it was possible that they might prove conclusively whether or not Chambers had ever known Hiss. If Hiss had lied on this point—and the committee could prove it—it would be a big feather in the committee's cap.

Nixon suggested that a subcommittee go immediately to New York to question Chambers in executive session. "Let's get him to tell us everything he knows about Alger Hiss," Nixon said. "Then we can see whether his story is a fabrication or not." Concurring with Nixon, Robert S. Stripling, the committee's chief investigator, noted that there was a witness in the Bentley case who lived in New York and who might also be questioned by the subcommittee.

Still unconvinced, Mundt nevertheless agreed. Then, as a cover up, in case the meeting with Chambers proved to be a dud, he told the press that the committee was going to New York to interrogate a "mystery witness" who might break the Bentley story wide open. The newspapers leaped for the "mystery" angle, ignoring the Hiss-Chambers aspect of the inquiry. As it turned out, it was the mystery witness who was the dud.

14

High Drama in a Hearing Room
II

THE EFFECT OF ALGER HISS' POINT-BLANK DENIALS
was electric. Partisans of the dapper young executive glee-
fully shouted "I told you so" from every housetop in Washington. The National Press Club bar was the scene of long
and fervent arguments between the pro-Hiss forces and the
pro-Chambers forces. Cocktail parties from Park Avenue to
Dupont Circle rang with an almost universal condemnation
of the House Un-American Activities Committee. The cry
of "red-baiting" which had been somewhat stilled in the land
since the cold war began was again heard loudly in liberal
circles. And the crypto-Communist smear factories began
working overtime with slanderous rumors on the moral and
sexual habits of Whittaker Chambers.

But while the uninformed and the misinformed traded
conversational gambits, Representative Nixon was prodding
at the two men in an effort to get facts. Though he was a
junior member of the committee and a freshman Congressman, he had in a sense taken the bit in his teeth when he
insisted on further hearings in New York. To all intents and
purposes, it was his show from that moment forward. Two
days after the first Hiss hearing, Nixon — accompanied by
Hébert, McDowell, Stripling, the committee's director of
research Ben Mandel, and several investigators—was meeting

in Room 101 of the United States Courthouse on Foley Square in New York. Nixon's subcommittee met secretly, in executive session, with Chambers. At 10:30 A.M. on Saturday, August 7th, Nixon called the meeting to order and began questioning Chambers.

"Mr. Chambers," Nixon said, "you are aware of the fact that Mr. Alger Hiss appeared before this committee, before the Un-American Activities Committee, in public session and swore that the testimony which had been given by you under oath before this committee was false. The committee is now interested in questioning you further concerning your alleged acquaintanceship with Mr. Alger Hiss so that we can determine what course of action should be followed in this matter in the future.

"Mr. Hiss in his testimony was asked on several occasions whether or not he had ever known or knew a man by the name of Whittaker Chambers. In each instance, he categorically said, 'No.' At what period did you know Mr. Hiss? At what time?"

Chambers. I knew Mr. Hiss, roughly, between the years 1935 and 1937.

Nixon. Do you know him as Mr. Alger Hiss?

Chambers. Yes.

Nixon. Did you happen to see Mr. Hiss' pictures in the newspapers as a result of these recent hearings?

Chambers. Yes; I did.

Nixon. Was that the man you knew as Alger Hiss?

Chambers. Yes; that is the man.

Nixon. You are certain of that?

Chambers. I am completely certain.

Nixon. During the time that you know Mr. Hiss, did he know you as Whittaker Chambers?

Chambers. No. He knew me by the Party name of Carl.

Nixon. Did he ever question the fact that he did not know your last name?

Chambers. Not to me.

Nixon. Why not?

Chambers. Because in the underground Communist Party the

principle of organization is that functionaries . . . shall not be known by their right names but by pseudonyms or Party names.

Nixon. Were you a Party functionary?

Chambers. I was a functionary.

Nixon. This entire group with which you worked in Washington did not know you by your real name?

Chambers. No member of that group knew me by my real name

Nixon. I understand you to say that Mr. Hiss was a member of the Party.

Chambers. Mr. Hiss was a member of the Communist Party.

Nixon. How do you know that?

Chambers. I was told by Mr. Peters.

Nixon. What facts did Mr. Peters give you?

Chambers. Mr. Peters was the head of the entire underground . . . Communist Party in the United States.

Nixon. Do you have any other evidence, any factual evidence, to bear out your claim that Mr. Hiss was a member of the Communist Party?

Chambers. Nothing beyond the fact that he submitted himself for the two or three years that I knew him as a dedicated and disciplined Communist.

Nixon. Did you obtain his Party dues from him?

Chambers. Yes, I did.

Nixon. Over what period of time?

Chambers. Two or three years, as long as I knew him.

Nixon. Party dues from him and his wife?

Chambers. I assume his wife's dues were there . . . Mr. Hiss would simply give me an envelope containing Party dues which I transferred to Peters. I didn't handle the money.

Nixon. How often?

Chambers. Once a month . . . He was rather pious about paying his dues promptly.

Nixon. Is there any other circumstance which would substantiate your allegation that he was a member of the Party?

Chambers. I must also interpolate there that all Communists in the group in which I originally knew him accepted him as a member of the Communist Party.

Nixon. Could this have possibly been an intellectual study group?

Chambers. It was in nowise an intellectual study group. Its primary function was not that of an intellectual study group. I certainly supplied some of that intellectual study business, which was part of my function, but its primary function was to infiltrate the government in the interest of the Communist Party.

Nixon. At that time, incidentally, Mr. Hiss and the other members of this group who were government employees did not have Party cards?

Chambers. No members of that group to my knowledge ever had Party cards, nor do I think that members of that group have Party cards.

Nixon. The reason is—

Chambers. The reason is security, concealment.

Nixon. In other words, people who are in the Communist underground are in fact instructed to deny the fact that they are members of the Communist Party?

Chambers. I was told by Peters that Party registration was kept in Moscow and in some secret file in the United States.

Nixon. Did Mr. Hiss have children?

Chambers. Mr. Hiss had no children of his own.

Nixon. Were there any children living in his home?

Chambers. Mrs. Hiss had a son . . . Timothy Hobson.

Nixon. Approximately how old was he at the time you knew him?

Chambers. It seems to me he was about ten years old.

Nixon. What did you call him?

Chambers. Timmie . . .

Nixon. What name did Mrs. Hiss use in addressing Mr. Hiss?

Chambers. Usually, "Hilly" . . .

Nixon. What nickname, if any, did Mr. Hiss use in addressing his wife?

Chambers. More often "Dilly" and sometimes "Pross." Her name was Priscilla . . .

Nixon. Did you ever spend any time in Hiss' home?

Chambers. Yes.

Nixon. Did you stay overnight?

Chambers. Yes, I stayed overnight . . from time to time.

Nixon. Did you ever stay longer than one day?

Chambers. I have stayed there as long as a week . . . I made that a kind of informal headquarters.

Nixon. I understand that, but what was the financial arrangement?

Chambers. There was no financial arrangement . . .

Nixon. Did the Hisses have any pets?

Chambers. They had, I believe, a cocker spaniel. I have a bad memory for dogs, but as nearly as I can remember it was a cocker spaniel . . . I remember they used to take it up to some kennel. I think out Wisconsin Avenue.

Nixon. They took it to board there?

Chambers. Yes. They made one or two vacation trips to the Eastern Shore of Maryland . . . At those times the dog was kept at the kennel.

Nixon. You state the Hisses had several different houses when you knew them. Could you describe any one of those houses to us?

Chambers. I think so. It seems to me when I first knew him he was living on 28th Street in an apartment house. There were two almost identical apartment houses. It seems to me that is a dead-end street and this was right at the dead-end and certainly it is on the right-hand side as you go up. It also seems to me that the apartment was on the top floor. Now, what was it like inside, the furniture? I can't remember.

Nixon. What was Mr. Hiss' library devoted to?

Chambers. Very nondescript, as I recall.

Nixon. Was there any special dish they served?

Chambers. No. I think you get here into something else. Hiss is a man of great simplicity and a great gentleness and sweetness of character, and they lived with extreme simplicity. I had the impression that the furniture in that house was kind of pulled together from here and there, maybe [they] got it from their mother or something like that, nothing lavish about it whatsoever, quite simple. Their food was in the same pattern, and they cared nothing about food. It was not a primary interest in their lives.

Mandel. Did Mr. Hiss have any hobbies?

Chambers. Yes; he did. They both had the same hobby—amateur ornithologists, bird observers. They used to get up early in the morning and go to Glen Echo, out the canal, to observe birds. I recall once they saw, to their great excitement, a prothonotary warbler.

McDowell. A very rare specimen?

Chambers. I never saw one. I am also fond of birds.

Nixon. Did they have a car?

Chambers. Yes, they did. When I first knew them they had a car. Again I am reasonably sure—I am almost certain—it was a Ford and that it was a roadster. It was black and it was very dilapidated. There is no question about that.

I remember very clearly that it had hand windshield wipers. I remember that because I drove it one rainy day and had to work those windshield wipers by hand.

Nixon. Do you recall any other car?

Chambers. It seems to me in 1936, probably, he got a new Plymouth.

Nixon. Do you recall its type?

Chambers. It was a sedan, a two-seated car.

Mandel. What did he do with the old car?

Chambers. The Communist Party had in Washington a service station—that is, the man in charge or owner of this station was a Communist—or it may have been a car lot.

Nixon. But the owner was a Communist?

Chambers. The owner was a Communist. I never knew who this was or where it was. It was against all the rules of the underground organization for Hiss to do anything with his old car but trade it in, and I think this investigation has proved how right the Communists are in such matters, but Hiss insisted that he wanted the car turned over to the open Party so it could be of use to some poor organizer in the West or somewhere.

Much against my better judgment and much against Peters' better judgment, he finally got us to permit him to do this thing. Peters knew where this lot was, and he either took Hiss there or he gave Hiss the address; and Hiss went there, and to the best of my recollection of his description of that happening, he left the car there and simply went away and the man in charge of the station took care of the rest of it for him. I think the records of that transfer would be traceable.

Nixon. Where was that?

Chambers. In Washington, D. C., I believe; certainly somewhere in the District.

Nixon. Do you recall other cars besides these two?

Chambers. No, I think he had the Plymouth when I broke with the whole business . . .

Nixon. Could you describe Mr. Hiss' physical appearance to us?

Chambers. Mr. Hiss, I should think, is about 5 feet 8 or 9, slender. His eyes are wide apart and blue or grey . . . I think they change . . . In his walk, if you watch him from behind, there is a slight mince sometimes . . . I remember he told me as a small boy he used to take a little wagon—he was a Baltimore boy—and walk up to Druid Hill Park, which was at that time way beyond the civilized center of the city, and fill up bottles with spring water and bring them back and sell it.

Nixon. Do you remember any physical characteristics of the boy?

Chambers. Timmie?

Nixon. Yes.

Chambers. Timmie was a puny little boy, also rather nervous.

Nixon. This is Mrs. Hiss' son?

Chambers. Mrs. Hiss' son by Thayer Hobson.

Nixon. Do you recall where he went to school?

Chambers. Yes; I do. I don't know the name of the school he was attending then, but they told me that Thayer Hobson was paying for his son's education, but they were diverting a large part of that money to the Communist Party.

Nixon. Hiss told you that?

Chambers. Yes, sir.

Nixon. Did he name the Communist Party as the recipient?

Chambers. Certainly.

Hébert. Hobson was paying for the boy's education?

Chambers. Yes; and they took him out of a more expensive school and put him in a less expensive school expressly for that purpose. That is my recollection.

Stripling. Do you remember anything about his hands?

Chambers. Whose?

Stripling. Alger Hiss'.

Chambers. He had rather long delicate fingers. I don't remember anything special.

Mandel. How is it he never wrote anything publicly?

Chambers. Well, he came into the underground like so many Communists did—this was a new stage in the history of American Communists.

Mandel. He was never in the open Communist Party?

Chambers. He was never in the open Communist Party, came in as an underground Communist.

Hébert. Did he have any other brothers or sisters besides Donald?

Chambers. He had one sister, I believe, living with her mother in Baltimore . . .

Stripling. Did he go to church?

Chambers. He was forbidden to go to church.

Stripling. Do you know whether he was a member of a church?

Chambers. I don't know.

Stripling. Do you know if his wife was a member of a church?

Chambers. She came from a Quaker family. Her maiden name was Priscilla Fansler before she was married. She came from the Great Valley, near Paoli, Pennsylvania.

Nixon. Did she tell you anything about her family?

Chambers. No, but she once showed me while we were driving beyond Paoli the road down which their farm lay.

Nixon. You drove with them?

Chambers. Yes.

Nixon. Did you make an affidavit concerning Mr. Alger Hiss?

Chambers. I made a signed statement. I should think it was about 1945. Before that I had reported these facts at least two years before to the FBI and nine years ago to Mr. Berle and mentioned Hiss' name.

Nixon. Nine years ago, are you certain that you did mention Hiss' name to Berle?

Chambers. I certainly mentioned Hiss' name to Berle.

Nixon. Have you seen Hiss since 1938?

Chambers. No; since the time I went to his house and tried to break him away, I have never seen him since.

Nixon. Would you be willing to submit to a lie detector test on this testimony?

Chambers. Yes; if necessary.

Nixon. You have that much confidence?

Chambers. I am telling the truth.

Nixon. Thank you. I have no further questions.

Hébert. I am interested in the houses he lived in. You said several houses. How many houses? Start from the beginning.

Chambers. As well as I can remember, when I first knew him he was living on 28th Street and when I went to see Mr. Berle it struck me as strange, because Mr. Berle was living in Stimson's house on Woodley Road near 28th Street. From there I am not absolutely certain of the order of the houses, but it seems to me he moved to a house in Georgetown—that I know; he moved to a house in Georgetown—but it seems it was on the corner of P Street, but again I can't be absolutely certain of the streets.

Hébert. It was on a corner?

Chambers. Yes; and as I recall, you had to go up steps to get to it.

Mandel. How many rooms were there in that house?

Chambers. I don't know offhand, but I have the impression it was a three-story house. I also think it had a kind of porch in back where people sat.

Then if I have got the order of the houses right, he moved to a house on an up-and-down street, a street that would cross the lettered streets, probably just around the corner from the other house . . .

Hébert. Still in Georgetown?

Chambers. Still in Georgetown. I have forgotten the reason for his moving. That was a smaller house and, as I recall, the dining room was below the level of the ground, one of those basement dining rooms; I think it had a small yard in back. I think he was there when I broke with the Communist Party . . . But I went to see him in the house he later moved to, which was on the other side of Wisconsin Avenue.

Hébert. The last time you saw him when you attempted to persuade him to break from the Party—

Chambers. That was beyond Wisconsin Avenue . . .

"When we took Chambers' testimony in New York on August 7th," Nixon has since said, "it was quite apparent from his detailed answers to the questions that we put to him that either he knew Hiss or that he had made a very thorough study of Hiss' life for the purpose of being able to testify against him. The second theory required, of course, that Chambers must have had a motive. And as Chambers himself put it to me in private conversation, the motive must have been one so strong that it would lead him to destroy his own career in the process."

Nine days elapsed between the Chambers testimony and Alger Hiss' second appearance before the committee. During this period, committee investigators feverishly attempted to corroborate statements of simple fact in Chambers' story. In instance after instance, the answers which Chambers had given were found to be substantially in agreement with the ascertainable facts. During this time, also, Nixon visited the Chambers farm at Westminster twice to see if he might develop other leads for investigation. Though he failed in this, the visits removed such doubts as he still entertained concerning the over-all veracity of Chambers' story.

"I realized in my conversations with him," Nixon told the

authors, "that when he discussed Hiss he was talking about
a man he knew rather than a man whose life he had studied.
On these occasions, I asked Chambers innumerable questions concerning his relationship with Hiss and his answers
to them, were in all cases, forthright and convincing. During
one talk, Chambers remarked about the fact that Mrs. Hiss
was a Quaker. Suddenly he snapped his fingers.

" 'Here's something which may be of interest,' he said,
'Mrs. Hiss usually used the plain speech when she was talking
with Alger in the home.' [The plain speech is the use of *thee*,
instead of *you*, which is part of Quaker custom.] I knew that
Chambers could not have known such intimate details unless
he actually knew Hiss."

The second scene of the second act of the drama was
played in the committee's hearing room in the Old House
Office Building on the afternoon of August 16th. Alger Hiss
arrived with a slight chip on his shoulder, the edges of his
suave manner rubbed off. Stories of Whittaker Chambers'
detailed testimony had percolated out of the committee's
hearing room. They had reached Hiss and worried him. His
friends—and he had many among the mighty—still continued
to rally about him. But among newspapermen in New York
and Washington, the first seeds of doubt as to Hiss' straight-
forwardness had been planted.

Another factor had also begun to condition the public
consciousness, as Hiss and Chambers assumed the proportions of heroic antagonists. Just as Richard Nixon had reasoned, so too did many others. For what possible motive
could a man, occupying a position of responsibility and importance on *Time,* one of America's major magazines, jeopardize his career in an attempt to smear an innocent man?
If Hiss were telling the truth, he was an innocent man whom
Chambers had never even met. If the men had met and
tangled, then Alger Hiss—whether he was a Communist or
not—had lied in denying the relationship. And if he had lied

about knowing Chambers, when to admit it would have been the wiser course—this seemed to hint at dark secrets.

Much of this reasoning was subconscious, particularly among people who had not yet taken sides in the widening controversy. For uppermost in many minds was the impeccable public character of Alger Hiss, his great persuasiveness, his distinguished record, and the loyalty of the exalted friends who surrounded him. To admit that he was a Communist was virtually an impossibility for liberal and conservative alike. To the liberal, it meant admitting that Hearstian charges against Reds in the New Deal had been true. To the conservative, it meant giving up the old stereotype about Communists if so clean-cut an American, so Rotarian a figure, could accept the devious ideology of the Marxists.

Perhaps this was why otherwise reasonable people were willing to resolve the paradox by ascribing to Chambers any and all the sexual and mental maladies which the Communist smear machine devised to discredit their ex-functionary. For if Chambers were mad, as the cocktail-party analysts insisted, there was no problem at all. But even this could not explain why his madness should have fixed itself on Alger Hiss. Perhaps it was with this in mind that Hiss testified as he did that August 16th.

After the formal preliminaries, in which Hiss was assured that the session was secret, Richard Nixon summarized the purpose of the committee: to determine which witness, Chambers or Hiss, was a perjurer.

"The committee," Nixon declared, "has the responsibility to resolve that problem . . . We have come to the conclusion that the individual who has come before the committee and has given false testimony must, if possible, answer for that testimony.

"For that reason we are going this afternoon to go into a number of items which I can assure you have a direct bearing on that problem . . . we want the record to be absolutely

straight on the conflicts between testimony presented by
Mr. Chambers and yourself . . .

"Now, when did you first hear of Whittaker Chambers?"

Hiss. The first time I ever heard of Whittaker Chambers to
the best of my knowledge was when two representatives of the
Federal Bureau of Investigation called at my office at 700 Jackson
Place, I think, in the month of May, 1947, and among the list
of names of people they asked me if I was acquainted with was
the name Whittaker Chambers . . . The name stuck in my
memory at the moment because it sounded like a distinctive and
unusual name, and I said, "No."

Nixon. You testified when you were before this committee that
in 1946 Mr. Byrnes had asked you to talk to him concerning
certain allegations made by members of Congress concerning
Communist affiliations, and at that time you saw Mr. Tamm of
the FBI.

Hiss. I rather think it was Mr. Ladd whom I actually saw . . .

Nixon. Did Mr. Ladd mention the charges to which Mr. Byrnes
had referred?

Hiss. No . . . My recollection is that I was asked very few
questions . . .

Nixon. You didn't hear the name Whittaker Chambers in 1939?

Hiss. No.

Nixon. Whittaker Chambers . . . has testified that he was
known by the name of Carl. Do you recall having known an
individual between the years 1934 and 1937 whose name was
Carl?

Hiss. I do not recall anyone by the name of Carl that could
remotely be connected with the kind of testimony Mr. Chambers
has given . . .

Nixon. Your testimony is then that you knew no person by the
name of Carl between 1934 and 1947?

Hiss. Merely by the name of Carl—absolutely.

Nixon. Do you know J. Peters?

Hiss. I do not.

Nixon. Now, Mr. Hiss, there is some testimony in your previous
record before the committee concerning your acquaintanceship
with Henry Collins . . . do you recall ever having gone to the
apartment of Henry Collins on St. Matthew's Court?

Hiss. I certainly wouldn't want to say I had never been there
because, as I testified before, I have known Mr. Collins since we

were boys. I have visited in his place of abode, whether it happened to be an apartment or a house, and he in mine certainly
since we again knew each other when I was in law school in
1929.

After some perfunctory questioning on Hiss' association
with Lee Pressman, Henry Collins, and others accused by
Chambers of Communist activity, Nixon got to the nub of
the matter. Picking up two pictures of Whittaker Chambers,
he asked Hiss if he could identify them in any way. Hiss was
voluble but hardly forthright.

Hiss. May I recall to the committee the testimony I gave in the
public session when I was shown another photograph of Mr.
Whittaker Chambers . . . I testified then that I could not swear
that I had never seen the man whose picture was shown me.
Actually the face has a certain familiarity. I think I also testified
to that.

It is not according to the photograph a very distinctive or
unusual face. I would like very much to see the individual face
to face. I had hoped that would happen before. I still hope it
will happen today.

I am not prepared to say that I have never seen the man whose
pictures are now shown me. I said that when I was on the stand
when a different picture was shown me. I cannot recall any person with distinctness and definiteness whose picture this is, but
it is not completely unfamiliar . . .

Nixon. Would your answer be any different if this individual
were described to you as one who had stayed overnight in your
house on several occasions?

Hiss. I think, Mr. Nixon, let me say this. In the course of my
service in government from 1933 to 1947 and the previous year
1929-1930 and as a lawyer, I have had a great many people who
have visited in my house.

I have tried to recall in the last week or so anyone who would
know my house whom I wouldn't know very well. There are
many people that have come to my house on social occasions or
on semibusiness occasions whom I probably wouldn't recall at all.

As far as staying overnight in my house is concerned . . . I
can't believe, Mr. Nixon, that anyone could have stayed in my
house when I was there . . . without my being able to recall the

individual; and if this is a picture of anyone, I would find it very difficult to believe that that individual could have stayed in my house when I was there on several occasions overnight and his face not be more familiar than it is . . . I don't want to suggest any innovation in your procedure, but I do want to say specifically that I do hope I will have an opportunity actually to see the individual.

Nixon. It is going to be arranged . . . I might say this, too: that Mr. Chambers, as you may be aware from newspaper accounts, appeared in executive session before us on Saturday . . . At that time we went into the situation with him, showed him pictures of you, and he declared without question you were the man.

For that reason we wanted to be sure that you had the same opportunity before we went into open session. Obviously, as you can see, an open session will involve a considerable amount of publicity, and we were thinking that if that could be avoided, that it should be avoided. It is quite apparent now, even so far as we have gone, that eventually that is going to occur, but I wanted to go into a few more questions here first . . . Your testimony now is that you have never been a member of the Communist Party?

Hiss. Never . . .

Nixon. Or of any underground organization connected with the Communist Party?

Hiss. Not any underground organization connected with the Communist Party.

Nixon. Do you have any children, Mr. Hiss?

Hiss. I have two children.

Nixon. Could you give us their ages?

Hiss. One will be twenty-two—he is my stepson—September 19 next. His name is Timothy Hobson. He has been my stepson since he was three years old. I was married in 1929. I have one other son who is now seven . . . He was born August 5, 1941. His name is Anthony Hiss . . .

Nixon then asked a series of questions about Mrs. Hiss to which Hiss replied:

Hiss. Her name was Priscilla Fansler, her maiden name. Her first marriage was to a Mr. Hobson . . . She was born in Evanston, Illinois, but spent most of her early life outside of Philadelphia . . . on the Main Line not far from [Paoli] . . . Her father was in the insurance business, and he acquired a small place—I suppose it could be called a farm—from which he commuted to his insurance business.

Nixon. Now, is your son Timothy still living with you?

Hiss. No; my son Timothy is now living on his own as an independent, earning male.

Nixon. Where is he at the present time?

Hiss. I think he is on his way back from California at the present time. He was expecting to return on the 16th, and I believe today is the 16th.

Nixon. Is he living in New York?

Hiss. He is living in New York.

Nixon. Could you give us the address of your son in New York?

Hiss. Mr. Nixon, you are asking me about a subject which is one of rather deep concern to me.

Nixon. I understand.

Hiss. My son served in the Navy, V-12. He went in as a very young man. When he left the Navy, he did not wish to go on with college. I did wish him to go on. He had had some college while in the Navy V-12 program. He feels the need of independence of his parents at the present time. He is being what people in Vermont call not only independent, but "indegoddampendent." That is a Vermontism.

I have an address from my son which I am told is not his present address. He has not told me or his mother in the past few months what his present address is. I expect he will do so. This is not the first time in the last year when he has changed address and told me after the event instead of before. I believe he tried to reach me by telephone the night before I testified here, because a phone call came in for me at the hotel from Los Angeles and I couldn't figure who it was and didn't know he was in Los Angeles at the time. I have since learned he was in Los Angeles and I believe he was calling me.

I learned from the same person who knew he was in Los Angeles that he would be back in New York on the 16th. I don't know of my own knowledge. I can give you the address in New York. I don't think you can reach him there.

I wonder if you would mind if I gave you instead the address of his doctor, because he has been consulting a psychiatrist in the last couple of years.

Nixon. Would the doctor know where he is?

Hiss. He will get in touch with the doctor as soon as he returns. The doctor has his other address, and I didn't think it appropriate to ask the doctor for his address. It is Dr. Abram Kardiner. You will understand why this is a very difficult subject to talk about because I love my stepson very deeply. Many people take an exaggerated view of what psychiatric assistance means.

Nixon. Mr. Hiss, could you give us the names of any servants you had during the period 1934 to 1937?

Hiss. Mr. Nixon, may I raise a question at this point?

Nixon. Certainly.

Hiss. You today and the acting chairman publicly have taken the attitude when you have two witnesses, one of whom is a confessed former Communist, the other is me, that you simply have two witnesses saying contradictory things as between whom you find it most difficult to decide on credibility.

Mr. Nixon, I do not know what Mr. Whittaker Chambers testified to your committee last Saturday. It is necessarily my opinion of him, from what he has already said, that I do know that he is not capable of telling the truth or does not desire to, and I honestly have the feeling that details of my personal life which I give honestly can be used to my disadvantage by Chambers then *ex post facto* knowing those facts.

I would request that I hear Mr. Chambers' story of his alleged knowledge of me. Now, I have been cudgeling my brains, particularly on the train coming down this morning, and I had three or four hours on the train between New York and Washington, as to who could have various details about my family. Many people could.

Mr. Nixon, I do not wish to make it easier for anyone who, for whatever motive I cannot understand, is apparently endeavoring to destroy me, to make that man's endeavors any easier. I think in common fairness to my own self-protection and that of my family and my family's good name and my own, I should not be asked to give details which somehow he may hear and then may be able to use as if he knew them before. I would like him to say all he knows about me now. What I have done is public record, where I have lived is public record. Let him tell you all he knows, let that be made public, and then let my record be checked against those facts instead of my being asked, Mr. Nixon, to tell you personal facts about myself which, if they come to his ears, could sound very persuasive to other people that he had known me at some prior time.

Nixon. The questions I have asked you to date, Mr. Hiss, if you will recall them, have all been facts that could be corroborated by third parties. Now . . . the question of who your servants were . . . is purely for the purpose of corroboration and it will be the intention of the committee, if possible, to find one of the servants to see whether or not they will corroborate the story.

Now, the second point I wish to make is this: of course, there is a very serious implication in your statement, and that is that the committee's purpose in questioning you today is to get information with which we can coach Mr. Chambers so that he can more or less build a web around you.

Hiss. Mr. Nixon, I meant no such implication.

But Alger Hiss was still not disposed to let the matter ride. Nor was he ready to give the committee an unequivocal denial or affirmation on the crucial point: did he or did he not know Chambers? Presented again with a photo of Chambers, he slipped into a double negative. "The face," he said, "is definitely not unfamiliar." Then he returned to the argument. "The issue is not whether this man knew me and I don't remember him. The issue is whether . . . I am a member of the Communist Party or ever was, which he has said and I have denied." His extreme caginess, however, strengthened the committee in its resolve to press him. Very subtly, the atmosphere changed. Representative J. Parnell Thomas and several of the other members, who had let the burden of questioning Hiss remain on Richard Nixon's shoulders, lost their hesitancy. Thomas, as chairman, began to lose his former obsequiousness. With a little annoyance in his voice, he asked:

"Mr. Hiss, would you be able to recall a person if that person positively had been in your house three or four times . . . in the past ten years . . . ?"

Hiss. I could not fail to recall such a man if he were now in my presence.

Chairman. You are positive . . .

Hiss. Exactly, if he hadn't had a face lifting . . .

Chairman. Now here is a man who says he spent a week in your house in the last fifteen years. Do you recognize him?

Hiss. I do not recognize him from that picture . . . but I would like to see him.

Chairman. I would like to have a more definite answer . . .

Hiss. I am not prepared to testify on the basis of a photograph. I want to hear the man's voice.

It was probably at this point that Hiss decided to change tactics. Perhaps he realized that, the shield of his dignity shattered, he would have to make a strategic retreat and to prepare the ground for a subsequent recognition of Chambers.

Chairman. If the man himself came in here, you would be able to say yes or no?

Hiss. I think I would, sir.

Chairman. You think you would.

Hiss. I can't believe a man would have changed as much as that, and I am absolutely prepared to testify that nobody, that man or any other man, had any such conversation with me in my house or anywhere else as he has testified to.

Stripling. What conversation did he testify he had with you in your house?

Hiss. Mr. Chambers, according to the record that I read, he said that he came to my house and pled with me to break with the Communist Party, and that I refused, and that I had tears in my eyes, and that the reason I gave was something about the Communist Party line.

Nixon. Mr. Hiss, let me explain this. Mr. Chambers, as indicated, did testify that he spent a week in your house. He also testified to other facts concerning his acquaintanceship with you —alleged facts, I should say—and I want to point out that the committee by getting answers to completely objective questions from you will be in a position to go certainly to third parties and to find out whether or not Mr. Chambers has committed perjury.

Now, on one point it is pretty clear that you have indicated that Mr. Chambers must have committed perjury because he said he spent a week in your house.

Now, these other matters to which Mr. Chambers has testified

involve the same type of testimony. I want to say when Mr.
·Chambers appeared, he was instructed off the record before that
that a material question would subject him to perjury. So consequently, as you see, a matter of membership in the Communist
Party is one thing because that is a matter which might be and
probably would be concealed, but a matter of objective items
concerning his relationship with you, his alleged relationship
with you, can be confirmed in some cases by third parties and
that, frankly, is the purpose of these questions.

Hiss. May I say one thing for the record?

Nixon. Certainly.

Hiss. I have written a name on this pad in front of me of a
person whom I knew in 1933 and 1934 who not only spent some
time in my house but sublet my apartment. That man certainly
spent more than a week, not while I was in the same apartment.
I do not recognize the photographs as possibly being this man.
If I hadn't seen the morning papers with an account of statements that he knew the inside of my house, I don't think I would
even have thought of this name. I want to see Chambers face to
face and see if he can be this individual. I do not want and I
don't think I ought to be asked to testify now that man's name
and everything I can remember about him. I have written the
name on this piece of paper. I have given the name to two friends
of mine before I came in this hearing. I can only repeat, and
perhaps I am being overanxious about the possibility of unauthorized disclosure of testimony, that I don't think in my present
frame of mind that it is fair to my position, my own protection,
that I be asked to put down here on record personal facts about
myself which, if they came to the ears of someone who had for
no reason I can understand a desire to injure me, would assist
him in that endeavor.

Nixon. This man who spent the time in 1933 and 1934 is still
a man with whom you are acquainted?

Hiss. He is not.

Nixon. And where were you living at that time?

Hiss. He was not named Carl and not Whittaker Chambers.

Nixon. Where were you living at that time?

Hiss. I have again written down here to the best of my recollection because I have not checked down with the leases—this is
something I did on the train coming down and the leases are in
my house in New York—where I believed I lived from June of
1933 until September 1943.

Again, Mr. Nixon, if I give the details of where I was, it is going to be very easy if this information gets out for someone to say then *ex post facto* "I saw Hiss in such and such a house." Actually, all he has to do is look it up in the telephone directory and find where it is.

Nixon. Your testimony is that this man you knew in 1933 and 1934 was in one of the houses you lived in?

Hiss. I sublet my apartment to the man whose name I have written down.

Nixon. But you were not there at the same time?

Hiss. I didn't spend a week in the same apartment with him. He did spend a day or two in my house when he moved in.

Nixon. This was the apartment you lived in between 1933 and 1934?

Hiss. It is exactly that apartment—1934 and 1935.

Nixon. Between 1934 and 1935?

Hiss. That is right.

Nixon. When you sublet your apartment? There was no other apartment and you can't testify as to what apartment that was?

Hiss. I can testify to the best of my recollection . . . I want to be sure Mr. Nixon definitely wants me to answer responsively in spite of my plea that I don't think he should ask me.

Stripling. Let the record show, Mr. Hiss, you brought up this *ex post facto* business. Your testimony comes as *ex post facto* testimony to the testimony of Mr. Chambers. He is already on record, and I am not inferring that you might know what he testified to, but certainly the United States attorney's office has several copies.

Hiss. If what I testify to in this committee today through no fault of any official . . . comes to his attention . . . he will again be able to testify *ex post facto* to my testimony of today . . .

Hébert. I will tell you right now and tell you exactly what I told Mr. Chambers . . . Either you or Mr. Chambers is lying . . . And whichever one of you is lying is the greatest actor America has ever produced. Up to a few minutes ago you have been very open, very cooperative. Now, you have hedged . . . Now, as to this inquiry which you make over and over . . . Mr. Chambers did not know or have any indication as to the questions we were going to ask him, and we probed for hours, and we literally ran out of questions . . . He could not have possibly

by the farthest stretch of the imagination prepared himself to
answer because he did not know where the questions were coming from . . .

You say you are in a bad position, but don't you think that
Chambers himself destroys himself if he is proven a liar? What
motive would he have to pitch a $25,000 position as the re-
spected senior editor of *Time* magazine out of the window?

Hiss. Apparently for Chambers to be a confessed former Communist and traitor to his country did not seem to him to be a
blot on his record . . . I am sorry but I cannot but feel to such
an extent that it is difficult for me to control myself that you can
sit there, Mr. Hébert, and say to me casually that you have heard
that man and you have heard me, and you just have no basis for
judging which one is telling the truth. I don't think a judge deter-
mines the credibility of witnesses on that basis.

Hébert. I am trying to tell you that I absolutely have an open
mind . . . The fact that Mr. Chambers is a self-confessed traitor
—and I admit he is—the fact that he is a self-confessed former
member of the Communist Party—which I admit he is—has no
bearing at all on whether the facts that he told—or, rather, the
alleged facts that he told—

Hiss. Has no bearing on his credibility?

Hébert. We have to have people like Chambers or Miss Bentley
to come in and tell us. I am not giving Mr. Chambers any great
credit for his previous life. I am trying to find out if he has re-
formed. Some of the greatest saints in history were pretty bad
before they were saints.

I don't care who gives the facts to me, whether a confessed
liar, thief, or murderer, if it is fact. That is all I am interested in.

Hiss. You have made your position clear. I would like to raise
a separate point. Today as I came down on the train I read a
statement—I think it was in the New York *News*—that a member
of this committee, an unidentified member of this committee, had
told the press man who wrote the article that this committee
believed or had reason to believe from talking to Chambers that
Chambers had personally known Hiss, not that Chambers had
had the conversation which is the issue here, that Chambers had
been in Hiss' home. That is not the issue before this committee
. . . I am not prepared to say on the basis of the photograph—

Hébert. We understand.

Hiss. —that the man, that he is not the man whose name I have written down here. Were I to testify to that, what assurance have I that some member of this committee wouldn't say to the press that Hiss confessed knowing Chambers?

In the first place, I have testified and repeated that I have never known anybody by the name of Whittaker Chambers. I am not prepared to testify I have never seen that man.

Hébert. For the record, the issue is whether Chambers did have the conversation with you, that is admitted, but the only way we can establish the fact that Chambers had the occasion to have the conversation with you is . . . to establish the fact that Hiss knew Chambers and Chambers knew Hiss, and this is very pertinent.

Chairman. Let's go on with this question.

Nixon. If Chambers' credibility on the question of whether he knew you or not is destroyed, obviously you can see that this statement that he had a conversation with you and that you were a member of the Communist Party, which was made on the basis of knowledge, would also be destroyed; and that is exactly the basis upon which this questioning is being conducted, I can assure you, because those are personal matters; whether you are a member of the Communist Party and whether he had a conversation with you individually is something that no third party can corroborate one way or the other. But these other facts are matters which third parties can corroborate. They won't prove, obviously, even if there is agreement on all facts, that this man knew you, but if there is disagreement on these facts, they will prove that Chambers is a perjurer and that is what we are trying to find out. If we prove he is a perjurer on the basis of his testimony now, the necessity of going into the rest of the matter will be obviated.

Hiss. But if he is able through my action to make a more plausible story of having known me or if he has in fact known me under circumstances very different from those he has testified to, I think in my own self-protection I should have a chance to see him. I think that for me to be asked details that may get back, through no fault of yours—I can only repeat if this committee asks me to go on with this specific line of inquiry, I will certainly do it.

The name of the man I brought in—and he may have no relation to this whole nightmare—is a man named George Crosley. I met him when I was working for the Nye committee. He was a writer. He hoped to sell articles to magazines about the munitions industry.

I saw him, as I say, in my office over in the Senate Office Building, with dozens of representatives of the press, people writing books, research people. It was our job to give them appropriate information out of the record, show them what had been put in the record. This fellow was writing a series of articles, according to my best recollection, free lancing, which he hoped to sell to one of the magazines. He was pretty obviously not successful in financial terms, but as far as I know, wasn't actually hard up.

Stripling. What color was his hair?

Hiss. Rather blondish, blonder than any of us here.

Stripling. Was he married?

Hiss. Yes, sir.

Stripling. Any children?

Hiss. One little baby, as I remember it, and the way I know that was the subleasing point. After we had taken the house on P Street and had the apartment on our hands, he one day in the course of casual conversation said he was going to specialize all summer in getting his articles done here in Washington, didn't know what he was going to do, and was thinking of bringing his family.

I said, "You can have my apartment. It is not terribly cool, but it is up in the air near the Wardman Park." He said he had a wife and little baby. The apartment wasn't very expensive, and I think I let him have it at exact cost. My recollection is that he spent several nights in my house because his furniture van was delayed. We left several pieces of furniture behind . . . and we put them up two or three nights in a row, his wife and little baby.

Nixon. His wife and he and little baby did spend several nights in the house with you?

Hiss. This man Crosley; yes.

Nixon. Can you describe his wife?

Hiss. Yes; she was a rather strikingly dark person.

Nixon. How tall was this man, approximately?

Hiss. Shortish.

Nixon. Heavy?

Hiss. Not noticeably. That is why I don't believe it has any direct, but it could have an indirect, bearing.

Nixon. How about his teeth?

Hiss. Very bad teeth. That is one of the things I particularly want to see Chambers about. This man had very bad teeth, did not take care of his teeth.

Nixon. Can you state again just when he first rented the apartment?

Hiss. I think it was about June of 1935 . . . I am sure, from my recollection, that the 28th Street apartment is definitely linked in time with my service on the Nye committee.

Stripling. What kind of automobile did that fellow have?

Hiss. No kind of automobile. I sold him an automobile. I had an old Ford that I threw in with the apartment and had been trying to trade it in and get rid of it. I had an old, old Ford we had kept for sentimental reasons. We got it just before we were married in 1929.

Stripling. Was it a model A or model T?

Hiss. Early A model . . .

Stripling. What color?

Hiss. Dark blue. It wasn't very fancy, but it had a sassy little trunk on the back.

Nixon. You sold that car?

Hiss. I threw it in. He wanted a way to get around and I said, "Fine, I want to get rid of it. I have another car, and we kept it for sentimental reasons, not worth a damn." I let him have it along with the rent.

Nixon. Where did you move from there?

Hiss. Again my best recollection is that we stayed on P Street only one year.

Nixon. Going back to this man, do you know how many days approximately he stayed with you?

Hiss. I don't think more than a couple of times. He may have come back. I can't remember when it was I finally decided it wasn't any use expecting to collect from him, that I had been a sucker and he was a sort of deadbeat; not a bad character, but I think he just was using me for a soft touch.

Nixon. You said before he moved in your apartment he stayed in your house with you and your wife about how many days?

Hiss. I would say a couple of nights. I don't think it was longer than that.

Nixon. A couple of nights?

Hiss. During the delay of the van . . .

Nixon. You don't recall any subjects of conversation during that period?

Hiss. We talked backwards and forwards about the Munitions Committee work. He told various stories that I recall of his escapades . . . He had been everywhere. I remember he told me he had personally participated in laying down the tracks of the street cars in Washington, D. C. . . . right with the road gang laying tracks . . .

Nixon. You gave this Ford car to Crosley? . . .

Hiss. I think I charged him exactly what I was paying for the rent and threw in the car in addition. I don't think I got any compensation . . .

Stripling. What kind of a car did you get [after the Ford]?

Hiss. A Plymouth sedan.

Stripling. Four-door?

Hiss. I think I have always had only two-door.

Stripling. What kind of a bill of sale did you give Crosley?

Hiss. I think I just turned over—in the District you get a certificate of title, I think it is. I think I just simply turned it over to him.

Stripling. Handed it to him?

Hiss. Yes.

Stripling. No evidence of any transfer. Did he record the title?

Hiss. That I haven't any idea. This is a car which had been sitting on the streets in snows for a year or two. I once got a parking fine because I forgot where it was parked. We were using the other car.

Stripling. Do those model Fords have windshield wipers?

Hiss. You had to work them yourself.

Stripling. Hand operated?

Hiss. I think that is the best I can recall.

Nixon. Do you recall the voice of this fellow Crosley?

Hiss. I was trying to recall that this morning. It was a low voice. He speaks with a low and rather dramatic roundness.

Nixon. There are matters which I wish to go into now to which Mr. Chambers has given categorical answers. I am going to put the questions objectively, as you can see. I am not going to try to lead you one way or the other. It will be very helpful as the two records look together to see how accurate he is in this case.

What were the nicknames you and your wife had?

Hiss. My wife, I have always called her Prossy.

Nixon. What does she call you?

Hiss. Well, at one time she called me quite frequently Hill, *h-i-l-l.*

Nixon. What other name?

Hiss. Hilly, with a *y.*

Nixon. What other name did you call her?

Stripling. What did you say?

Hiss. She called me Hill or Hilly. I called her Pross or Prossy almost exclusively. I don't think any other nickname.

Nixon. Did you ever call her Dilly?

Hiss. No; never.

Nixon. Where did you spend your vacations during that period?

Hiss. My son went to a camp over on the Eastern Shore of Maryland . . . When he was at camp we spent two summers, I think, during this period in Chestertown, Maryland.

Nixon. On the Eastern Shore?

Hiss. On the Eastern Shore of Maryland. He went to a camp of friends of ours who lived just outside of Chestertown. For two summers we took a small apartment.

Nixon. Did you have pets?

Hiss. We had a brown cocker spaniel we had before we came to Washington, was with us all during that period, and lived to be so old she died of old age.

Nixon. What did you do with the dog when you went on your vacations, do you recall?

Hiss. I think we took Jenny over on the Eastern Shore. I think we took her on the Eastern Shore when we went there. She did spend some time in the kennels when we were away.

Nixon. You can't recall for sure?

Hiss. We had a very good vet out near Rock Creek Park.

Nixon. Do you know his name?

Hiss. No; but I could easily ascertain it.

Nixon. That is where you would have left the dog, boarded the dog?

Hiss. Yes; at that time I think we left her there.

Nixon. What hobby, if any, do you have, Mr. Hiss?

Hiss. Tennis and amateur ornithology.

Nixon. Is your wife interested in ornithology?

Hiss. I also like to swim and also like to sail. My wife is interested in ornithology, as I am, through my interest. Maybe I am using too big a word to say an ornithologist because I am pretty amateur, but I have been interested in it since I was in Boston. I think anybody who knows me would know that.

McDowell. Did you ever see a prothonotary warbler?

Hiss. I have right here on the Potomac. Do you know that place?

Nixon. Have you ever seen one?

Hiss. Did you see it in the same place?

McDowell. I saw one in Arlington.

Hiss. They come back and nest in those swamps. Beautiful yellow head, a gorgeous bird . . . Henry Collins is an ornithologist . . .

Nixon. As a boy, Mr. Hiss, did you have any particular business that you engaged in?

Hiss. I had two businesses. One of which I was most proud was the delivery of spring water in Baltimore. Baltimore people didn't think they had very good municipal water . . . We had to go to Druid Hill Park . . . where there were good springs and some of us had water routes and we carried water and delivered it to customers . . . I also raised pigeons and sold squabs . . .

Stripling. Did you ever go riding with Crosley in this automobile (you say you gave him)?

Hiss. I think I drove him from the Hill to the apartment.

Stripling. Did you ever take him to Pennsylvania?

Hiss. No. I think I once drove him to New York City when I was going to make a trip to New York City anyway.

Nixon. Was Mrs. Hiss along?

Hiss. That I wouldn't recall. She may have been. I think I may have given him a lift when I went to New York.

Stripling. Did you go to Paoli?

Hiss. If Mrs. Hiss was along, yes.

Chairman. Route No. 202?

Hiss. Route 202 goes through that part of Pennsylvania, and that is the route we would take.

Nixon. Did you ever drive to Baltimore with Crosley?

Hiss. I don't recall it. I think he moved to Baltimore from here, as a matter of fact, but I don't recall that I ever drove him.

Nixon. How did you know that?

Hiss. I think he told me when he was pulling out. He was in my apartment until the lease expired in September.

Nixon. What year?

Hiss. I think it was September, 1935, and I think I saw him several times after that, and I think he had told me he moved from here to Baltimore.

Nixon. Even though he didn't pay his rent you saw him several times?

Hiss. He was about to pay it and was going to sell his articles. He gave me a payment on account once. He brought a rug over which he said some wealthy patron gave him. I have still got the damned thing.

Nixon. Did you ever give him anything?

Hiss. Never anything but a couple of loans; never got paid back.

Nixon. Have you ever heard of him since 1935?

Hiss. No; never thought of him again until this morning on the train.

Stripling. You wouldn't say positively George Crosley and this person are the same?

Hiss. Not positively.

Stripling. You would not say positively?

Hiss. I think they are not. That would be my best impression from the photographs.

In thinking this morning what I thought was that Crosley is the only person I know who has been in my house who knows the lay-out of any house or apartment I lived in.

Nixon. He knows the lay-out of only one house?

Hiss. Only one house.

Nixon. Mr. Chambers, of course, as I say, was very convincing in his testimony and you certainly are very convincing in yours.

Now, frankly, the committee has a difficult problem here and I wonder if under the circumstances for the assistance of the committee in this matter you would be willing to take a lie-detector test on this.

I might say before you answer, so you will have full knowledge of what the committee knows, Mr. Chambers was asked that question and said he would take a lie-detector test.

Alger Hiss had expected this question. He had been told that Chambers had shown no hesitation whatsoever in agreeing to take a lie-detector test. And he knew that to refuse would prejudice his case—with the committee and with the public.

"Shall I answer now?" he asked Mr. Nixon. The young Californian told him to go ahead. Hiss' answer was oblique; he discussed the pros and cons of the lie detector, questioned its value as a scientific determinant of truth. Then, still ducking the answer, he continued to talk:

Hiss. I would like to know who the administrator is, whether this is being done by someone in the Bureau who is an expert or an individual so-called expert, what kind of a test it is. In other words, I don't think I ought to, on the basis of the advice I have had, to try to answer it out of hand until I know and you know.

I would be surprised if this committee would want to rely on something that isn't scientific.

Nixon. Certainly. In answer to your question, the committee has contacted Mr. Leonardo Keeler . . . probably the outstanding man in the country. The test Mr. Keeler has is the polygraph machine. It is the only one, I think, that has any broad acceptance at all.

Finally, Hiss laid it on the line. He could not agree then and there to take the test, but he would take the matter under advisement and give the committee his answer in several days. From there on in, the testimony rambled back and forth over ground already covered. Still giving with one hand and taking with the other, Hiss continued to build up his character of the "deadbeat" George Crosley, while refusing to state categorically that Crosley was Chambers. When Nixon asked him if the matter of the unpaid rent for the Hiss apartment would be sufficient motive for Chambers' testimony against Hiss, he answered:

"No, that is why I can't believe it was the same man. I can't imagine a normal man holding a grudge because somebody had stopped being a sucker."

It was at this point that Robert Stripling casually and ineptly shifted to a question which, though valueless in a court of law, was extremely pertinent. Was it reasonable to believe that so acute a man as Alger Hiss could have been closely associated with avowed Communists and pro-Communists as Henry Collins, John Abt, and Lee Pressman without having the slightest idea of their politics? A trial lawyer could have made much of this question, but Stripling immediately vitiated the effectiveness of his sally by drawing in other, extraneous issues. And like the lawyer that he was, Hiss seized on the minor points and so demolished them that the major question was forgotten. As a result, the second act of the great drama petered out.

But though it was obscured in desultory questioning, including many assurances by the committee that Hiss would be furnished a transcript of his testimony, the big curtain line was there: Alger Hiss and Whittaker Chambers would be brought face to face.

15

The Great Confrontation

THE STAGE WAS NOW SET FOR THE GREAT THIRD ACT OF
the House committee's dramatic hearings. Fortified by Alger
Hiss' lame recollection that he had probably known Whittaker Chambers as George Crosley, Representative Nixon and
the other members of the committee decided to move
quickly. Almost immediately after Hiss' appearance, the committee resolved to go ahead with the long-promised confrontation. Representative McDowell wired Hiss asking him
to appear before a subcommittee at the Hotel Commodore
the following day. Reluctantly, Hiss agreed. A similar wire
was sent to Chambers, and he indicated his willingness.

But Chambers misunderstood one thing; he thought that
this hearing was to take place in Washington. On the afternoon of August 17th, he turned up on the steps of the Old
House Office Building. By sheer accident, he ran into Nixon,
McDowell, Stripling, J. Parnell Thomas, and other members
of the committee staff just as they were leaving for New York.

This created a serious problem.

Alger Hiss had charged that the committee was in cahoots
with Chambers, that it had been leaking secret testimony to
Chambers in order to damage Hiss. If Chambers were seen
riding up from Washington with committee members, it
might well be taken as evidence that Hiss' charges were true.
The committee was on the receiving end of bludgeoning
criticism from the Truman Administration and from large

segments of the press. Touchily, the subcommittee agreed that it would be wiser for Chambers to ride in another car. Throughout the trip, therefore, Chambers sat with W. P. Bannister, the committee's stenographic reporter.

At 5:35 P.M., in Room 1400 of the Hotel Commodore, the great confrontation scene began. Accompanied by a friend, a highly perturbed Alger Hiss made his greetings. After being sworn, he sat down in an easy chair with his back to the entrance of the suite. As usual, Richard Nixon carried the ball for the committee. His first words were addressed to Hiss.

Nixon. It is quite apparent at this stage in the testimony, as you indicated yesterday, that the case is dependent upon the question of identity. We have attempted to establish the identity through photographs of Mr. Chambers and that has been inadequate for that purpose.

Today, we thought that since you had in your testimony raised the possibility of a third party who might be involved in this case in some way and had described him at some length to the committee that it would be well to, at the earliest possible time, determine whether the third party is different from the two parties or the same one, and so consequently we have asked Mr. Chambers to be in New York at the same time so that you can have the opportunity to see him and make up your own mind on that point . . .

Hiss. I would like the record to show that on my way downtown from my uptown office, I learned from the press of the death of Harry White, which came as a great shock to me, and I am not sure that I feel in the best possible mood for testimony. I do not for a moment want to miss the opportunity of seeing Mr. Chambers. I merely wanted the record to show that.

I would like to make one further comment. Yesterday, I think I witnessed—in any event, I was told that those in the room were going to take an oath of secrecy. I made some comments before I answered certain questions of Mr. Nixon which I had not intended as a reflection on the committee but which some members of the committee thought implied that I was referring merely to the possibility of leakage of information. I would like this record to show at this stage that the first thing I saw in the morning paper, the *Herald Tribune,* was a statement that the committee yesterday had asked me if I would submit to a lie-detector test . . . There were other statements in the press which I read coming down which referred to other bits of my testimony which could only have come from the committee. They did not come from me . . .

McDowell. The Chair would like to say something. I, too, was greatly disturbed when I read the morning paper. Obviously, there was a leak, because the story that appeared in the various papers I read was part of the activities of yesterday afternoon. I have no idea how this story got out. In my own case, I very carefully guarded myself last night, saw and talked to no one except my wife in Pittsburgh. It is regrettable and unfortunate . . .

Nixon. Mr. Russell, will you bring Mr. Chambers in?

Louis J. Russell, the committee investigator, left the room via the bedroom of the suite. When he returned with Chambers, he walked through the front door. Hiss, who had his back to the entrance, did not move or turn his head. His face remained expressionless. Chambers walked around Hiss' chair and sat down on a divan opposite Hiss. The two men were face to face at last.

Nixon. Mr. Chambers, will you please stand? And will you please stand, Mr. Hiss? Mr. Hiss, the man standing here is Mr. Whittaker Chambers. I ask you now if you have ever known that man before?

Hiss. May I ask him to speak? Will you ask him to say something?

Nixon. Yes. Mr. Chambers, will you tell us your name and your business?

Chambers. My name is Whittaker Chambers. (*At this point, Mr. Hiss walked in the direction of Mr. Chambers.*)

Hiss. Would you mind opening your mouth wider?

Chambers. My name is Whittaker Chambers.

Hiss. I said, would you open your mouth? You know what I am referring to, Mr. Nixon. Will you go on talking?

Chambers. I am senior editor of *Time* magazine.

Hiss. May I ask whether his voice, when he testified before, was comparable to this?

Nixon. His voice?

Hiss. Or did he talk a little more in a lower key?

McDowell. I would say it is about the same now as we have heard.

Hiss. Would you ask him to talk a little more?

Nixon. Read something, Mr. Chambers. I will let you read from . . .

Hiss. I think he is George Crosley, but I would like to hear him talk a little longer.

McDowell. Mr. Chambers, if you would be more comfortable, you may sit down.

Hiss. Are you George Crosley?

Chambers. Not to my knowledge. You are Alger Hiss, I believe.

Hiss. I certainly am.

Chambers. That was my recollection . . . [reading from *Newsweek*]. Since June . . .

Nixon (interposing). Just one moment. Since some repartee goes on between these two people, I think Mr. Chambers should be sworn.

Hiss. That is a good idea.

McDowell. You do solemnly swear, sir, that the testimony you shall give this committee will be the truth, the whole truth, and nothing but the truth, so help you God?

Chambers. I do.

Nixon. Mr. Hiss, may I say something? I suggested that he be sworn, and when I say something like that I want no interruptions from you.

Hiss. Mr. Nixon, in view of what happened yesterday, I think there is no occasion for you to use that tone of voice in speaking to me, and I hope the record will show what I have just said.

Nixon. The record shows everything that is being said here today.

Stripling. You were going to read.

Chambers (reading from *Newsweek* magazine). Tobin for Labor. Since June, Harry S. Truman had been peddling the labor secretaryship left vacant by Lewis B. Schwellenbach's death in hope of gaining the maximum political advantage from the appointment.

Hiss. May I interrupt?

McDowell. Yes.

Hiss. The voice sounds a little less resonant than the voice that I recall of the man I knew as George Crosley. The teeth look to me as though either they have been improved upon or that there has been considerable dental work done since I knew George Crosley, which was some years ago.

I believe I am not prepared without further checking to take an absolute oath that he must be George Crosley.

Nixon. May I ask a question of Mr. Chambers?

Hiss. I would like to ask Mr. Chambers, if I may.

Nixon. I will ask the questions at this time. Mr. Chambers, have you had any dental work since 1934 of a substantial nature?

Chambers. Yes, I have.

Nixon. What type of dental work?

Chambers. I have had some extractions and a plate.

Nixon. Have you had any dental work in the front of your mouth?

Chambers. Yes.

Hiss. That testimony of Mr. Chambers, if it can be believed, would tend to substantiate my feeling that he represented himself to me in 1934 or 1935 or thereabout as George Crosley, a free-lance writer of articles for magazines . . .

Nixon. Can you describe the condition of your teeth in 1934?

Chambers. Yes. They were in very bad shape.

Nixon. The front teeth were?

Chambers. Yes, I think so.

Hiss. Mr. Chairman . . . I would like a few more questions asked. I didn't intend to say anything about this, because I feel very strongly that he is Crosley, but he looks very different in girth and in other appearances—hair, forehead, and so on, particularly the jowls.

Nixon. What was Crosley's wife's name?

Hiss. I don't think I recall.

Nixon. You did testify that she on several occasions was in your home overnight.

Hiss. That is right.

Nixon. And that you have ridden with her in a car as well as with him.

Hiss. I don't recall testifying to that.

Nixon. Do you testify she didn't?

Hiss. I don't recall.

Nixon. But she did stay overnight in your home on several occasions?

Hiss. She did. I don't think I said several occasions.

Nixon. How many times did you say?

Hiss. My recollection is that at the time George Crosley sub-rented my apartment on 29th [sic] Street his wife and he and infant spent two or three or four consecutive nights in my house because the van had not come with their furniture, and we left only certain pieces of furniture behind to accommodate them.

Nixon. In regard to the rental agreement that was entered into with Mr. Crosley, do you recall approximately the rental that was charged and agreed to?

Hiss. My recollection is that I said I would be glad to let him have the apartment for the cost to me. It was a rather moderate rental.

Nixon. Could you say within certain limits?

Hiss. My recollection—I can't remember just what I paid for the apartment that far back—my recollection is it was under $75 a month. It was a very reasonable rental. That is one of the reasons I had taken it.

Nixon. For how long was this rental agreement?

Hiss. . . . Sometime in the spring, according to my recollection, of 1934.

Nixon. Or did you say 1935?

Hiss. That is my best recollection.

Nixon. You are testifying, as I understand, that the lease to Mr. Crosley was for the three summer months approximately.

Hiss. As long as he wanted to stay during the summer period while I still had the use of that apartment . . .

Nixon. Then the total rental value for the period was, if it were for two months; it would have been approximately $150; three months, approximately $225.

Hiss. It was contingent upon the number of months he would occupy the remaining unexpired term under my lease.

Nixon. Did he ever pay any rent at all?

Hiss. My recollection is that he paid no cash, that he once paid in kind.

Nixon. No cash at all?

Hiss. He also borrowed some cash in addition.

Nixon. How much did he borrow, approximately?

Hiss. I don't think it got over $35 or $40 in different trans-actions, not all at once. I hope it didn't.

Nixon. You had known Mr. Crosley, your testimony is, for about eight months before you entered into this agreement?

Hiss. Five or six months.

Nixon. Then you had had several conversations with him during that period?

Hiss. I think I must have seen him as often as I did any other newspaperman who was particularly interested. I think I saw him ten or eleven times.

Nixon. Never saw him socially during that period?

Hiss. Never saw him socially.

Nixon. And then there was some conversation about a car. What was that?

Hiss. There was. Mr. Crosley said that while he was in Washington he wondered if he could get a rented car or something, because he would like to have it while his family were with him, get out week-ends, something like that.

I said, "You came to just the right place. I would be very glad to throw a car in because I have been trying to get rid of an old car which we have kept solely for sentimental reasons which we couldn't get anything on for trade-in or sale." I would be very glad to let him have the car because we wanted somebody to make real use of it. We had had it sitting on the city streets because we had a new one.

Nixon. It was a '29 Ford?

Hiss. One of the first model A Fords.

Nixon. The year of this transaction would be 1935?

Hiss. That would be my best recollection.

Nixon. A six-year-old Ford?

Hiss. That is right.

Nixon. You just gave him the car with this $225 rental?

Hiss. As part of the total contract. That is my best recollection.

Nixon. Then before he moved into the apartment I understand that you allowed him and his wife to stay with you in your home?

Hiss. My recollection of that—and this is repetitious—

Nixon. We are repeating it for his benefit as well as to see if he can recall the incident.

Hiss. I am glad he has no other way of finding out about it, Mr. Nixon.

My recollection on that point is that . . . we put them up the way one would be apt to try to be helpful to people you were subletting. You develop a kind of pseudo-friendliness over a transaction of that kind.

Mr. Crosley, his wife, and infant were put up in my house for two or three days while the moving van was coming; it may have been four, may have been two. It was more than one night. I imagine my wife would testify it seemed even longer than that.

Nixon. Were those the only two apartments in which Mr. Crosley saw you?

Hiss. To the best of my knowledge, yes.

Nixon. When did you see him after that period of the rental agreement?

Hiss. I saw him several times in the fall of 1935, as I recall it.

Nixon. What were the occasions of those visits?

Hiss. Some occasions—he would call—no; I think he came to my house once or twice after that because of this establishment of a personal relationship. I remember on one occasion he came and brought me a rug which was part payment. He hadn't yet sold his articles, he was hard up, he was going to make payment. My recollection is I never got paid a single red cent in currency.

Nixon. What kind of a rug was it?

Hiss. It was about the color of this rug [*indicating rug on floor*]. I still have it. A fairly sizable rug. My recollection is Mr. Crosley said some wealthy patron had bestowed it upon him as a gift.

Nixon. On these other occasions on which Mr. Crosley stayed with you; did he ever stay overnight?

Hiss. I wouldn't be sure of my recollection. It is quite possible he may have said that he couldn't get a reservation. Mr. Crosley was apparently in the habit of having difficulties. He may very well have said that he couldn't get a hotel reservation, could I put him up. Mr. Crosley, not being someone who paid his debts, may very well have added to his obligations in that way. That I wouldn't be sure of.

Nixon. You testified on one occasion you took him on a trip, as I understand it, ferried him to New York.

Hiss. My recollection is that on one occasion when my wife and I were going to drive to New York in any event, Mr. Crosley asked for a ride. I may have mentioned when I was talking to him that I was going to New York, or he may have said he was going to New York, and I said so was I.

Nixon. Was that after the time of this rental agreement?

Hiss. I am afraid I can't recall.

Nixon. No further questions of Mr. Hiss at this time.

Stripling. Mr. Hiss, you say that person you knew as George Crosley, the one feature which you must have to check on to identify him is the dentures.

Hiss. May I answer that my own way rather than just "yes" or "no"?

Stripling. Well, now, I would like to preface whatever you are going to say by what I say first.

I certainly gathered the impression when Mr. Chambers walked in this room and you walked over and examined him and asked him to open his mouth, that you were basing your identification purely on what his upper teeth might have looked like.

Now, here is a person that you knew for several months at least. You knew him so well that he was a guest in your home.

Hiss. Would you . . .

Stripling. I would like to complete my statement—that he was a guest in your home, that you gave him an old Ford automobile, and permitted him to use or you leased him your apartment, and in this, a very important confrontation, the only thing that you have to check on is this denture; is that correct?

There is nothing else about this man's features which you could definitely say, "This is the man I knew as George Crosley," that you have to rely entirely on this denture; is that your position?

Hiss. Is your preface through? My answer to the question you have asked is this:

From the time on Wednesday, August 4, 1948, when I was able to get hold of newspapers containing photographs of one Whittake Chambers, I was struck by a certain familiarity in features. When I testified on August 5th and was shown a photograph by you, Mr. Stripling, there was again some familiarity of features. I could not be sure that I had never seen the person whose photograph you showed me. I said I would want to see the person.

The photographs are rather good photographs of Whittaker Chambers as I see Whittaker Chambers today. I am not given on important occasions to snap judgments or simple, easy statements. I am confident that George Crosley had notably bad teeth. I would not call George Crosley a guest in my house. I have explained the circumstances. If you choose to call him a guest, that is your affair.

Stripling. I am willing to strike the word guest. He was in your house.

Hiss. I saw him at the time I was seeing hundreds of people. Since then I have seen thousands of people. He meant nothing to me except as one I saw under the circumstances I have described.

My recollection of George Crosley, if this man had said he was

George Crosley, I would have no difficulty in identification. He denied it right here.

I would like and asked earlier in this hearing if I could ask some further questions to help in identification. I was denied that.

Stripling. I think you should be permitted—

Hiss. I was denied that right. I am not, therefore, able to take an oath that this man is George Crosley. I have been testifying about George Crosley. Whether he and this man are the same or whether he has means of getting information from George Crosley about my house, I do not know. He may have had his face lifted.

Stripling. The witness says he was denied the right to ask this witness questions. I believe the record will show you stated "at this time." I think he should be permitted to ask the witness questions now or any other motion should be granted which will permit him to determine whether or not this is the individual to whom he is referring.

Hiss. Right. I would be very happy if I could pursue that. Do I have the Chair's permission?

McDowell. The Chair will agree to that.

Hiss. Do I have Mr. Nixon's permission?

Nixon. Yes.

McDowell. Here is a very difficult situation.

Nixon. The only suggestion I would make in fairness to Mr. Chambers is that he should also be given the opportunity to ask Mr. Hiss any questions.

McDowell. Of course.

Hiss. I will welcome that.

Nixon. Mr. Chambers, do you have any objection?

Chambers. No.

Hiss. Did you ever go under the name of George Crosley?

Chambers. Not to my knowledge.

Hiss. Did you ever sublet an apartment on 29th Street from me?

Chambers. No; I did not.

Hiss. You did not?

Chambers. No.

Hiss. Did you ever spend any time with your wife and child in an apartment on 29th Street in Washington when I was not there because I and my family were living on P Street?

Chambers. I most certainly did.

Hiss. You did or did not?

Chambers. I did.

Hiss. Would you tell me how you reconcile your negative answers with this affirmative answer?

Chambers. Very easily, Alger. I was a Communist and you were a Communist.

Hiss. Would you be responsive and continue with your answer?

Chambers. I do not think it is needed.

Hiss. That is the answer.

Nixon. I will help you with the answer, Mr. Hiss. The question, Mr. Chambers, is, as I understand it, that Mr. Hiss cannot understand how you would deny that you were George Crosley and yet admit that you spent time in his apartment. Now would you explain the circumstances? I don't want to put that until Mr. Hiss agrees that is one of his questions.

Hiss. You have the privilege of asking any questions you want. I think that is an accurate phrasing.

Nixon. Go ahead.

Chambers. As I have testified before, I came to Washington as a Communist functionary, a functionary of the American Communist Party. I was connected with the underground group of which Mr. Hiss was a member. Mr. Hiss and I became friends. To the best of my knowledge, Mr. Hiss himself suggested that I go there, and I accepted gratefully.

Hiss. Mr. Chairman.

Nixon. Just a moment. How long did you stay there?

Chambers. My recollection was about three weeks. It may have been longer. I brought no furniture, I might add.

Hiss. Mr. Chairman, I don't need to ask Mr. Whittaker Chambers any more questions. I am now perfectly prepared to identify this man as George Crosley . . .

Stripling. You will identify him positively now?

Hiss. I will on the basis of what he has just said * positively identify him without further questioning as George Crosley.

Nixon. Mr. Hiss, another point that I want to be clear on. Mr. Chambers said he was a Communist and that you were a Communist.

Hiss. I heard him.

Nixon. Will you tell the committee whether or not during this period of time that you knew him, which included periods of three nights, or two or three nights, in which he stayed overnight

---

* Of all the people who acknowledged having known Chambers, *Hiss was the only one* who insisted he could not recognize him.

and one trip to New York, from any conversation you ever had, had you any idea that he might be a Communist?

Hiss. I certainly didn't.

Nixon. You never discussed politics?

Hiss. Oh, as far as I recall his conversations—and I may be confusing them with a lot of other conversations that went on in 1934 and 1935—politics were discussed quite frequently. May I just state for the record that it was not the habit in Washington in those days, when particularly if a member of the press called on you, to ask him before you had further conversation whether or not he was a Communist. It was a quite different atmosphere in Washington then than today.

I had no reason to suspect George Crosley of being a Communist. It never occurred to me that he might be or whether that was of any significance to me if he was. He was a press representative and it was my duty to give him information, as I did any other member of the press. It was to the interest of the committee investigating the munitions industry, as its members and we of its staff saw it, to furnish guidance and information to people who were popularizing and writing about its work.

I would like to say that to come here and discover that the ass under the lion's skin is Crosley, I don't know why your committee didn't pursue this careful method of interrogataion at an earlier date before all the publicity. You told me yesterday you didn't know he was going to mention my name, although a lot of people now tell me that the press did know it in advance. They were apparently more effective in getting information than the committee itself. That is all I have to say now.

McDowell. Well, now, Mr. Hiss, you positively identify—

Hiss. Positively on the basis of his own statement that he was in my apartment at the time when I saw he was there. I have no further question at all. If he had lost both eyes and taken his nose off, I would be sure.

McDowell. Then, your identification of George Crosley is complete?

Hiss. Yes, as far as I am concerned, on his own testimony.

McDowell. Mr. Chambers, is this the man, Alger Hiss, who was also a member of the Communist Party at whose home you stayed?

Nixon. According to your testimony.

McDowell. You make the identification positive?

Chambers. Positive identification.

Hiss had begun his testimony with relative calm. But as the hearing progressed, he had grown sharper and sharper with the committee, snapping out his answers in a manner hardly consistent with the charm and tactfulness of his approach in the earlier hearings. He was no longer the suave, young diplomat, generously aiding the committee in arriving at the true facts. Instead, he was out to prove himself an innocent victim. Except for the accusation that Hiss was a Communist, Chambers had spoken of him with respect and affection. Hiss had countered by attempting to destroy Chambers' character in any way possible—to make him out a cheap "deadbeat" who sponged off people.

Now, white-faced with anger, Hiss got up and walked in the direction of Chambers.

"May I say for the record at this point," he burst out, "that I would like to invite Mr. Whittaker Chambers to make those same statements out of the presence of this committee without their being privileged for suit for libel?" Looming threateningly over Chambers, he said vehemently, "I challenge you to do it, and I hope you will do it damned quickly." He was now so close to Chambers that Russell stepped forward to restrain him.

"I am not going to touch him," he said violently to the investigator. "You are touching me."

Chambers sat quietly, imperturbably, through the whole outburst.

Russell. Please sit down, Mr. Hiss.
Hiss. I will sit down when the chairman asks me.
Russell. I want no disturbance.
Hiss. I don't . . .
McDowell. Sit down, please.
Hiss. You know who started this . . . Mr. Chairman, would you be good enough to ask Mr. Chambers for the record his response to the challenge that I have just made to him?
McDowell. That has nothing to do with the pertinency of the matter that the committee is investigating, and I don't feel I should.

Hiss. I thought the committee was interested in ascertaining truth . . .

Stripling. I am concerned with the statement you made before the committee of Congress in the presence of quite a few hundred people that you didn't even know this person. You led the public and press to believe you didn't know such a person.

Hiss. Will you show where that is?

Stripling. Yes . . . Reading here from your statement, I have just started in on it, but here is one sentence:

"So far as I know, I have never laid eyes on him, and I should like to have the opportunity to do so."

Hiss. That is correct. I did not say that I have never seen this man. I said, so far as I know I have never seen Whittaker Chambers . . .

Stripling. You are fully aware that the public was led to believe that you had never seen, heard, or laid eyes upon an individual who is this individual, and now you do know him.

Hiss. Mr. Stripling, you are stating your impression of public impression.

Stripling. Absolutely . . .

Nixon. You never knew this man under the name of Carl?

Hiss. I did not.

Nixon. You never paid this man any money for Communist Party dues?

Hiss. I certainly did not.

Nixon. This is the man you gave the car to?

Hiss. The car?

Nixon. Yes.

Hiss. C-a-r—yes.

Chambers. May I ask a question?

Nixon. Yes.

Chambers. Did you ever pay dues to J. Peters?

Hiss. I certainly did not.

Chambers. To Henry Collins?

Hiss. I certainly did not; not even for the Audubon Society did I pay dues to Henry Collins.

Nixon. Did you ever discuss your hobby, ornithology, with this man?

Hiss. I may very likely have. My house has pictures very similar to that [*indicating picture on wall*]. This is an appropriate hearing room.

McDowell. It was a complete coincidence.

Hiss. Anyone who had ever been in my house would remark that I had an interest in birds.

Nixon. Do you know if this man you knew as Crosley was an ornithologist?

Hiss. Not to my knowledge.

Nixon. You have never given Crosley anything you recall besides the car?

Hiss. I have no such recollection. I don't consider I gave him the car, but threw it in with the whole transaction.

McDowell. Mr. Hiss, did you ever have a dinner or a meal with George Crosley?

Hiss. I think we fed him when he was in the house for a couple of days. That is my custom with people staying under my roof.

McDowell. You are not sure?

Hiss. I know I have had lunch with him, because it was my practice, and still is, that if someone wants to talk to me about a matter that requires relatively lengthy discussion, a luncheon discussion has a termination. If they come to see you in your office, it is not quite so easy to terminate it at your own convenience.

McDowell. Did this fellow have any characteristics or habits that you can recall now?

Hiss. No; not of significance, except his bad teeth.

McDowell. Would you know whether—aside from his bad teeth, would you know whether he was a heavy drinker, or modest drinker, or non-drinker?

Hiss. I have no information about that.

McDowell. Did you ever take a walk with him?

Hiss. That I couldn't be sure. I certainly must have walked to lunch if we went to lunch from the Senate Office Building. We had to walk quite a distance to get to any restaurant from the Senate Office Building.

McDowell. It would appear to me, Mr. Hiss, of all the newspapermen that you were in contact in your highly important jobs with the Nye committee that you must have formed some sort of an affection for this man to go through all of the things that you did to try to occupy your home, take over your lease, and giving him an automobile . . .

Stripling. Mr. Nixon, did you ask the witness whether or not George Crosley ever wrote an article for *American Magazine?*

Nixon. Yes. He testified to that yesterday that it was your understanding that one of the magazines for which he wrote was *American.* Am I correct in this?

Hiss. Yes; that was my understanding from him.

Stripling. Did you ever see any article which appeared in *American Magazine*?

Hiss. I never did. I noticed Mr. Crosley was not marketing his articles with the success he had expected.

Stripling. Mr. Chambers, did you ever write for *American Magazine*?

Chambers. No, I never did.

Stripling. You never had any articles published in *American Magazine*?

Chambers. Not at all.

Stripling. Did you ever represent yourself as a free-lance writer writing articles for *American Magazine*?

Chambers. No, I never did.

McDowell. Mr. Hiss, might I say it is my custom—I too have almost constant contact with newspapermen and writers and students as you described a good bit ago—it has been my custom, although not the rule or law, that I always find out who they are writing for, who they represent, who they work for, if they are free-lance writers whether they have written anything.

Can you recall ever finding out any particular thing that Mr. Chambers or Mr. Crosley had written?

Hiss. No; I didn't, Mr. McDowell.

McDowell. Or where his things had been published other than *American Magazine*? . . .

Hiss. I never saw anything he produced. He was a singularly unproductive writer . . .

Nixon. Do you have anything to say for the record?

Chambers. I don't think so.

Hiss. I wouldn't think so. I am not surprised.

Chambers. If you want to question me, I would be glad to answer any questions.

Nixon. I suggest we adjourn . . .

Stripling. Did you ever pay any Communist Party dues to Mr. Whittaker Chambers, whom you now have identified as George Crosley?

Hiss. I did not and I did not pay Communist Party dues to anybody, not being a member of the Communist Party.

Chambers. May I ask a question?

Nixon. You may.

Chambers. Did you ever meet me in the company of Harold Ware?

Hiss. I did not.
Chambers. Or J. Peters?
Hiss. I did not . . .
Chairman. Any more questions to ask of Mr. Hiss?
Nixon. I have nothing.
Chairman. That is all. Thank you very much.
Hiss. I don't reciprocate. '
Chairman. Italicize that in the record.
Hiss. I wish you would.

Reviewing the printed record of this first encounter for the February, 1949, *Progressive*, James A. Wechsler touched on many points with remarkable intuition. "When it is over and when we finally glimpse the total truth," he wrote, "I suspect that the hotel-room confrontation . . . will make even more dramatic reading than it does now; and that re-reading the record of this encounter one will pause at several places, thinking: 'Of course, that was it. I should have seen it all there.'" Then, though he had never discussed the case with Hiss or Chambers, Wechsler put his finger unerringly on their opposing motivations, the inner workings of their minds:

"There are those who believe that Chambers was in effect imploring Hiss to acknowledge the degree of guilt already ascribed to him—mere association with the Communist ring," Wechsler wrote, modestly ascribing to others what few perceived, "so that it would not be necessary to unfold the papers which presumably damaged both men, transforming the case from the level of Communist affiliation to the more desolate plane of espionage. According to this view, Hiss misinterpreted Chambers' initial failure to produce the documents as assurance that he never would; and Chambers was equally confident that Hiss, correctly understanding his gesture, would never sue for libel."

Alger Hiss did not know it then, but the committee finally had enough direct testimony in its hands to place him dangling from the hook. Merely by letting Hiss talk, they had got from him the very facts and contradictions which his astute legal mind had refused to furnish in earlier appearances before the committee. It was a feat of major proportions, for it split the case wide open.

Actually, what the committee had done was simple: it had merely let Hiss know that Chambers had made some damaging disclosures. In order to clear himself, Hiss had tried to pattern an innocent story to guilty facts. But since he had not known just what Chambers had said, he had been forced to work in the dark. He had guessed pretty well, but not well enough. And he had forgotten that records existed—apartment leases, bills of sale on cars, etc. It was these trivia which caught him.

Between the first, secret confrontation and the public confrontation in the caucus room of the Old House Office Building, the committee's investigators began checking these cold, unbendable facts of record. They found that in all cases where Chambers' story was verifiable, it checked; and where Hiss' story could be matched with the record, it fell down. On August 25, 1948, in a room packed with spectators and the press, Hiss and Chambers were once more brought face to face. For the record, it can be stated that when the hearings got under way, most of the press was pro-Hiss.

It was a dramatic moment, supercharged with emotion, when J. Parnell Thomas called the hearing to order. Chambers, as usual stolid and resigned, seemed again more a spectator than a participant. Hiss, accompanied by counsel, was in a fighting mood, ready to put on a superb exhibition of broken-field running. No longer the urbane young executive, his comments were acrid. Perhaps he realized, or sensed, that time was running out for him. But neither sharp answers nor skillful dodging could help him. The facts were on the line.

Very gently, Nixon and Stripling led him on. They dragged out letters from utilities companies and landlords to show that Hiss' recollection of when he had turned over the 28th

Street apartment to Chambers was faulty. Justifiably, Hiss answered that no man could be expected to remember the exact day in which he moved from one apartment to another —when it had all occurred ten years previously. Then Stripling went over the story of the old Ford car which Hiss claimed he had given to Chambers. And once again, Hiss stated categorically that he had given the car to Chambers in May or June of 1935, *after* he had purchased a new Plymouth. The audience wondered what these petty details were building up to. They found out pretty quickly when the committee sprang its trap.

In quick succession, Nixon and Stripling showed that Hiss had lied from start to finish about the car. Using documentary proof, they showed that at the time Hiss had allegedly given the Ford to Chambers, he had no new Plymouth. They showed that he had bought the Plymouth in September, 1935. His story then, that he had owned the two cars simultaneously, that the Ford had been parked in the snow for months because the Hisses had no use for it, and that he had "thrown it in" when he sublet his apartment to Chambers—this whole story fell apart.

Then Hiss did a shocking thing. It was shocking because it was so completely out of the character he had built up for himself. He began denying what was down in black and white in the record of his previous testimony. Denying, denying, denying, he said he had never testified that the car had been given to Chambers in the spring of 1935. He had merely given him temporary use of the car, he now claimed. As to when this occurred, he grew vaguer and vaguer—and, as his own testimony was impeached, more irate. Perhaps he had given the car to Chambers *after* the deadbeat and welsher had moved out without paying rent and without repaying a number of small loans. Perhaps he had given Chambers the car a long time after. That must be it.

But even this story was shot full of holes. Once Hiss had clutched it firmly to his bosom, the committee tossed its next bombshell—a bill of transfer showing that in 1936, Alger Hiss had transferred the car to the Cherner Motor Company which in turn had transferred it to one William Rosen who gave a false address. Hiss' signature, notarized by a Department of Justice lawyer, was on the transfer. And, the committee showed, all records of that transaction had mysteriously disappeared. All this circumstantially bore out Chambers' earlier story that Hiss had given the car to the Communist Party for the use of some "poor" organizer. (The following day, Rosen appeared before the committee but refused to "incriminate" himself on the subject of the transfer or on his membership in the Party.)

It was at this point that the pro-Hiss faction in the press section began melting away. Many of them just sat in the hearing room and suffered; the man they had believed in was a liar; if only on a minor point, he was a liar; and if he had lied about the car—well . . . Yet Hiss continued to batter his head against the factual evidence, to deny that he had ever seen Chambers after 1935. When Richard Nixon summed up in several hundred devastating words, Hiss' absurd contradictions, the witness decided that the time had come for a counterattack. Only this could now save him.

First he attempted to dazzle the committee with a statement in which he hauled out the names of a galaxy of important Americans. They would testify to his good character, Hiss said bravely. This was but one of Hiss' many attempts to invoke his own theory of innocence by association. By mingling with a crowd of the blameless, he hoped to assume a protective coloration. The committee let him run on for a while, then peppered him with a few more minor contradictions. On various occasions, he had testified that he had never heard of Whittaker Chambers until some time in 1948. But he had also testified that he had heard of him in 1947. Which date was correct? He had testified once that Chambers had never repaid any of the loans Hiss had made him. He had also testified that Chambers had repaid $15 or $20.

He had stated that he knew no Communists. Yet among his friends were men identified with the Communist Party, men who had refused to affirm or deny this connection.

For that one, Hiss had an easy answer. He never cross-examined his friends as to their political beliefs. If these people were Communists, he had not known it, despite their blatant affiliation with Communist causes. Stripling caught him here: if he could not tell whether or not Lee Pressman—notorious for his views—was a Communist, how could he claim that his powerful friends, in any conscience, could vouch for him? Harried by his own inconsistencies, Hiss now did a very clever thing: he asked that the committee put a series of questions to Whittaker Chambers. They were good questions, combining a fishing expedition into Chambers' past, a well-calculated smear of Chambers himself, and the overt hint that Hiss was the victim of a gigantic frame-up.

As he began listing these questions, beginning with "Where does he now reside," Hiss' lawyer began handing out copies to the press.

Hiss. I would ask that you ask him to list the various places where he has lived since 1930, indicating the length of time he has lived at each place, and the name he has used at each place. As far as I am concerned, that is all a matter of the record of the committee as to where I have lived, and the name I have used.

Next, what name was he given when he was born? What names has he used at any time since his birth for any purpose?

Ask him to give his complete employment record during his membership in the Communist Party, since his resignation from the Communist Party, stating the name of each employer, stating his occupation, and his compensation, also the name by which he was employed in each instance.

I would like him to give a complete bibliography of all his writings. He says that he was a writer. Give the writings under any and every name he has used.

I would like him to be asked whether he has ever been charged or convicted of any crime.

I would like him to give the full particulars, if so, as to where, when, and for what.

I would like him to be asked whether he has ever been treated for a mental illness.

Hébert. Mr. Chairman, may I interrupt there to tell Mr. Hiss that at least one question has been asked Mr. Chambers, No. 7. I asked him in New York whether he had ever been treated for any mental illness, whether he was ever in a mental institution or not, and he replied in the negative and added also he was not an alcoholic. So, you can strike that. That was asked already.

Hiss. Was that the extent of the committee's inquiry into that subject?

Hébert. The committee's inquiry into that was because a typical Communist smear is: when a man gets up to testify, and particularly a former Communist, is to say he is insane or an alcholic or something else is wrong with him.

Immediately after Mr. Chambers testified before this committee, the committee heard reverberations already of the fact that he was a mental case; in fact, it said it came from *Time* magazine by his own associates, so I have always believed the only way to find out anything to start off with is to ask the individual involved, and I asked Mr. Chambers a direct question. "Mr. Chambers, were you ever in a mental institution or treated for any mental disease?" I wanted to know, and I wanted to ask him, and then check back from there.

Chairman. I might say—

Hébert. I asked him, and he denied it, and said, "No," and also added to that that he was not an alcoholic, which was another charge that was made against him.

I may say to you now, Mr. Hiss, that I do not accept Mr. Chambers' word on his own statement. I intend to check that, too.

Hiss. So do I.

Chairman. I might say, Mr. Hiss, and also to the members of the committee, that Mr. Chambers will take the stand directly after you finish on the stand today.

Nixon. Mr. Hiss, excuse me, do you have any evidence that you would like to present at this time that Mr. Chambers has been in a mental institution? You made the charge that he has been.

Hiss. I have made no such charge.

Nixon. Then, you do not mean that by your statement?

Hiss. I mean that I am making no charges. I am seeking information.

Nixon. The charge appeared yesterday from your letter, as you recall—the suggestion of Mr. Chambers' being a mental case.

Now, do you have any evidence to present to the committee that he is?

Hiss. I have made no such charge. I just read the record here—the letter into the record. I asked the question, "Is he a man of sanity?"

Nixon. Will you answer the question as to whether you have any evidence of his having been in a mental institution?

Hiss. I have had various reports made to me to the effect that he has been.

Nixon. What reports have you had?

Hiss. I have had reports made by individuals.

Nixon. What individuals?

Hiss. They are so far only hearsay. The reports that came to me were from individuals, individual members of the press, so far, that they had heard rumors to that effect.

Nixon. What members of the press?

Davis [Hiss' counsel]. Mr. Mundt, can he finish his statement? I understood we were not to be interrupted. Let them take notes and then ask the questions after he finishes.

Chairman. All right, go ahead and finish the questions.

Hiss. I would like the committee to ask him if he has ever been treated for mental illness, where, and when, and by whom.

I would like him to be asked where, when, and to whom he has been married. How many children he has; where does his wife now reside.

I would like him to be asked to describe the circumstances under which he came in contact with this committee and *to make public all written memoranda which he may have handed to any representative of the committee.**

I would like to know whether he is willing, as I said at the outset of these questions, to make before this committee, in a manner free from the protections of this committee, the statements so that I may test his veracity in a suit for slander or libel.

Before the committee got around to asking Chambers for his answers, Representative Mundt made one telling jab at Hiss' contention that it would have been "inconceivable" for him to have remained all those years in the State Department and still be a member of the Communist Party. "This is not inconceivable to me without in any way attempting at this

* Italics ours.

time to indict the credibility of Mr. Hiss," Mundt said. "But I wish to point out that John Peurifoy, Assistant Secretary of State in charge of security, has notified Congress that 134 members of the Communist Party had weasled their way into the State Department alone and had been removed for disloyalty reasons. So it is not at all inconceivable that the number could just as well have been 135 as 134."

On the stand and under oath, Chambers imperturbably answered Hiss' questions. He listed his various Party names, described where he had lived, denied that he had ever been convicted of a crime or been committed to a mental institution. He repeated much of his account of the friendship between the Chamberses and the Hisses. He testified that he had appeared before the committee under subpoena and had made no attempt to invite that subpoena. He was, as always, painfully forthright. There was one question which he did not wish to answer. He did not want his address made public, for obvious reasons: Communists have long memories and they forgive little.

When the hearing adjourned, it had come to no official conclusion. Nor had the question, Who is lying? been answered definitely. But whereas after the first public hearing members of the press and spectators had rushed to shake hands with Hiss and speak to him, at the end of this session Alger Hiss and his lawyer walked out alone.

16

Libels and Pumpkins

FROM THE TIME THAT THE HOUSE UN-AMERICAN Activities Committee took the pursuit of the Bentley-Chambers case from the hands of a do-nothing Justice Department, President Truman and his Attorney General had been free in expressing criticism of the congressional investigation. No evidence of importance, they insisted, had been produced. Mr. Truman made his first charge that the hearings were merely a pre-election "red herring" shortly after Hiss' initial appearance before the Committee in August, 1948.

And reading from left to right, editorial writers and radio commentators vented their spleen on Committee procedures by minimizing the headline-making disclosures. Even after the hearing of August 25th, when Hiss clearly contradicted his previous testimony, reporters quoted Justice Department sources as stating that Alger Hiss would never be charged with perjury. Curiously enough, official bile was directed exclusively at Whittaker Chambers—perhaps because he had had the bad manners to put official Washington's nose out of joint.

On August 27th, Chambers appeared as guest on the "Meet the Press" radio program. His inquisitors—and they were exactly that—included Lawrence E. Spivak, editor of the *American Mercury* magazine which conducts the show; James B. (Scotty) Reston of the New York *Times* Washington bureau; Edward T. Folliard of the Washington *Post*; and

Tom Reynolds of the Chicago *Sun-Times*. With very little preamble, Folliard went straight to the point.

"Are you willing to say now [in answer to the Hiss challenge] that Alger Hiss is or ever was a Communist?" he asked.

The emotional impact was great when Chambers, in his low-pitched voice and in a mood heavy with the weariness of weeks of questioning, replied flatly:

"Alger Hiss was a Communist and may be now."

"Are you prepared to go to court to answer a suit for libel or slander?" Folliard pressed.

"I don't think Hiss will go to court," Chambers answered.

Chambers had been prepared for these questions. He had known, from the derogatory attitude of the Administration, that only by destroying the immunity which blanketed his charges before a congressional committee could he give weight to his unsubstantiated word. But he was totally unprepared for the overt hostility of questions such as Reynolds' gratuitously offensive:

"Do you find it easier to make a living now than when you were a member of the Communist Party?"

Nor could he understand why Reynolds attempted continually to needle him into making wild charges against Hiss. Fortunately for Chambers, the questions came so thick and fast that, in his state of fatigue, his entire attention was concentrated on answering circumspectly and to the point. It was not until later that he realized the implication of Reynolds' bludgeoning questions.

But now the fat was in the fire. The next day, newspapers featured the story of Chambers' defy. Both press and public waited to see if Hiss' challenge had been a bluff or the cry of a man who really wanted to clear his name. Would he sue for libel? As weeks went by, that question built up to a crescendo. "If Hiss isn't a Commie, why doesn't he sue?" Said the Washington *Post*, "Mr. Hiss himself has created a situation in which he is obliged to put up or shut up." Only

Whittaker Chambers doubted that Hiss would ever put his innocence or guilt to a court test. Very subtly, the attitude toward Hiss, even among his staunchest partisans, began to change.

One month after the broadcast, Hiss finally filed a $75,000 suit * in a Baltimore Federal court, charging Chambers with making "untrue, false, and defamatory" statements against him. Explanations for the delay came from both camps. Pro-Hiss spokesmen pointed out that his attorney, William L. Marbury, had been abroad as a member of the American delegation to a Geneva tariff conference since August 6th, and that the weeks following his return on September 14th had been taken up by a study of the record.

The anti-Hiss forces pointed out that Hiss was in a cleft stick. As president of the Carnegie Endowment for Peace, he was responsible to a conservative and eminent board of trustees which so far had been unequivocal in its public support of him. If he sued and lost, he risked not only his $20,000-a-year job but his entire future. On the other hand, if he did not sue, it would be taken as a tacit admission of guilt. Chambers himself believed that the delay was merely a canny wait to determine two things: (1) would the clamor die down, and (2) would any concrete proof be offered by the ex-courier. It was Marbury who made the final decision and fixed the amount of damages.

"I welcome Mr. Hiss' daring suit," Chambers told reporters when the charges were filed. "But I do not believe that Mr. Hiss or anybody else can use the means of justice to defeat the ends of justice."

There was no turning back now for Alger Hiss. With his lawyers, he plunged into the business of preparing for the court test. Scores of letters were sent out to former associates, asking them if they would testify as character witnesses. In a remarkable number of cases, the answers were in the

---

* Originally $50,000, damages were upped to $75,000 when Chambers repeated his charge.

affirmative and included warm statements of support. However, Gardner Jackson and Judge Jerome N. Frank, who had known Hiss well, rebuffed him. Joseph Freeman, an ex-Communist who had worked on the *New Masses*, was approached by Hiss' lawyers and asked if he would testify that Chambers used the pen name of George Crosley. Freeman refused.

"Chambers did not use that name on the *New Masses*," he is reported to have said flatly. "And," he added, "Chambers is incapable of telling an untruth."

Hiss' lawyers were not disconcerted. They hired John A. Broady, an investigator with a reputation for ruthlessness, to search into Chambers' past and to try to prove Communist-inspired stories that the *Time* editor was a sexual invert and that he had been committed to a mental hospital at some period in his life. Broady's detectives worked hard but they could find nothing. Finally, Broady dropped the assignment in disgust.

From Lionel Trilling, whose novel *The Middle of the Journey* had been based on rumors he had heard about Chambers, Hiss' lawyers got even less. When they called on Trilling, an English professor at Columbia College, he told them that, yes, he had known Chambers in the twenties. Chambers had been "domineering." But he had no first-hand knowledge of his activities, and he could testify to nothing.

In mid-November, Chambers was called to a pretrial hearing in Baltimore. Present also were Marbury, Harold Rosenwald, and Chambers' lawyer, Richard Cleveland. The questions flung at Chambers, especially by Rosenwald, who glared balefully at the *Time* editor throughout, were of such a nature that he left the hearing convinced "that Hiss was determined to destroy me—and my wife, if possible."

Back home on his Westminster farm that night, Chambers realized that he had for the third time in his life reached a point of crisis. Ever since his break with the Communist Party, he had sought to destroy the theory without hurting

the people who espoused it. Though he had spoken freely
when asked, he had also tried hard to shield the dupes and
to damage as few people as possible. As a Quaker, he could
do little else. But as a thinking man, he knew that it would
be folly now to continue to hold back evidence—no matter
whom it hurt.

In a *Time* cover story on Reinhold Niebuhr, the Protestant
philosopher, Chambers had written, "Between God's purpose
in eternity and man's purpose in time there are unbridgeable
differences." To protect himself and his family, and to scotch
Hiss' plans, he would have to do something that, in God's
eternal scheme, would be "wrong." It was in this frame of
mind that, for the first time in ten years, he thought of the
"life insurance" he had put by against Communist vengeance.
He decided to disinter the evidence of his past.

The next morning, Chambers sent a telegram to his nephew
Nathan Levine in Brooklyn. "Have my things ready." It was
a very bewildered young man who met Chambers. Only after
considerable conversation did he recall the package of papers
and its hiding place. From the top of the disused dumbwaiter shaft in his mother's home, Levine hauled out the
bulky manila envelope. While Levine attempted to remove
the grime, Chambers carried the package into the kitchen.
When Levine followed him there, Chambers had already
opened the package and was looking over its contents. "My
God," Chambers exclaimed. "I didn't know this was still in
existence." There were forty-seven typed copies of official
documents, three rolls of microfilm, four memos in Hiss's
writing and five memos in Harry White's writing.

"It's a strange thing," Chambers remarked not long afterward. "But I didn't remember what was in the package. I
thought there were just a few memos in Alger's handwriting.
When I saw what I had, I was amazed."

But in "finding" this documentary bonanza, Chambers had
also created serious new problems for himself. In the past,
he had carefully refrained from admitting that there were

any documents. Repeatedly he had stated that the only issue between Alger Hiss and himself was the question of Communist Party membership. In talking to the FBI, in discussing his former Communist affiliation with his superiors on *Time*, he had carefully skirted the espionage angle. In his testimony before the Un-American Activities Committee, he had moved perilously close to perjury by giving the impression that the primary purpose of his elite group was infiltration.

The only giveaway had been his convincing statement that on breaking with the Party, his life had been in danger. Everyone with experience or sophistication in the ways of the Communist underground apparatus realized immediately that Chambers' role had been more than that of a Party functionary. The Communists were a vengeful lot, but had they attempted to kill every man who broke with the Party, the world would be full of the dead and dying.

Now, he would have to reveal the treasonous nature of his old activities. "But I always knew that sooner or later I would have to do that," he has said. "This was the time."

When, on November 17th, he sat down in Marbury's quiet, book-lined office for the second pretrial hearing, there was no indication on his face that he was ready to spring the trap.

"Do you have any documentary proof of your assertions?" Marbury asked him badgeringly after some questioning.

"Only these," said Chambers blandly, laying a thick sheaf of papers on the table. There was a moment of dead silence. Then, as Marbury reached for the incriminating papers, Chambers' lawyer said:

"Let's identify these papers by reading the first and last words of each one into the record." It was a long, but tense, process. " 'Tokyo . . . February 12, KENNEDY.' 'Paris . . . February 15, 1938 . . . Secretary of State . . . Signed BULLITT.' 'Vienna . . . February 13, 1938 . . . Secretary

of State . . . Signed WILEY.' 'Rome . . . March 29 . . .
The Embassy learns . . . Signed PHILLIPS.' 'Warsaw . . .
March 29 . . . I learn following in strictest confidence . . .
Signed BIDDLE.' "

As Cleveland introduced all forty-seven documents and the
handwritten memos into the record, Marbury stood by the
window looking out blankly while Rosenwald paced up and
down, stopping every now and then to stare at Chambers with
a look of implacable hatred. And now the deed was done;
there was no turning back; a poet sitting in that room might
have heard, faintly, the flapping wings of the Furies.

Both Marbury and Cleveland agreed that the matter had
gone far beyond a defamation of character suit. Judge W.
Calvin Chestnut, who had sat on the case, was called in and
all three decided that the Justice Department should take
over. The opposing attorneys telephoned Alexander Campbell, head of the Criminal Division, sketching in the general
nature of the material which Chambers had so unexpectedly
produced.

Taking Dean Shedler, the Department's Chief of Public
Information, with him, Campbell rushed up to Baltimore for
a conference with Cleveland, Marbury, Harold Medina, Jr.,
(a Time Inc., lawyer), and Judge Chestnut. The documents
were sealed in the interest of national security, and the court
reporter who had been taking down the depositions was instructed to provide no copies of the transcript. And everyone
concerned was enjoined to keep the events of the day completely secret. Then the administrative wheels began to
grind. The FBI examined the papers and began a thorough
check of existent documents. Simultaneously, it grilled Hiss
and Chambers *privatim et seriatim*. A few days later, Campbell directed United States Attorney McGohey to order the
grand jury, which had been meeting in New York, reconvened for December 8th.

Two weeks after the documents had been turned over to

the Justice Department, neither the Un-American Activities
Committee nor the Washington press corps knew that something was afoot. Then, a perplexing and curious thing happened. On December 1st, Jerry Kluttz carried an item in his
Washington *Post* column, Federal Diary, to the effect that
the pretrial hearings had uncovered "some very startling information as to who is a liar." But on the same day, the Washington *Daily News* disclosed that "the Justice Department is
about ready to drop its investigation of the celebrated Alger
Hiss-Whittaker Chambers controversy."

"One Department source," the story read, "said that on the
basis of available evidence, officials in charge of the case
believe it would be unwise to take it before the grand jury.
But he emphasized that this attitude could change overnight
if the House Committee or the Department's investigators
dig up some new evidence."

These conflicting stories were enough to set Bert Andrews
of the *Herald Tribune* busy beating at doors. He got little
satisfaction from Alex Campbell, Chief of Criminal Division
of the Justice Department. "I just can't comment on these
stories. I just can't answer any questions about the Hiss-
Chambers case," Campbell said frankly; "Number 1. This is
too hot. Number 2. I just can't say anything about it." To all
other questions, he gave an emphatic "No comment."

Certain that he was on to something, Andrews made a
series of phone calls—to Judge Chestnut, Marbury, Cleveland,
Hiss, and Chambers. From each of them he got evasive
answers which further tantalized him. With the kind of
persistence and imagination which make a top-notch reporter,
Andrews decided to prod history a little: he sent a wire to
Richard Nixon, at sea on the S.S. *Panama*, bound for Central
America and a vacation.

"Information here is that Hiss-Chambers case has produced new bombshell [he wired]. Chambers has been questioned in libel suits by Hiss. Indications are that Chambers

has produced new evidence. All concerned are silent . . . In view your committee's role can you tell me whether committee will reopen its investigation?"

Decisively taking the initiative, Nixon wired back: "Have asked Stripling to investigate and advise me re new evidence. Will reopen hearings if necessary to prevent Justice Department cover up . . ." At Nixon's direction, Stripling drove out to Westminster that same day. He found Chambers in overalls, finishing the evening's milking. Had he withheld evidence from the committee, Stripling asked bluntly. Chambers admitted it but refused to go beyond that. If he discussed the events of the pretrial hearing, he would be in contempt of court.

This was enough for Nixon. Commandeering a Coast Guard plane, he had himself removed from the *Panama* and flown back to Washington. While he was en route, the committee was busy. The day after Kluttz's item had started the ball rolling, Chambers received a phone call from the committee asking him to come down to Washington. He was met with a subpoena calling for all documents or material in his possession. Chambers knew that he had nothing to gain by denying the existence of other material; he readily agreed to surrender it.

That night committee investigators William Wheeler and Donald T. Appell followed Chambers' car up the long, winding approach to Chambers' farm. By the light of the electric bulb on the back porch, they saw that a number of squash lay with their necks pointing toward a pumpkin. Chambers picked it up.

"Here's what you're looking for," he said.

The two bewildered investigators leaned over to examine the pumpkin. It had appeared intact and growing on the vine. But closer scrutiny showed that the top had been neatly sliced off and then carefully replaced. From the hollowed-out base came three rolls of undeveloped film encased in light-proof metal cylinders and sealed with tape. One of the cylinders had been smashed and Chambers remarked that it was probably light-struck. Two other rolls, already developed, were wrapped in oil paper.

Chambers had placed the microfilm in the pumpkin for good and sufficient reason. Ever since Hiss had begun his defamation of character suit, prowlers had been seen near the Westminster farm. Were they Comintern agents? Were they detectives hired by Hiss? Or were they tramps who happened around coincidentally at this time? Chambers had no way of knowing. So when he had gone up to Washington, he had hidden the microfilm. On the principle of Poe's purloined letter, he had placed the precious cylinders where they could lie in plain view without being discovered. "The pumpkin," he said afterward, "was the last flare-up of my conspiratorial nature."

He had no way of knowing that antagonistic commentators would play that pumpkin for all it was worth, as if it had been the funniest thing in the world. They would howl about the "pumpkin papers" as if ridicule could make them disappear. By linking "pumpkin" with "espionage" they hoped to make all of Chambers' disclosures sound preposterous. After all, who ever heard of a spy with a pumpkin? But the contents of those cylinders were too explosive to remain funny.

When Stripling examined the developed film through an enlarger, he knew immediately that the secret State Department papers pictured there had given the committee the kind of evidence which would finally crack the Hiss-Chambers case. And there was plenty of this evidence. Carefully developed at the Veterans Administration photography laboratory, the prints made a pile over four feet high.

The following Sunday, December 5th, Nixon was back in Washington directing the committee's operations. His first act was to have Stripling determine the date of manufacture of the precious microfilm. On Monday morning, Stripling called in Maurice Lewis, the Eastman Kodak representative for the Washington area. Lewis examined the film, jotted down its serial number, and checked with his company in Rochester.

An hour later, Lewis called with a piece of disconcerting news. The film had been manufactured in 1947. Committee members hit the ceiling. How could Chambers have hidden the one-year-old film ten years ago? Could his entire story of the documents be a fabrication, put together at the last minute to clear himself of libel? For an hour and a half, the committee stewed. Chambers was called in and challenged to explain the inexplicable. Then Lewis called again, apologetically. Rochester had just phoned him, he said, to correct the earlier statement. The film had been made in 1937 after all. Nixon sighed with relief and plunged ahead with the investigation.

While other members of the committee basked happily in the headlines, enjoying the kind of public approbation it seldom got, Nixon was consulting with former Undersecretary of State Sumner Welles and Assistant Secretary John E. Peurifoy, the Department's security officer. Would it be safe to publish the documents? Or did their contents, after ten years, still involve the national security? Both Welles and Peurifoy agreed that to publish the papers at the time might be risky. The committee contented itself with vague descriptions of what the pumpkin papers contained.

The hullabaloo that followed forced the Justice Department's hand. Campbell instructed McGohey to reconvene the grand jury on Monday, December 6th, instead of on the 8th as previously ordered. Subpoenas were issued to Chambers, Hiss, and others, hoping to forestall their appearance before the Un-American Activities Committee. But this did not deter Nixon. On the day the grand jury began hearing its witnesses, he showed up in New York, accompanied by other members of the committee.

McGohey met them at the train and followed them to the Commodore Hotel, pleading that Chambers and Hiss be left alone while they were under grand jury subpoena. But Nixon, who had little faith in the Justice Department's motives, insisted that he would not be deterred from holding an executive session in New York. The committee's intervention had brought the case to its climax, he argued, despite the hostile lack of cooperation from the Administration. What proof had he that the Attorney General meant to press the case to an indictment? As the argument became heated, both McGohey and Nixon lost their tempers.

When the discussion descended to expletives, Stripling threw open the hotel window and said bitterly, "We might as well let them hear about it on Fifth Avenue." This quieted the shouters. When the committee and McGohey emerged from the room, they were talking "cooperation" and Nixon had agreed to hold off his projected interview with Chambers. But the antagonism between the Justice Department and the Un-American Activities Committee was too ingrained to be talked out of existence.

Its causes were many. There was, to begin with, the natural lack of confidence which has always existed between the legislative and the executive branches of the government. There was, also, a particular antipathy toward the committee which went back to the days of Representative Martin Dies. The Administration had good reason to believe that the committee had abused its investigatory powers time and again, not to root out Communists but to tar the New Deal. Men like David Saposs, of good reputation and sound anti-Communism, had been hounded by the Dies Committee merely because they spoke with a slight accent and were Jews. In the case of Chambers, the Justice Department claimed that in its eagerness to make headlines the committee had been willing to jeopardize by premature revelations any chance of breaking the spy case and jailing the culprits.

On the other hand, the committee could argue convincingly that the Justice Department was primarily interested in suppressing evidence of espionage in order to save the Administration generally, and the State Department particularly, from embarrassment. The committee could cite example after example—starting with the Amerasia case—to show that the Administration had no real desire to root out Communist elements in the government. On one point, the committee could speak with no fear of contradiction. From the start, the Justice Department had clearly indicated that it was more interested in nailing Chambers—the star witness— than in bringing Hiss and the other culprits to trial. Whatever might be said of its publicity-seeking proclivities, the committee had been the first to force into the open aspects which the FBI had failed to uncover of the most serious case of espionage in American history.

When the grand jury reconvened on Monday, December 6th, the mere names of the witnesses made copy for the newspapers: Alger and Donald Hiss, Whittaker Chambers, Mrs. Priscilla Hiss, and so on. But names and conjectures were all that reporters had to go on. The real stories began the following day when the House Committee resumed its sessions. Ironically, the testimony most damaging to Hiss came from three former associates: ex-Undersecretary of State Sumner Welles, Assistant Secretary John Peurifoy, and Assistant Secretary Francis B. Sayre.

Welles made it very clear that "under no consideration whatever" could *any* documents be removed "for any purpose from the [State] Department." He made it equally clear that the release of the pumpkin papers to unauthorized hands in 1938 would be "in the highest degree prejudicial, and in the highest degree dangerous, to the nation's interest." Some of the documents were still too confidential, ten years later, to be released. The distribution of these documents, within the State Department, he added would have been "extremely

restricted," to be "kept under lock and key." To have delivered the documents to a foreign power would have meant to
deliver also the means of breaking our most secret codes.

Peurifoy nailed the lid down even tighter on Hiss. In
answer to a direct question, he agreed that removal of the
documents in question from the Department would be *prima
facie* evidence that they had been taken for a purpose detri-
mental to the United States.

"Would it be a violation of the law for [a State Department
official] to copy [a document] for his own personal use?"
Rankin asked.

"Well, he might make a paraphrase, dictate it to a stenog-
rapher, in order to pass it to another official, but if you mean
taking a pencil and writing it out, I would say that would be
a very unusual procedure."

Presented with the four memoranda in Hiss' handwriting,
Peurifoy answered unequivocally: "I would regard anyone
making notes of what I have seen here, in personal handwriting, and taking them out of the Department, as violating
all the security regulations of the Department."

"Would there be any reason for an individual to make a
memorandum such as you have just looked at, in his own
handwriting?" Hébert pressed.

"No sir; not in my judgment," Peurifoy answered.

"You would have to assume that he did it for some ulterior
motive?"

"I think that is right," said the Assistant Secretary. "Under
the Yardley Act . . . a person would be liable to a $10,000
fine, and I think up to ten years imprisonment for doing such
a thing."

Sayre's testimony, taken in secret session and never published, did Alger Hiss no good. What the former Assistant
Secretary of State said was doubly damaging because he was
thoroughly reluctant to testify against a friend. Yet by indirection, he seemed to point the finger straight at Hiss. Stat-

ing categorically that only he, the two unquestionably loyal office secretaries, and Alger had access to the files, Sayre noted that in his office these files "were kept locked always." Reluctantly, he admitted that three of the documents could have been removed only from his office and only by Hiss or the two secretaries. The Q. & A. on the documents was particularly devastating.

Nixon. Did Mr. Hiss, at his home, have as one of his duties the paraphrasing of these documents and bringing them back to you in this way?
Sayre. The answer is "No."

Little by little, as the questioning progressed, doubts began to grow in Sayre's mind. "It is a crime of such gravity that I yet can't believe that Alger Hiss would indulge in it. Maybe he did."

"Do you agree there was nothing important or nothing wrong with turning this stuff over?" Nixon asked, commenting on press reports that the State Department was not too horrified by the theft of the documents.

Sayre. I violently disagree, not only because of the substance of these cables, but because some of them were in the highly confidential codes; . . . And for these telegrams to get out at the time they did meant that other governments could crack our codes and that, I think, is indescribably horrible.
Rankin. In other words, if they got these documents, if they were absolutely insignificant from the point of view of international importance, they could crack the codes without trouble.
Sayre. The other point is that some of these cables reveal sources from which information was obtained, sources planted in foreign countries. Now you make a cable of this kind known, you cut off that source of information from another country, and you kill what you have been working on for years.

Two days later, Henry Julian Wadleigh, a slender man in shell-rimmed glasses, who had already testified before the grand jury, came before the committee in Washington. His face gaunt and his hands shaking, Wadleigh chain-smoked throughout the one and a half hours he sat on the stand. But though he retired behind the now-overworked formula of "I refuse to testify on the grounds that I may incriminate myself," his nervousness was such that newspaper reporters agreed he would surely crack. Within forty-eight hours, he had told his story to the grand jury.

The same newspaper which carried the story of Wadleigh's performance also carried another Administration blast at the committee. Even the concrete evidence which had finally been produced did not restrain the President from repeating his "red-herring" charges. The committee was "dead," he said with a certain degree of relish.

All this, of course, was window dressing. The real action was taking place elsewhere. Both the FBI and the grand jury were attempting to answer one big question: could Hiss be linked with the Chambers pumpkin papers? An early examination of these papers had revealed that they had been typed on a 1928 Woodstock typewriter. Such a machine had been given Priscilla Hiss by her father. It was known that this typewriter had been in the possession of the Hisses in 1938. But between *a* Woodstock and *the* Woodstock, there was a sizable gap.

While the grand jury attempted to extract testimony from recalcitrant witnesses, the FBI went about its work. First it was learned, by checking procurement records, that no Woodstocks had ever been used in Hiss' office. This cleared up one point: the documents had been typed outside of the State Department. The big problem was now to find the Hiss Woodstock. Failing that, the FBI hoped to unearth letters or papers typed on the Hiss machine at the time of the espionage activities.*

---

* The Hisses were asked to submit specimens of typing from any machines they had owned. They replied that they had not yet uncovered any samples from the Woodstock. This despite the fact that Mrs. Hiss had already received from Bryn Mawr a three-page report to the alumnae association which she had typed on the Woodstock.

On Friday December 10th, the foreman of the grand jury notified United States Attorney John F. X. McGohey that the jurors could find no indictment.* Instead they intended to issue a report condemning the Un-American Activities Committee for its interference in Justice Department matters. But over the week-end, the FBI struck pay dirt. On Monday morning, with dramatic suddenness, it turned over to McGohey two papers typed on the original Woodstock—a letter written by Hiss to his insurance company and one Mrs. Hiss had written to the headmaster of her son's school. Both were dated 1937. Matched against the typing on the pumpkin papers, the type faces and the type peculiarities of the two sets were found to be identical.†

But while the trap was being baited, the grand jury was also seeking corroborative evidence from others named in Chambers' charge. Each of these witnesses, as he went in, glanced at an apparently unconcerned Hiss, waiting in the anteroom. When Hede Massing emerged, she went over to Alger. He gave her a calm smile as she repeated the substance of her incriminating testimony.

"Very interesting," he said. "Thank you for coming. No doubt you think you are doing the government a service, but I never saw you before."

With the trap ready for springing, Alex Campbell called in Hiss and Edward McLean, one of his lawyers. "I'm convinced you committed espionage," Campbell told the ex-official. "You've seen Chambers, Wadleigh, and others go in and confess. If you do the same, it will go easier with you." Smilingly, Hiss continued to deny all. "I'm also convinced that you committed perjury," Campbell continued.

"What you say doesn't interest me, Mr. Campbell," Hiss

* On the same day in Radio City offices of *Time*, Chambers resigned his senior editorship in order not to embarrass the magazine further. Quickly and gratefully his resignation was accepted.

† On Monday, too, Hiss submitted his resignation to the board of trustees of the Carnegie Endowment for International Peace. It was tabled, and Hiss was given a leave of absence with pay.

said, breaking in before McLean could speak. "I've nothing
to confess. I told no lies. I just don't know what you're talking about." Five days later, on Wednesday, December 15th,
Hiss was called in and sworn. Most meticulously, the grand
jury moved ahead.

"Mr. Hiss, you have probably been asked this question before, but I'd like to ask the question again," McGohey began.
"At any time did you, or Mrs. Hiss in your presence, turn any
documents of the State Department or of any other government organization over to Whittaker Chambers?"

Hiss' denial was by now routine. "Never. Excepting, I
assume, the title certificate to the Ford."

"To nobody else did you turn over any documents, to any
other person," a juror asked.

"And to no other unauthorized person," Hiss answered.

Now the questioning shifted. "Mr. Hiss, Mr. Chambers has
testified that he obtained typewritten copies of official State
Department documents from you," he was told.

"I know that."

"Did you ever see Mr. Chambers after you went into the
State Department?"

"I do not believe I did," Hiss answered. "I cannot swear
that I did not see him some time, say, in the fall of '36 . . ."

"Can you say definitely that you did not see him after
January 1, 1937?"

"Yes, I think I can definitely say that," Hiss said. The trap
snapped shut.

Next the typewriter evidence was presented to him. How
could he account for the fact that the purloined documents
had been copied on a machine which was in his possession at
the time? Could he explain away two hundred pages of type-
script? Hiss' answer came quickly.

"I am amazed; and until the day I die I shall wonder how
Whittaker Chambers got into my house to use my typewriter," he said blandly.

The jury laughed out loud.

If Hiss was to be believed, Chambers had somehow made his way into the house on various occasions, avoiding all members of the family, and busily copied two hundred pages of documents which should not have been there in the first place. The jury acted with despatch. The statute of limitations prevented it from bringing espionage charges against Hiss. It did the next best thing; it handed down a perjury indictment, charging that Hiss has (1) lied under oath by denying that he transmitted copies of secret documents to Whittaker Chambers, and (2) lied again by claiming that he had not seen and conversed with Chambers after January 1, 1937.

The following day, a thin and sober-faced Alger Hiss stood before Judge John W. Clancy in a third-floor courtroom of the United States Courthouse in New York.

"How do you plead?" the clerk asked.

"Not guilty to both counts," said Hiss firmly in a voice so resonant that it carried to every part of the courtroom. With bail fixed at $5,000, special assistant Attorney General Raymond P. Whearty said to the judge, "Now I ask that the defendant be photographed and fingerprinted as a condition of bail."

Accompanied by two FBI agents, the bright young careerist who had sat next to Roosevelt and Stalin at Yalta left the court for the sixth-floor room where he would be "mugged" like a common criminal. It was a cold day, a day of driving rain, and the shiver of tragedy was in the air. In Washington, Representative Mundt would say "I hope that nobody anywhere will ever refer to this case again as a red herring."

In New York, as the winter gloom settled over the city, Whittaker Chambers said quietly, "I would be less than human if I could take any pleasure in Alger Hiss' personal troubles." This was the measure of the man.

17

The Trial of Alger Hiss

THERE WAS NO PROFESSIONAL DETACHMENT ABOUT the reporters who waited in the third-floor corridor of New York's Federal Courthouse on May 31, 1949. They broke up into little groups, arguing quietly or angrily over the innocence or guilt of Alger Hiss. There was tension and anxiety in the air. After six postponements, dragged out over five and one half months, the Hiss perjury trial was about to begin. When special assistant Attorney General Thomas J. Donegan and Assistant United States Attorney Thomas F. Murphy appeared, they were immediately surrounded by reporters. Would it be a long trial, they asked. Did the government have a good case?

"We've got plenty of cogent evidence," Tom Murphy told them.

Shortly before 11:30 A.M., Alger and Priscilla Hiss sauntered toward the courthouse doors. With them was their chief counsel, Lloyd Paul Stryker, red-faced, crop-haired, ebullient. As the defense and the prosecution moved to their tables within the pen of the courtroom, there was a stir and a rustle. "All rise," a bailiff commanded, and Judge Samuel H. Kaufman took his seat at the bench. A small, sharp-faced man, his role in the trial was to stir up heated controversy. His record as a Truman appointee, the fact that he was trying his first important case, and his possible political indebtedness to Stryker were to be raked over in the newspapers. But at this moment, he was just a judge, torn between affability and sternness.

Before him lay the stage on which the crucial scene in the long drama was to be played. The actors had their roles. The script was yet to be written. There was Tom Murphy, 6 feet 4 inches tall and proportionately broad, soft-spoken and deliberate, an outsize moustache shielding a gentle face. He was a veteran of the Justice Department's criminal division, but this case focussed on him the attention of the nation's press. And there was Stryker whose reputation as a master of cross-examination glittered. He had won and lost important cases, but the pyrotechnics of his performance never failed to entrance the audience. In the protracted duel to come, each lawyer would use his witnesses as foils.

He would prove, said Murphy in his opening statement, that Alger Hiss had taken documents wholesale from the State Department. He would show that these were typed on Hiss' Woodstock typewriter for transmittal to Colonel Boris Bykov in New York. The government did not have the typewriter, but it did have letters typed by Mrs. Hiss and experts would prove that they had been written on the same machine as the documents. "We will corroborate Mr. Chambers' testimony by the typewriter and the handwriting of the memos," he said. "Until you have heard Mr. Chambers' complete story you will not be in a position to test his credibility . . . I want you to watch the color of Mr. Chambers' face . . . If you don't believe Mr. Chambers' story, we have no case."

Stryker paced back and forth restlessly as he outlined his case. In typical slam-bang fashion, he pictured the virtues of Alger Hiss, invoking the shades of Oliver Wendell Holmes and Franklin D. Roosevelt. He waved the flag, rhapsodized over "the land I love and you love" and marshalled an impressive array of clichés to make his points. Chambers was "a thief," "a moral leper," a "perjurer," a "furtive, secretive, deceptive man" engaged in a "nefarious, low-down conspiracy," he said—his voice ranging from a shout to a sibilant whisper.

The accusations against the Hisses were "concocted" by Chambers and by his wife Esther. Side by side, Alger and Priscilla sat stony-eyed and stony-jawed. Now and then a wisp of an enigmatic expression passed over Mrs. Hiss' face. But in the ebb and flow of Stryker's tirade, the two Hisses seemed remote and abstracted.

Then the real trial began. Under Murphy's questioning, Whittaker Chambers began telling the long story of his involvement in the Communist movement, of his submergence into the Soviet underground, of his association with Alger Hiss. He told of his break with the Party and his long, hard struggle to rise in the community of free men. This was his background, his introduction to the jury. Of more immediate pertinence was the groundwork of evidence which he lay for the government. He described Hiss' willingness to turn over documents, he told of visits to the Hiss home and of returned calls by the Hisses. He stunned the defense by testifying that he borrowed $400 from Hiss in November, 1937, to buy a car. A Washington bank executive testified later in the trial that on November 19, 1937, Mrs. Hiss withdrew that sum from her account. And an officer of the Schmidt Motor Company testified that four days after Mrs. Chambers bought a Ford sedan from him, paying $486 in cash.

Chambers told the court that on orders from Bykov he had given Alger a Bokhara rug in 1937—in payment for services rendered to the Soviet Union. Hiss had admitted receiving a rug, but he claimed that it had been given to him in 1935. Later in the trial, Professor Meyer Schapiro testified that he had purchased and shipped to Washington four Bokhara rugs for Chambers. He had been paid in cash for them. A rug dealer identified the sales slip. It was dated December 23, 1936. Chambers also described trips he had taken with the Hisses, the arrangement of their various homes, all with the same intimate detail which had been so convincing during the House committee hearings.

When Stryker took up the cross-examination, he was aided

in his biting, scratching attack by the witness himself. For Chambers was in a pentitential mood. His past in the underground had to be expiated, and despite the indignity of Stryker's onslaught, Chambers was willing to say, "*Mea maxima culpa.*" Calmly he admitted that as a Communist he had lied and cheated.

"You were an underhanded enemy of this country doing what you could to aid a foreign country and overthrow our Constitution by force and violence?" Stryker stormed.

"Yes," Chambers answered. Drawing from the record of five months' pretrial testimony during which Chambers had discussed with Hiss' attorneys every peccadillo as well as the grave misdeeds in Chambers' life, Stryker systematically assailed the witness. A lie to the Columbia College dean suddenly emerged as a monstrous and symbolic crime against society. Then Stryker drew up his big guns.

"When you testified [first] before the grand jury, you were asked whether there was any espionage . . . And you answered there was not?" Chambers acknowledged this. "So you testified falsely and committed perjury . . ." Stryker thundered. "That is right," said Chambers impassively. Turning to each other, Alger and Priscilla smiled triumphantly. Under this rancorous cross-examination, Chambers admitted that he had withheld part of the truth on six instances. But his explanation, on redirect examination, made clear why he had not told everything about Hiss' activities:

"There are degrees of injury," he said slowly, "and I sought to keep [Mr. Hiss] from the ultimate consequences of what [he] had done . . . Rather than reveal the extent of his activities and those of others, I chose to jeopardize myself."

Perhaps the crowning indignity for Chambers was the presence within the pen of Dr. Carl A. L. Binger, a psychiatrist engaged by the defense to "analyze" him. Taking copious notes, Binger stared down his nose at Chambers "as if to give him a double whammy," as an FBI man remarked.

When Chambers stepped down, a series of witnesses

identified letters and papers, typewritten as late as May,
1937, by Mrs. Hiss and bearing the signatures of Alger or
Priscilla. These were produced to compare their type characteristics with those of the copied documents—proof that all
had been written on the Hiss Woodstock. One after another, these witnesses wove a circumstantial net about the
defendant.

Then the government struck another body blow at the
defense contention that Alger Hiss had never seen Chambers
after January 1, 1937: it called Mrs. Esther Chambers to the
stand. She bore the imprint of Quaker simplicity. Her toughened hands gave a clue to her present occupation as manager
of a 300-acre farm. "It was impossible for anyone to feel that
Mrs. Chambers was telling anything but her best recollection, after agonized searching, of the truth," the late H. R.
Knickerbocker said in his broadcast that night. "She is a
small woman, forty-nine years old, whose body is hardened
by toil and whose soul had been purified by suffering, if it
were ever anything else but pure. She wore a gray suit, ill-
fitting, and a black hat which framed an intense, angular face
totally devoid of make-up but not of beauty. She had a spiritual beauty in her pale face which was not even impaired by
spectacles . . . Her struggle to master her emotions, her profound simplicity, her pain at being forced to hurt old, dear
friends was enough to move even the ones being hurt. . . .
How could such a woman as Esther Chambers be false?"

Speaking softly but with the authority of sincerity, she
recalled with a wealth of detail some of her many meetings
with Alger and Priscilla. She recalled the color and pattern
of the wall paper in one Hiss home, listed the furniture on
each of three floors, and told of the chintz bedspread which
Mrs. Hiss had bought at a sale. She described other Hiss
homes and gave personal details of their home life. She remembered a New Year's party at the Hiss home on December
31, 1936—coinciding with the date set in the indictment. She

mentioned a wedding anniversary party earlier that month to which the Hisses brought champagne—although here she admitted that her memory was somewhat vague.

"What was your last name?" Judge Kaufman asked.

"We never had a last name [to the Hisses]," Esther Chambers answered.

"Your husband testified that you were known as Crosley," the judge challenged.

"Oh, no!" spectators cried out, correcting Kaufman. He looked angrily at them but subsided as he had on other occasions when his recollection of testimony had been vague.

Despite the great strain which possessed her, Mrs. Chambers spoke almost chattily of the days in 1935 when the Chambers couple had moved into the 28th Street apartment and later when the two families had tried joint housekeeping in the Hisses' P Street home. "Pleasant as it was to be together, we decided we'd better have separate households," she said quietly.

When the Chamberses moved to Baltimore, the Hisses gave them a patched rug, a table, and a toy cabinet which Timmie had outgrown. On one visit to the Hiss home, she testified, the Chambers baby "wet the floor. Priscilla gave me a lovely old linen towel to use as a diaper." In return, Esther Chambers painted pictures for the Hisses, including a landscape and a portrait of Timmie. (In her testimony, Mrs. Hiss insisted that the portrait had been painted in one night.)

Then for two days a snarling and shouting Stryker tried to force Mrs. Chambers into contradicting her direct testimony. Pale but in control of herself, the witness fought back. Though she once wavered on a date, the main body of her story—that the Hiss and Chambers families had been close friends—remained undamaged. At the same time, she fiercely defended Whittaker against Stryker's ceaseless assault. "My husband is a decent citizen and a great man," she said sharply. "If he does what he believes is the right thing to do at the moment, I believe he is a great man . . . His beliefs may change, and his did." When she stepped down from the stand, her testimony was there to plague the defense.

On a specially built platform over the witness box, the prosecution next mounted blow-ups of the copied State Department documents. One document was withheld from the jury. The State Department still considered it too secret. Hour after hour Murphy compared the copies with the originals, brought down from Washington by a State Department employee. Murphy's purpose was a dual one: to show that the top-level diplomatic papers had passed across Alger Hiss' desk and to tear down a statement by the defendant that the documents were not highly confidential. But only students of history, interested in United States foreign policy during the Munich era, could find any excitement in this painstaking demonstration. The jury looked bored and somnolent, and Stryker wandered out into the corridor to smoke or chat with reporters.

A little life returned to the courtroom when Miss Eunice A. Lincoln, private secretary to Assistant Secretary of State Francis Sayre (Hiss' boss in the crucial years), took the stand as the government's twenty-ninth witness. Her role was small but significant: she identified the four memos as being in the handwriting of Alger Hiss, and she seriously punctured defense hints that the incriminating papers had been stolen from Hiss by Henry Julian Wadleigh.

"Did Mr. Wadleigh ever come to your office and take any files out?" Murphy asked Miss Lincoln.

"I don't recall that he did," she answered. "He did not come to the office frequently, and when he did it was usually with others, for conferences."

The really damning testimony came from Ramos S. Feehan, an FBI handwriting and typewriter expert. Feehan explained that all but one of the documents had been copied on the same typewriter, according to the government, the old Woodstock belonging to Priscilla Hiss. Comparing the copied documents with letters written by the Hisses at the time, he stated categorically that they had all been typed on the same machine. The defense conceded the point. Before Feehan could testify on the four memos, Stryker conceded that they were in Hiss' handwriting.

There was a brief interlude as the defense, with the permission of the government, put two character witnesses on the stand. They were John W. Davis, Democratic Presidential candidate in 1924, and Dr. Stanley Hornbeck, Hiss' superior in the Department's Far Eastern Division. Both men lauded the defendant. But in cross-examination Davis admitted that he had never heard of Hiss until 1945, and Hornbeck recalled a warning he had received from an unnamed friend that Hiss was a Communist fellow-traveler. Hornbeck declared that he had disregarded the warning.

Then the prosecution really jolted the courtroom: it called Henry Julian Wadleigh. A tall, carelessly dressed, shock-haired man, he was the first person to corroborate in open court Chambers' story of the Soviet spy ring.*

"I began to take out documents and give them to unauthorized people as soon as I joined the State Department in 1936, mostly to a man identified to me recently as David Carpenter [a copy reader on the *Daily Worker*] . . . I selected documents from those that came to my desk," Wadleigh said calmly, almost brashly.

"Were there some occasions when you gave the documents to Whittaker Chambers?" Murphy asked. Yes, he had. Had he given Chambers any of the documents now in evidence? No, said Wadleigh. These were "rich finds" and he would have remembered them. Had he taken any papers from Hiss' office to transmit to the Russians? He had not, Wadleigh insisted. "The only material I used was that which came across my desk." He had also gotten a rug from Chambers in 1937.

* The son of an Episcopalian minister, a graduate of Oxford, a State Department official, Wadleigh was on a social and intellectual par with the defendant.

All the next week, the defense sought to chip away at the government's case. A string of witnesses, their testimony calculated to cast doubt on Chambers' story, were called by Stryker and his associate, Edward McLean.

J. Kellogg Smith, director of a Maryland camp, testified that his friends the Hisses had never left Chestertown, Maryland, during the bulk of the summer of 1937—the time when Chambers claimed that they joined him on a trip to Peterborough, New Hampshire. But under cross-examination, Smith admitted that the notes he was reading from, giving the vacation dates, had been obtained "word for word" from Alger Hiss. Mrs. Lucy E. Davis, who operated the guest house in Peterborough where the Hisses and the Chamberses had allegedly stopped overnight, swore that she had never seen the defendant or his wife. There was no record of their tenancy.

Next the defense threw in two prize packages—Supreme Court Justices Stanley Reed and Felix Frankfurter. (Taking a day off from Mt. Olympus, a newspaperman cracked about Frankfurter.) Their appearance as character witnesses left shattered precedents strewn about the courtroom. Judge Kaufman rose from the bench to shake hands and was visibly impressed at being able to do so. Each reaffirmed the public reputation of Hiss. When Murphy asked Frankfurter whether he had ever put his stamp of approval on Lee Pressman, Kaufman sustained defense objections to the question, and the matter was dropped.

In contrast with the two judicial dignitaries, the next two witnesses were former servants of the Hisses. The first, Mrs. Claudia Catlett, had spontaneously recognized Chambers in FBI headquarters the previous February. Now she would admit only that she had seen him once, in 1936, and then under the name of "Crosby, like in Bing." The famous Woodstock typewriter, she said, had been given to her two sons in 1936 or 1937—the first date in obvious contradiction to the evidence of Hiss letters already admitted in the case.

Her son Raymond backed her up admirably in direct testimony, rattling off names and dates with ease. But under cross-examination, his story fell apart when he admitted that he had not the faintest notion of the month or year that he got the typewriter. After some surly remark at prosecutors in general, he clammed up. This, more than the sudden appearance of the machine in court—dragged out from under the defense table—was the big sensation of the day.

Perry Catlett knocked an even greater hole in the story. When he and Raymond received the typewriter in 1937, he testified, they had taken it to a Woodstock shop on K Street and Connecticut Avenue in Washington to try to have it repaired. "What if I tell you that the shop on K Street wasn't opened for business until September, 1938?" Murphy shouted. Perry weighed the question. "I don't know the time," he said in defeat.

There was a stir when Alger Hiss, a neat figure in a tan summer suit, took the stand. A hush settled over the courtroom as Stryker stalked over to his star witness.

"Mr. Hiss," he said in a ringing voice, "are you now or have you ever been a member of the Communist Party . . . or a fellow-traveler?"

Hiss (firmly). I never have been and I am not.
Stryker (showing him handwritten memos). Are these in your handwriting?
Hiss. Yes, they are.
Stryker. Did you in . . . 1938 or any other time in your life deliver those exhibits to Whittaker Chambers?
Hiss. I did not.
Stryker. Did you in your lifetime ever deliver any kind of State Department documents . . . to Chambers?
Hiss. I did not.

Stryker turned triumphantly to the jury and to the press and shot his cuffs. Then for fifty minutes he led Hiss through a detailed account of his life, from his childhood in Baltimore

to his job as general secretary of the San Francisco Conference. The picture that emerged was of a faithful public
servant who worked long and earnestly to serve his country.
Hiss went into great detail about his work in the State Department. "My duty was to advise Mr. Sayre on various matters coming across his desk. There was a great volume of
paper work . . . So I weeded out material for him. In the
course of this I made memos of fairly lengthy papers, sum-
marizing them." Touching on his role at Yalta and at Dumbarton Oaks, Hiss drew a self-portrait of a behind-the-scenes
operator, a friend of Franklin D. Roosevelt, and the host
at international conferences. "I am very proud," he said
modestly.

As Hiss spoke, his sharply delineated face was calm. Occasionally a pleasant smile punctuated his testimony. Only in
the way he clenched his hands, gripped the arms of the witness chair, or crossed and uncrossed his legs was there any
indication of nervousness. His soft voice reached only partly
across the packed, tense courtroom. To hear him people
leaned forward, cupping their ears. He described "this person representing himself as a free-lance writer—'George
Crosley,'" who had lived in his apartment, welshed on the
rent, borrowed his car, borrowed money, and then disappeared. Once Crosley and Mrs. Crosley had stayed over for
two nights at the Hiss home in Georgetown. During that stay,
Hiss said, Mrs. Crosley painted a picture of his stepson
Timmie.

Then Stryker moved in on the all-important State Department documents. Following the questions, Hiss reported that
the doors of his office were always open. The public and newspapermen drifted in and out at will. ". . . Mr. Wadleigh
came in several times . . ."

Had Chambers given him a rug? Yes, said Hiss, in the
spring of 1936. What about the alleged $400 loan made to
Chambers late in 1937? Hiss took a bankbook out of his
pocket. Yes, he admitted, $400 had been withdrawn from the

Hisses' joint bank account. But it was used to purchase some new furniture for their Volta Place house. He could not explain how the Chamberses were aware of the withdrawal. Then, he took back his grand jury testimony that the Woodstock typewriter had been in his possession through 1938. The Catlett testimony had refreshed his recollection, he stated. He had given it away in 1937.

Prim in an oyster-colored summer suit and a chaste brown tie, Alger Hiss lounged in the witness chair. Only the quick movement of his eyes betrayed his tense alertness. Prosecutor Murphy leaned heavily against the lectern near the jury box. Tugging at his cavalryman's outsize moustache, he seemed more mournful than aggressive. For two days Murphy tried to make the nimble-witted Hiss admit that he turned State Department documents over to Whittaker Chambers or that he saw the former *Time* editor after January 1, 1937. He moved slowly and ponderously after an assailant who usually eluded him. He could pin inconsistencies on Hiss, but he could not get Hiss to admit that he had offered many differing explanations of each crucial point.

In his testimony before the House Un-American Activities Committee, Hiss declared that he gave his 1929 Ford to Chambers in the spring of 1935 as part of a deal in which he sublet his apartment to the Communist underground agent. At the time of the deal, Hiss claimed, he already had bought a Plymouth. But, Murphy pointed out, when he learned that the Plymouth was not purchased until August, 1935, Hiss changed his story. He now said that he gave Chambers the car during 1936, *after* Chambers had welshed on several debts and *after* he had gone off without paying rent on the sublet apartment.

Murphy dragged from the defendant the admission that his own experts agreed the documents were typed on the Hiss Woodstock—a vital part of the government's case. But as the prosecutor sought to grapple with a swift legal mind which wrapped every sentence and every phrase in qualifications, he usually found himself hugging thin air. When Hiss stepped off the stand, he was still prim, still unshaken.

There was drama, sharp and quick, when Priscilla Hiss took the stand. Speaking in a lilting voice so clutched by nervousness that it could barely be heard, she told a story which in all essentials jibed with her husband's. Point by point, she contradicted the tightly packed account of inter-family intimacies told by both Whittaker and Esther, flatly denying such minor things as Esther's remark that Priscilla did not like ice-cream.

Now it was Murphy's turn. Like a Great Dane handling a kitten, he gently led her into two glaring contradictions which left her visibly shaken. While living with Alger Hiss in New York in 1932, had she been a member of the Socialist Party? "No," said Mrs. Hiss.

"Maybe I can refresh your recollection," Murphy said softly. He showed her photostats of Board of Elections registrations in 1932, calling her attention to her name alongside a Socialist Party designation.

"Mrs. Hiss," he added, "don't you know that the records of the Socialist Party's Morningside Branch list you as a member?" She did not, Mrs. Hiss whispered.

Murphy had the aid of defense counsel in springing the next trap. To prove that she had seen the Hisses in 1937, Mrs. Chambers testified that Priscilla told her she planned that year to take a nursing course at the Mercy Hospital in Baltimore. Under Stryker's questioning, Mrs. Hiss had triumphantly denied taking any such course. Murphy recalled the testimony of the two women. Then he read into the record a letter to the University of Maryland written by Mrs. Hiss in May, 1937, applying for enrollment in an in-organic chemistry course as a prerequisite to a Mercy Hospital course she had planned to take. It was as great a shock to Stryker as it was to Mrs. Hiss.

Moving on, Murphy had other puzzlers for Mrs. Hiss. Why had she testified to the grand jury that Mrs. "Clytie" Catlett was dead when the woman was alive? Why, if she had charge accounts in numerous department stores and an active checking account, had she drawn $400 cash for "family shopping" in November of 1937? She had told the grand jury that the Woodstock was in her possession in 1938. Why had she changed her testimony, alleging that she had given it to the Catlett children in 1937? When Mrs. Hiss left the stand, she seemed on the verge of hysteria.

Before the defense rested, it called one last important witness—Dr. Carl A. Binger. Against the prolonged objections of Murphy, Judge Kaufman allowed Binger to take the stand. Then, for forty-five minutes, Stryker posed a hypothetical question on Chambers' sanity. The judge refused to allow Binger to answer, and he was dismissed. "A grave injustice has been done to the government," Murphy roared.

The government had hoped to clinch the case by placing on the stand Mrs. Hede Massing, the first wife of Kremlin agent Gerhart Eisler and herself a former Communist agent who had known Hiss in the spy underground. But Judge Kaufman, already under fire for his handling of the case, refused to let her testify. She was not a legitimate rebuttal witness, he insisted. Frustrated and outraged, Murphy tried to call in a witness to contradict Hiss' testimony about the Ford car. Again Kaufman ruled him out.

During the long, heat-seared days of the trial, the question had echoed in the courtroom and on city streets where smothered New Yorkers glanced at the screaming headlines. "Who is lying? Hiss or Chambers?" Finally, Stryker gave his answer. Striding forcefully to the enclosure where the jury sat, he began his long summation. Short, erect, and white-thatched, the red-faced lawyer stormed in denunciation of Whittaker Chambers and orated grandly in praise of his client. As he moved from climax to climax, every spade was a glorious instrument or a dirty shovel, never merely a spade.

The jury members were "citizen-judges of the fact," the

"soldiers of justice," a great "orchestra of justice," he said, pacing back and forth. He himself was the Arturo Toscanini. His defense would be like the "four-or-five note theme of Beethoven's *Fifth Symphony*," repeated over and over again, now softly, now thundering. It was a simple theme, taken from a phrase in the prosecutor's opening statement, "If you don't believe Whittaker Chambers, the government has no case."

"We are trying one question here, and only one," Stryker said passionately. "Did Mr. Hiss furnish, transmit, and deliver to Chambers restricted documents in February and March, 1938. That is the sole question . . . There is only one man in the whole world who says Mr. Hiss furnished documents to him, and that man is Whittaker Chambers . . . I would not believe Chambers on a stack of Bibles if the FBI stacked them as high as this building . . . Roguery, deception, criminality have marked this man Chambers as if with a hot iron. He shows the pattern of an unusual personality and his life is filled with strange incidents . . ."

Why had Chambers accused Hiss of stealing documents from the State Department for transmission to the Russians? To help defeat the Democrats, Stryker answered. "It was a wonderful red herring to take the public's mind off the 80th Congress." How did Chambers get the documents and the handwritten memos? "Some other rogue or thief got [them] after Mr. Hiss was done with them in his office." How about the Woodstock which had been used to type the documents? "Mr. and Mrs. Hiss did not have that typewriter . . . when most of those documents were typed," said Stryker.

"This isn't a case; it's an outrage," he shouted. Then, turning to the defendant, he said slowly and huskily: "Alger Hiss, this long nightmare is drawing to a close. Your fate, your life, is in good hands." And he bowed to the jury. The summation, lasting four hours and thirty-five minutes stretched out over two days, had been a virtuoso performance.

When Murphy rose to sum up the government's case, it was

impossible to guess how he would reply to the dramatic oratory of the defense counsel. Throughout the trial Murphy's approach had been painstaking and a little pedestrian. Now, to the surprise of the spectators his voice rang out dramatically. He described first, the physical evidence submitted to the court, "the undisputed facts."

"We have shown you here," he said, "the typewriter, the original State Department documents, and the documents in this case—three solid witnesses." He then pointed out that the defense had not disputed three facts: Whittaker Chambers had in his possession copies, some verbatim, of original, secret, confidential State Department documents; the documents were all dated in the first three months of 1938; all but one of the typewritten documents were copied on the Hiss typewriter. Next he moved on to the parade of fifteen character witnesses called by the defense to "prove" the absurdity of the charges the jury was to weigh.

"Mr. Stryker said that he was going to call the shade of Oliver Wendell Holmes and have the ghost of that revered Justice testify on behalf of the defendant. And I said to myself, if he is going to call the shade of Justice Holmes, there are a couple of shades that I would like to call here. One man's name was Judas Iscariot and the other's Major General Benedict Arnold."

Then he went on. "But let me dwell just a moment on reputation. I daresay that Judas Iscariot had a fairly good reputation. He was one of the Twelve. He was next to God, and we know what he did. Benedict Arnold came from a fine family . . . He was made a major general and sold out West Point. He wasn't caught. But if he had been caught, don't you think he could have had George Washington as a reputation witness . . .

"Mr. Stryker first told you, in his opening, to beware of Whittaker Chambers. He said he was a moral leper, a thief . . . If Mr. Stryker calls Mr. Chambers a moral leper, what is the defendant Hiss? What is the name for a government

employee who takes government papers and gives them to an
espionage agent? . . . Inside of that smiling face, the heart
is black and cancerous. He is a traitor . . ."

Murphy proceeded to a slashing analysis of the defense.
"Now this trial has been in progress since May 31 . . . and
not once have I been able to find out what the defendant
charges here was the motive of Chambers. What was his
motive? What was the motive of the senior editor of *Time*—
getting $30,000 a year—to come forward with these papers?
Well, this morning I heard something about a political campaign. Mr. Stryker did not say in so many words that that
was the motive. He skirted around that a little bit. Let us
see now, what was the senior editor of *Time* going to get as a
result of injecting himself in a political campaign? I assume
we will have to agree that he was not going to get a $30,000
job in the government. Do you know what members of the
Cabinet get? . . . Nothing like $30,000. What was he going
to get if his side won, and what was his side? Could it be
some political advantage? There is no testimony that the man
ever concerned himself with politics after 1938. He was in-
tensely interested in politics prior to 1938. He was interested
in Communist politics, with his friend Alger Hiss.

"No motive has been proved. No motive has ever been
suggested on the witness stand here . . .

"How did Mr. Stryker know all about the intimate life of
the Chamberses? Do you think it was the result of some very,
very mysterious investigation that he and his colleagues conducted? . . . Wasn't it obvious to you, as I told you in my
opening, that there was not a blessed thing that the defense
did not know before this trial commenced? They had examined Mr. and Mrs. Chambers under oath in Baltimore—for
some 1300 pages. That examination commenced, I think, in
the early part of November, 1948, and concluded in the latter
part of March, 1949 * . . . They had the testimony of the
House committee in printed form . . . And armed with all

---

* Having been continued even after Hiss was indicted.

that they came into court and tried to impress you with the fact that all of this information was obtained by virtue of their own industry, secretly . . . They knew everything. They even had the typewriter . . .

"Do you remember how shocked Mr. Stryker was when Mr. Chambers told about the $400 loan. 'That's the first time you testified to that,' he said . . . and what did they do with it? They fumbled; they dropped the ball on that one . . . Where is Chambers' testimony corroborated? In what respect do we know as rational human beings that he told the truth? In what respect do we know that Hiss lied? You determine where the lie is in this case by examining and placing side by side the testimony of the Hisses and the Chamberses. One that struck me as being very cogent was the description of the houses, the inside lay-out of the rooms. Bear in mind, the Hisses say that neither of the Chamberses were in 30th Street or Volta Place. We have a description from Mrs. Chambers and from Mr. Chambers concerning the inside of the houses." Then Murphy read the meticulous description of the two Hiss homes from the record of Esther Chambers' testimony. "Is it possible in the nature of things for [Mr. Chambers and Mrs. Chambers] to describe two houses in such detail and not have been there? Is it humanly possible? Consider that when you ask yourself who is lying."

With a fine edge of irony, Murphy described the confrontation of Chambers by Alger Hiss, the cagey way in which Hiss approached an identification of Chambers. He mocked the fact that Hiss could not recognize Chambers until the latter had opened his mouth. "Well, Chambers opened his mouth and he looked in, and having looked, he wanted then to know the dentist's name. See, that would be important. He also wanted to know when the dental work was done. That would help him recognize his man." It was not until Chambers said, "You and I, Alger, were Communists together," Murphy recalled significantly, that Hiss "recognized" his antagonist. This was the story of the confrontation and not what Hiss said when testifying, "I recognized him without hesitation . . ."

"Now about the car," Murphy continued. "Let us assume that Hiss could not honestly remember what year it was that he gave the car away. There is no doubt in your mind that you would remember to whom you gave it . . . He first testified that the giving of the car was to clinch [the sublease of his apartment to Chambers]. No written lease, nothing like that, just an oral agreement, no rent in advance. This Harvard man, a brilliant law student, then a lawyer, practicing law with the Nye committee, permitted a man whom he did not know too well, did not know where he worked, did not know where he could reach him, permitted him to become a subtenant of his without a written lease, without demanding the money in advance, and then, to clinch the bargain in 1935, gave him a Ford.

"Later on he said he gave him 'the use' of the Ford. That is Mr. Hiss' forte. He is able to distinguish, to combine truth with half-truth, a little bit to color it, a little bit more to testify, and then, if placed in a corner, to rely upon the truthful part, and you have to be pretty good to do that, and he is pretty good.

"Now, he said he gave the car in 1936. That is, he completely divested himself of the car in 1936, in the summer, because he promised to give it to him in April of the year before. It was a promise made and a promise fulfilled. Of course the guy gypped him a little bit in between, beat him out of the rent, touched him for $30 or so, a complete moocher, but he made a promise, and, by God, when the man said, 'Where is the car?' 'Here it is.' And he gave him the car.

"But what does the assignment of title say? The assignment of title, which was introduced in evidence here, says, 'For value received the undersigned hereby sells, assigns and transfers unto Cherner Motor Company, 1781 Florida Avenue, N. W., the motor vehicle described on the reverse side of this certificate, and the undersigned hereby warrants the title' and so forth, and the signature of the assignor: 'Alger Hiss.' 'Sworn to July 23, 1936. W. Marvin Smith, Notary Public.' As a matter of fact, I think Mr. Hiss testified that he wrote in the name Cherner Motor Company himself. That is what he said under oath on July 23, 1936. That is what he said he did with that Ford automobile. He assigned, transferred, and sold that car to Cherner Motor Company, and Judge Kaufman would not let me prove what happened after that.

"One thing more to add to the list of things that will help you decide who lied. Mr. Chambers testified that he bought four Oriental rugs with money he received from Bykov. He had his friend, Professor Meyer Schapiro from Columbia, buy them for him. . . . Mr. Hiss says he did get *a* rug from Chambers. . . ."

Moving on to the all-important typewriter, Murphy declared that after Chambers had produced the memos and documents, "it became very, very important" to find the Hisses' Woodstock typewriter. "Hiss wanted to help this government of yours and mine. He wanted to track down and nail this horrible story of treason . . . Yes, sir, he wanted to help. So what did he do? He told FBI agents that [he and Mrs. Hiss] had an old typewriter, yes they had it, but they disposed of it in 1938 to a second-hand dealer in Georgetown.

"That was to help the FBI find the typewriter . . . So the FBI looked and they looked and they could not find it. But they did find . . . letters written by the Hisses on that typewriter, and their expert looked at them, just as a ballistics expert looks at a bullet, and said, 'Yes, those documents except the one we know as No. 10, were all written on the same typewriter that these specimens were written on.' It brought us a little closer to Alger Hiss. Now in looking for this typewriter, the FBI also had some other help from the Hisses. You can see how that first help saved the government a lot of money and time, but he wanted to help. That was the only thing he wanted to do in December, was to help the FBI.

"Mrs. Hiss told the grand jury that their maid, Claudia Catlett, was dead. You can see how that would help. You could just eliminate her from the list of people to see. But they found [the typewriter]. How? They went to the same sources that we did. The FBI agents saw the Catlett boys at the end of January, 1949, and they denied knowing anything about a Hiss typewriter. That is what they told the FBI. But what did they tell the Hisses? That little Catlett boy said he went to Donald Hiss the day after and said the FBI agents were around inquiring about a typewriter and then things started to buzz.

"We find Mr. Rosenwald, a fellow classmate [of Hiss], out in Detroit in the end of January. And then we know the story, how through the smaller of the Catlett boys the typewriter was traced through his family, through the sister, and finally [to Detroit] into Mr. Lockey's hands, and then Mr. Lockey sold it to Mr. McLean, and the receipt says April 19, 1949, for $15. So you can see how this helped. Now the Hisses knew that the typewriter formed a connecting link between Chambers and them. They knew that from the period from May or June, 1937, until his defection in April of 1938 that that typewriter was going all the time, and if there ever was going to be a charge against the Hisses, that would be the immutable witness forever against them. So what did they do? Did they sell it? Of course not. If they sold it, there would always be a record as it passed from one person to another. They got rid of it by giving it to the Catletts.

"Until [Hiss] was indicted he never once mentioned it to his lawyers. Of course, he never told the grand jury either, but he did tell one of the Catlett boys. He said, 'If the FBI ever comes looking for a typewriter, don't telephone me but tell my brother Donald.' In other words, he could let it sit. If the agents did not find the Catletts, all well and good . . . I submit that two things must be clear; one, that the typewriter was in the possession of the Hiss family until at least

Mr. Chambers' defection, until he left the Party; and two, that the Catletts had the typewriter for some time after that . . .

"Now another item, the $400. You know the story. Mr. Chambers says that Hiss gave him $400 and he used that to help pay for a car. The car was bought . . . in November, 1937. He used it in his break from the Party. Now if his statement was untrue there, of course, could not be any $400 withdrawal from the bank. But if his statement was true and there was an exact $400 withdrawal, he is psychic. He did not have the bank account. He did not say $350, he did not say $500, or $425, but an even $400. What did they do with it? Mrs. Hiss said she bought all of these items for her Volta Place house. I, too, am going to ask the ladies on the jury, is that the way you do it when you have a checking account and a charge account, and you have not moved in? Do you take the $400 out in one lump? Do you go around and buy curtains and items for the house to be delivered later and pay for them in cash? If you are going to have them delivered later you might as well pay by check. Is that $400 explanation reasonable to you or is it just another lie, another peg upon which you can tell which side credibility lies?

"The government's Exhibit 17 is the one that hurts. That is the one that scored. That is a pretty good typing job. And what did she say in there? She said she was going to the university in order that she might take courses at Mercy Hospital. That is what Mrs. Chambers testified that Mrs. Hiss talked of, 'taking courses.' Now why did it hurt? Because [Mrs. Chambers] too must have been psychic to know about that plan, or else, if she was not psychic, she was chumming with Mrs. Hiss, and I submit that is how she knew it.

"And again, finally, you are the second jury to hear this story. The grand jury heard the same story. The grand jury heard this traitor and Mr. Chambers, and that grand jury indicted Hiss. It indicted Hiss because he lied. He lied to them, and I submit he lied to you. The grand jury said that he lied twice on December 15th. And as a representative of 130,000,000 people of this country, I ask you to concur in that charge of the grand jury. I ask you as a representative of the United States Government to come back and put the lie in that man's face."

When Murphy had finished, Judge Kaufman took over. After he had finished his charge, the jury filed out of the courtroom to begin its deliberations. Four times the jury reported that it could arrive at no verdict. Each time the judge asked them to go back and try again. But the deadlock in the jury room could not be broken. As the hours passed, Hiss put aside a statement he had been writing to be issued following his acquittal.

Frayed of temper and weary of discussion, the jury returned to the courtroom on the evening of their second day's deliberation and reported that there was no hope of agreement among them. After fourteen hours and forty-four minutes, it was still split—eight for conviction and four for acquittal. The long ordeal had ended in a deadlock after twenty-seven days and 803,750 words of testimony.

Alger Hiss, gray-faced and grim, stalked out of the courtroom without a word or a formal handshake for Stryker. But down on his farm in Westminster, Maryland, Whittaker Chambers said softly: "I did what I had to do . . . Time will bring out the truth."

Judge Samuel H. Kaufman had barely dismissed the jury before criticism of his conduct of the case burst into the open. In Washington, Representative Nixon called for an investigation. Kaufman's "prejudice for the defense and against the prosecution was so obvious . . . that the jury's 8–4 vote for conviction came frankly as a surprise to me," he declared.

Above the fight, one fact remained unobscured. With every advantage on his side, with one of the country's shrewdest trial lawyers and a sympathetic judge, Alger Hiss could not clear himself of the charges made by Whittaker Chambers.

18

Two Strikes Are Out

BETWEEN THE FIRST AND SECOND HISS TRIALS, JULIAN
Wadleigh wrote his emotional, egocentric series of articles
for the New York *Post* syndicate. Retailing his experiences in
the Communist underground, they had the effect of corrob-
orating Whittaker Chambers on all essential details. But their
romantic inaccuracies * were to plague the prosecution in the
second trial. Much more happened, however, than the citizen
could read in his evening paper.

The real activity was subterranean, and much of it shaped
the course of the impending litigation. The FBI, living up to
its most glorious reputation, went all out to find witnesses
who might plug up whatever holes there had been in the first
government exposition of the evidence. Fanning out to the
four corners of the country, it tracked down the slimmest of
leads and came home triumphant. On the most vagrant teaser
—that the Chamberses had employed a Negro maid named
Edith in Baltimore during 1935 and 1936—they were able to
turn up Mrs. Edith Murray after six months of search. Another witness who brought the defense up short, Sergeant
George Norman Roulhac, was located in the Aleutians. Mrs.
Gladys Tally was brought in from St. Louis to confound the
Hisses on several minor but psychologically vital bits of testimony.

* Wadleigh insisted among other things that Colonel Bykov was one-
armed.

The defense itself was not sleeping. Having dropped Lloyd Paul Stryker for reasons never explained, Hiss engaged Claude B. Cross, a lawyer of high reputation but negligible criminal court experience. No surprise witnesses could be produced, but the defense worked most lovingly on one project. From the start, Hiss' lawyers made it clear that an attempt would again be made to use psychiatric evidence to prove that Chambers was an unreliable witness. Simultaneously, Hiss' friends ranged Boston, New York, Westchester, and Washington spreading as "explanation" for the ex-diplomat's predicament a story so preposterous and obscene that it could not be published in a family newspaper. That this "explanation" explained nothing did not deter those who spread it; their intention was to implement the Stryker theory of the "moral leper."

Despite this vicious rumor-mongering, a subtle change in atmosphere was taking place. The Justice Department—which to outward appearances at least had not seemed enthusiastic over Prosecutor Tom Murphy's herculean efforts to win a conviction—suddenly woke up. Perhaps the violent criticism of Judge Kaufman's behavior in the first trial had shaken a few policy makers. Perhaps it was tied in with the Truman Administration's general drift away from the New Dealers and the emergence of a jealous Fair Deal group in Washington which did not relish a link with the Rooseveltian past. At any rate, the difference in attitude was perceptible in the United States Courthouse on New York's Foley Square.

Another factor changed the balance of forces in the second trial. Tom Murphy had been thrown into the first trial too late to grasp fully the highly complex evidence, the little by-ways of fact and fancy that made up the case. The mass of material to be absorbed was fantastic in its aggregate, and Murphy had done surprisingly well in his first presentation. Between the two trials he was given a chance to assimilate what experts on Communist subversion were familiar with only out of their long experience. Murphy had grown in stature during the long, bitter duel with Stryker. A big man of immense potentialities, the abortive first trial had served him as a limbering up time. Now he was ready, willing, and anxious to cope with the best the defense could throw at him. Like any man of courage and intellectual means, he rose to the challenge.

When Murphy stepped into court on November 19, 1949, he was fully dedicated to the job ahead. And he could devote his entire energy to proving his case. On the bench sat Judge Henry W. Goddard, a veteran of twenty-three years in the Federal courts, who ruled his domain with a rigorous impartiality which could only be matched by his obvious desire to have all the facts laid before the jury. Throughout the trial, Judge Goddard gave both sides the widest latitude in the calling of witnesses and in eliciting testimony in both direct and cross examination. As a result, the acrimonious atmosphere of the first trial was lacking.

Murphy outlined what Chambers' testimony would be, but he stressed the importance of the documentary proof—the "immutable" typewritten documents and the memos in Hiss' handwriting. Cross, a small, stocky man, gray of voice and appearance, told the jury that he would prove that the documents had been stolen by Wadleigh and an unnamed employee of the State Department's Far Eastern Section. Clearly the defense had profited by a close study of the first trial record and the glaring deficiencies of Hiss' case had been noted. Throughout the trial, the press (and presumably the jury) waited impatiently to learn the name of this mysterious "real" thief. The question mark grew greater with the days. It was never converted into the exclamation point which would hammer home a defense victory.

Whittaker Chambers' testimony, richer in incident,* and therefore more damning than his first Federal court recital, was marked by a sharp change in attitude. Where once the

* Where Kaufman had limited Chambers generally to "yes" and "no" answers, Judge Goddard preferred full explanation.

government's star witness had sat in penitential stoicism, he now demonstrated that he was through with accepting the unwarranted slurs of a cross-examining attorney. Though he answered frankly and without reservation, an element of calm irony characterized his sparring with Cross. Often the defense chief was forced to retire, red-faced, annoyed, and definitely the loser. At one point, Chambers blandly invited Cross to press him on a point—what one of the Hiss maids had said to him when the two were brought face to face by the FBI. Cross stepped into the trap.

"She said that she didn't remember me, but that Lee Pressman and Nathan Witt were frequent visitors at the Hiss home," Chambers said. In anguish, Cross objected to the answer that he had demanded, but the judge let it stand. By subpoenaing Chambers' 1935 "David Breen" passport application he made mischief for his client. He could not explain satisfactorily how the defense had knowledge of the passport. And the passport photo showed Chambers sporting a bushy

---

LONDON   Underground Espionage Agent
  (1) *Dr. Philip Rosenbliett*—Formerly of (41st St. & B'way, NE)
        Dr. Greenberg—MD (West 70th NY)
        Brother-in-law
        American leader of British Underground C.
        Head in America Mack Moren (alias Philipovitch—allegedly Yugoslav)—real name—?
    Rosenbliett—in U.S.
        connected with Dr. Isador Miller—Chemist's Club—41st St. Chemist, Explosive Arsenal, Picatinny, N.J.
        war "front" behind Mack Moren existed—in Miller's employ
        Knew Pressman—his alias was "Cole Philips"—
           Introduced him to Mack Moren, buying arms for Spanish (Loyalist) Gov't.—
        Pressman—as counsel—helped Moren—made a flight to Mexico with him; forced down at Brownsville, Tex. in late '36 or early '37—probably fall of '36.
    Pressman
        Underground organized by the late Harold Ware; Pressman was in his group—(1932-3??) Pressman then in the A.A.A.—
        Nathan Witt—Secretary of the NLRB—head of the underground group after Harold Ware—
        John Abt—followed Witt in that group—Tax Div'n—Dep't of Justice & now in CIO (M. Ware's widow—Jessica Smith Ed. Soviet Russia).

moustache. Cross tried to make much of the fact that Chambers had never mentioned the moustache. All he proved was that neither Alger nor Priscilla had mentioned it either, although the witness had worn a moustache *during the entire period in which Hiss admitted knowing Crosley.*

The defense's demand that the government produce notes made by A. A. Berle after his conversation with Chambers in 1939 and those made by a State Department security officer in 1945 were a boon to the prosecution. Deliberately coy about these notes, Murphy grudgingly produced them. But instead of proving what the defense hoped they would prove—that Chambers had never made accusations of espionage before November, 1948—they strengthened the government's case. *

When Esther Chambers took the stand, she described a New Year's eve celebration in which the Hiss and Chambers

---

* The Berle notes also cast serious doubts on his House committee testimony that Chambers merely described "a Marxist study group" to him. The text, beginning on page 254:

Mr. Abt—Sister: Marion Bacharach—Secretary—Communist from Minnesota.
(Jessica Smith: With Reuters in 1926—friend of Louis Fischer)
Meeting place: John Abt's house—15th St.
Charles Krivitsky—alias Charles Kramer—(CIO)worked in La Follette Committee—Physicist.
Vincent Reno—Now at Aberdeen Proving Grounds—Computer—Math. Assist. to Col. Zornig (Aerial bomb-sight Detectors) Formerly CP organizer under alias "Lance Clark."
Philip Reno—in Social Security (??)—was head of Underground Trade Union Group Political leader
Elinor Nelson, treasurer of Fed. Employees' Union—(Fed. Workers' Union, CIO—headed by Jake Baker)
Reno connected with Baltimore Party ·
organizer—Benjamin (Sunday) Friedman alias Field—then California—then Russia—now organizer for Baltimore & Washington of Above-Ground Party—Underground connections—
STATE
Post—Editorship, *Foreign Service Journal.* Was in Alexandria Unit of CP—in "Underground Apparatus"—
Duggan—Laurence—(Member CP??)
(Wadleigh) Wadley—Trade Agreement Section
Lovell—Trade Agreement Section
Communist Shop Group
Elinor Nelson—Laurence Duggan—Julien Wadleigh—

families greeted 1937 together. But she had been not too certain of the year. It could be 1936 or 1937. By pounding away
at her, Cross forced her to set the date definitely as 1936.
When Hiss was on the stand, Cross triumphantly produced a
letter (postmarked December 30, 1936) which the defendant
had written to Mrs. Hiss, then visiting in Chappaqua, com-
miserating with her because Timmie had come down with
chicken pox. Mrs. Hiss in turn testified that because of the
illness, she and Timmie had remained in Chappaqua "until
about two weeks after the New Year." Obviously, the defense
argued, the celebration Mrs. Chambers described could never
have occurred. When this point boomeranged, the effect was
devastating. Dr. Margaret Mary Nicholson, a prominent
Washington pediatrician, was sworn by the government and
produced her records to show that Mrs. Hiss and Timmie had
visited her office on January 2, 1937. This not only made the
New Year's party a possibility, but because the defense had

West European Div'n—*Field*—still in—
   (Levine says he is out went into I.E.O.
   Then in committee for Repatriation
   His leader was Hedda Gompertz
Laughlin Currie: Was a "Fellow Traveler"—helped various Com-
   munists—never went the whole way.

———

S.E.C.
   Philip Reno—used to be
TREASURY
   Schlomer *Adler* (Sol Adler?)
   Counsel's Office
   Sends weekly reports to CP (Gen. Counsel's Office)
   Frank Coe—now teacher at McGill.
      There are two: brother—One of them in CP's "Foreign Bureau"
      —Bob Coe

———

Known from Peters—formerly in Bela Kun
   Govt. Agricultural Commissariat—called Gandosz (?) Then to
   Russia—then here, in Business Office of Communist paper "Uj
   Elori"—then, after 1929—head of CP Underground, lived in
   Hamilton Apts., Woodside, L.I.—under alias "Silver"—& lectured
   in Communist camps—
   Friend: "Blake" of "Freiheit"—real name—*Wiener*—American:
   Polish Jew.—

worked so hard to knock down the story, made it psychologically a distinct probability.

Dr. Nicholson's records were also of value to the government by demonstrating that another sworn assertion of Mrs. Hiss—that she could not have taken an automobile trip to Peterborough, New Hampshire, with the Chamberses during the summer of 1937 because she had not once left Chestertown, Maryland—was false. According to the records Mrs. Hiss and Timmie had visited Dr. Nicholson's office in Washington repeatedly that summer. Further, Dr. Nicholson stated that defense counsel had known of these visits during the time of the first trial.

But the first really staggering blow to the defense, similar to the effect of Wadleigh's testimony in the first trial, had come when Judge Goddard permitted Mrs. Hede Massing to take the stand for the government. Mrs. Massing told the court how in 1935 she had met Hiss at the home of Noel

---

Peters was responsible for Washington Sector
Went to Moscow—where is he now?—
Wife—a Comintern courier—
West Coast—Head: "The Old Man"—Volkov is his real name—
daughter a Comintern courier. He knows the West Coast
underground—Residence: San Francisco or Oakland—

———

Alexander Trachtenberg—Politburo—
member of the Exec. Committee
Head of GPU in U.S.
Works with Peters—
Plans for two Super-battleships—
secured in 1937—who gave—
Karp—brother-in-law of Molotov—working with Scott Ferris,
got this released—
Now: Naval Architect working on it, why??
Field was original contact
He introduced Duggan to Gompertz (Hedda)
Duggan's relationship was casual—
Shall excuse?—Where is Hedda Gompertz?—
Duggan & Field supposed to have been both members
of party.—
Donald Hiss
(Philippines Adviser)
Member of CP with Pressman & Witt—

Field, a member of her spy ring, and how she and Hiss had
argued over Field—she to keep him in her apparatus and Hiss
to bring him into the Hiss-Chambers underground group.
For the first time in a court of law, Hiss had been linked to
the Communist netherworld by a witness other than Chambers. And for the first time in either trial, Alger Hiss showed
agitation over the testimony of a witness. Try as he might,
Cross could not break up Mrs. Massing, and she left the stand
with her story unshaken. The name of Field was to crop up
later when Murphy produced a letter from Hiss to the Kremlin agent, written in 1948. That Field had disappeared mysteriously behind the Iron Curtain in 1949 did not help the
defense.

There were other witnesses: the experts who testified that
the documents had been typed on the Hiss Woodstock; Miss
Eunice Lincoln; William Rosen, who received the famous
Hiss Ford car in 1936 (he stood on constitutional grounds
and refused to answer questions); and Felix Inslerman, who
microfilmed purloined documents for the spy ring.

There was little change in the defense case. A series of
nineteen character witnesses * took the stand to affirm that
Hiss' reputation for "loyalty, veracity, and integrity," had
been excellent. But even in this, Hiss suffered setbacks.
Stanley Hornbeck, as in the first trial, was forced to admit
that at least two occasions he had been warned that Hiss

---

* Frankfurter and Reed were conspicuously not among them.

Labor Dep't.—Asst. to Frances Perkins—
Party wanted him there—to send him as arbitrator in Bridges
trial—
Brought along by brother—
Alger Hiss
Ass't. to Sayre—CP—1937
Member of the Underground Com.—Active
Baltimore boys—
Wife—Priscilla Hiss—Socialist—
Early days of New Deal
NOTE—When Loy Henderson interviewed Mrs. Rubens his report immedi-
ately went back to Moscow. Who sent it? Such came from Wash-
ington.

was a Communist. This time he—reluctantly—named his informant: Ambassador William C. Bullitt. Francis Sayre denied any knowledge of the four memos Hiss swore he had prepared at Sayre's direction. He volunteered that there was a difference of opinion as to Hiss' character. Equally damaging was his testimony that at one time Hiss had recommended Noel Field as a possible aide when Sayre was High Commissioner of the Philippines. Other witnesses admitted that they had known Hiss for a relatively short time.

Hiss' testimony was, as usual, marked by evasion, niggling, and bickering over details. Turning his famous smile on and off, he was eloquent on all immaterial matters. When confronted by discrepancies between present and previous testimony, he insisted that his memory had been refreshed or that his recollection had been faulty. Still the urbane man of charm, he persisted in his account that he had known Chambers as a deadbeat free-lance writer named George Crosley. Despite Sayre's flat denial that the memos in Hiss' handwriting had been prepared as part of State Department routine, Hiss placidly clung to that explanation. Now and then he delicately wiped his face, his little finger crooked just a trifle. He stepped down unshaken, but then no one had expected that he would give any ground.

Like a frightened somnambulist, Mrs. Priscilla Hiss faced her ordeal on the stand. The burden she had borne since August 3, 1948, had pressed its imprint on her face. Her prominent eyes looked opaque, the pupils dilated. And in a sing-song voice, like a small girl reciting her lessons, she entered her denials of the minutely telling account which Esther Chambers had placed on the record. Almost by system, she called black whatever Mrs. Chambers had called white. Was the wall paper in the Hiss Volta Place living-room mulberry colored? No, she said, it was grayish tan. Had she visited the Chamberses in Baltimore? No, she had not visited them anywhere. Had there been any intimacy between the two families? No, Mr. Crosley had been purely a business acquaintance of Mr. Hiss. What about the $400 which Chambers said he had borrowed from the Hisses? Very elaborately, Mrs. Hiss explained how the money had been used to purchase curtains and other furnishings for the Volta Place house. However, she could account for only $200 of the sum under discussion.

This was in direct testimony. Under cross-examination, she shrivelled up. Her memory left her. She remembered next to nothing. Denying, denying, denying, she fell into one trap after another. Murphy showed that at the time she had made the $400 withdrawal for furnishings, she was also charging purchases and drawing checks steadily and that the withdrawal had so depleted their funds that Priscilla had borrowed $300 early in December. Her claim that these purchases had been delivered to the Volta Place house in November of that year because they had the key long before they moved into it on December 29, 1937, was carefully underlined by the prosecutor.

(Later in the trial, he demolished that testimony by showing that the house was not rented until December 8th and that the Hisses had not even seen the house until at least the 5th of that month. By calling Mrs. Gladys M. Tally, daughter of the owner of the house, he also showed that Mrs. Chambers' description had been accurate and Mrs. Hiss' false.)

Both Alger and Priscilla had sworn repeatedly that she was "not a typist." "I'm a longhander," she had tinkled. Hadn't Mrs. Hiss passed a typing course at Columbia University? Murphy asked. Mrs. Hiss withdrew into vagueness. She had no recollection of *passing* any such course, she said. Murphy introduced Columbia University records to prove that she had. Still Mrs. Hiss refused to accept cold fact. She refused to accept documentary proof that she had been a member of the Socialist Party? Or that her brother Thomas Fansler had been a member? What about her insistence that she had never in her life seen second sheets (the documents were typed on onion skin)? Why, the only times she had ever seen paper of that kind was as wrapping for dresses—tissue paper. Not even when she was office manager at *Time* magazine? Not even then. Murphy let the point ride. Denying, denying, denying, Mrs. Hiss left the stand. ("She just lost the case for Hiss," said a reporter.)

Then the defense played what it thought was trump. It called Dr. Carl A. L. Binger to the stand. Friends of Hiss in the spectators' section brightened. This was the psychiatric testimony which would forever destroy Whittaker Chambers. For sixty-nine minutes Cross read his hypothetical question, a compound of every rumor, irresponsible allegation, garbled fact, and unpleasant truth about Chambers that could be assembled. Assuming these things to be true, said Cross, what would be your diagnosis. "A psychopathic personality," said Binger. And what were the symptoms of a psychopathic personality? Cross asked. Binger listed twelve symptoms: repetitive lying, stealing, withholding truth, insensitivity for the feelings of others, play-acting and assuming false names, bizarre and unusual acts, vagabondage, instability of attachments, panhandling, abnormal emotionality, paranoid thinking, and pathological accusations.

So eager to prove his point was Binger that he was reprimanded by Judge Goddard. "You are here as a witness, not as an advocate," said the judge severely.

"Mr. Chambers is suffering from a condition known as psychopathic personality," the saturnine psychiatrist said in smooth, rolling periods, "a disorder of character, the outstanding features of which are amoral and asocial behavior." One of the symptoms of this ailment was "a tendency to make false accusations." A psychopathic personality, somewhere between the neurotic and the psychotic, could not be believed. "He is under constant compulsion to make his fancies come true." Lying was another symptom, and Chambers' lies had begun in 1919, Binger testified. After consulting his notes, he admitted to an error in dates. Half an hour later, Binger cited inability to remember precise dates as an important indication of mental disorder.

Binger—a tall, fleshy-nosed individual who had lolled at ease under direct examination—was brought up abruptly by the persistent questions of Prosecutor Tom Murphy. Holding up to scrutiny each of Binger's findings, Murphy's cross-examination employed respectful incredulity, broad sarcasm, and common-sense indignation. Behind it were months of exhaustive reading in the field of psychiatry.

Would Dr. Binger's diagnosis explain how the stolen State Department documents offered by Chambers had been typed on the Hiss Woodstock typewriter? No, said Binger. Wasn't it true—and here Murphy read copiously from standard psychiatric texts—that the term "psychopathic personality" was a meaningless, catch-all phrase and "not a diagnostic entity"? Binger agreed. As to Binger's qualifications as an expert, wasn't it true that the doctor had not been certified as a psychiatrist until 1946, that he had never held a residency in any mental hospital, that he had not passed an examination in order to be certified, and that he had been turned down at least once by the American Psychiatric Association? Binger conceded that all this was so.

For two days, Murphy went over Binger's testimony. In some cases, Binger allowed that his assumptions might not be true; in others he excused the paucity of symptoms by explaining that though individually they might be negligible, he was concerned with the "total life pattern."

Hadn't he testified that one of Chambers' symptoms was that he looked at the ceiling frequently when on the witness stand? Yes. Did Dr. Binger know that in fifty minutes, he himself had looked up at the ceiling fifty-nine times? There was a roar of laughter in the courtroom.

Murphy. Wouldn't you say it was important for a psychiatrist to have detailed information concerning the early childhood relationships [in order to form a diagnosis]?

Binger. Certainly.

Murphy. You had the subject's name, the city of his birth, that he had a father, a mother, and a brother, and that's all you had until [Chambers' sixteenth year]?

Binger. That was all the information I had up to that time.

Murphy drew from Binger that he was a friend of Hiss, that his wife and Mrs. Priscilla Hiss had attended the same college and taught at the same school. He got Binger to state that description of his testimony as "impartial" would be "not accurate."

Taking up the symptoms one by one, Murphy asked for evidence to back them. Were ten lies in twenty years an example of repetitive lying? Might be, said Binger. Could he name one case of panhandling in Chambers' life? "You win on that point," Binger said laughing. Were a nineteen-year successful marriage and ten years as a *Time* editor evidence of instability of attachment? "That's cogent evidence of stability," Binger admitted. Retreating on all points, however, he still refused to modify his analysis. But Murphy had done his work well. His questioning was of such probing perception that it could become a textbook model on the cross-examination of psychiatric witnesses.

When Dr. Henry A. Murray, a Harvard clinical psychologist, took the stand, Murphy had a different sort of antagonist. Though he had never set eyes on Whittaker Chambers, Murray insisted that it was enough to read a man's writing in order to arrive at a diagnosis. Though he himself was afflicted with a nervous twitch and gesticulated almost compulsively, Murray brushed this aside as not symptomatic of any disturbance.

Under cross-examination, Murray refused to accept the possibility that prosecution descriptions of the Communist underground espionage apparatus were valid. Though he had helped assess candidates for the Office of Strategic Services' own underground, he could not believe that such things went on in the United States. That a Communist espionage agent might flee from the wrath of the NKVD, once he had broken, seemed "preposterous" to Murray.

That was on a Friday. As court recessed for the week-end, Murphy looked gloomy. But that evening the FBI got a phone call from a friend of a former *Time* writer. He reported that Murray had come to see the journalist during the previous November, and only on reading newspaper accounts of the doctor's testimony had he realized the significance of his visit. He reported that Murray had asked about Chambers' personal habits and had grown very irate when the writer refused to accept Murray's statement that Chambers was a "pathological liar."

"You're just trying to whitewash Chambers," Murray had said then.

In court the following Monday, Murphy carefully got Murray to repeat several times that he had based his diagnosis solely on a selected list of Chambers' writings and on the hypothetical question "and nothing else." When had he made up his mind, Murphy asked. Not until Christmas, Murray answered. When Murphy quoted the *Time* writer's words, showing that the doctor has started out convinced of his diagnosis even before he had made any study, and that he had lied to the court about his investigations, the effect of Murray's testimony was vitiated.* When he left the stand, there was little doubt that the two psychiatric witnesses had done more for the prosecution than for the defense.

What had been accomplished? The Catletts, on whom both Stryker and Cross depended mightily, had made bad witnesses. They were shaky in their dates and surly under cross-examination. Hiss had hoped to convince the jury by their testimony that the Woodstock was in their possession during late 1937. But Perry Catlett had nullified his own testi-

---

* After the close of the trial, Dr. Murray's political record was unveiled. According to a congressional report, he had been a sponsor of the Waldorf-Astoria "peace" conference in 1949.

mony by acknowledging that the typewriter had been given to him by Mrs. Hiss after his family moved to a house on P Street. Surprisingly enough, a defense witness—an employee of the Washington gas company—pinned down that date. It was in the middle of January. Sergeant Roulhac, signer of the lease for that house and who had lived with the Catletts, made the Hiss case even worse by testifying that he had not seen the machine until mid-April in 1938, *after* the last date on any of the documents.

In a blaze of indecisiveness, the defense called another brace of character witnesses and rested its case.

Then Murphy covered himself with glory. On the Tuesday of the week the trial ended, he called in his rebuttal witnesses with a canniness and an eye for the dramatic worthy of a master. First he put on an FBI man, a typist, who rapidly copied one of the documents right before the jury. The Hiss contention that they had given the typewriter away because it was a wreck vanished into thin air. Then he called his surprise witness. She was Edith Murray, the Chambers' maid in 1936. A small, personable, and friendly-faced woman, Mrs. Murray was simple honesty personified. In a clear, quiet voice she told the court that she had worked for Mr. and Mrs. Lloyd Cantwell (a Chambers pseudonym) when they lived at Eutaw Place in Baltimore. The Cantwells had only two visitors "that I know of," she said, a lady and her husband.

"Stand up out of that chair," Murphy told her gently, "and point her out." Suddenly, the import of what she was about to do hit the courtroom. Reporters stopped taking notes and strained forward. Standing up, Mrs. Murray pointed unhesitatingly at Priscilla Hiss. "This lady, right there," she said. Mrs. Hiss turned deathly white, but not a muscle of her face twitched. For the first time in a court of law, a witness had testified to the friendship between the Hisses and the Chamberses—a friendship running well past the time when both Alger and Priscilla had sworn they had stopped seeing Crosley.

Almost conversationally, Mrs. Murray continued: "She came and stayed overnight one time when Mrs. Cantwell was pregnant and had to go to the doctor in New York." Chambers had been away, and Priscilla had come up from Washington to take care of his small daughter. "The little girl's name was Eleanor or Ellen; we used to call her Peegee." What did she call the visitor, Murphy asked. "Miss Priscilla," said Edith. And could she identify the man? Edith Murray stood up again and pointed out Hiss who smiled as if unseen hands had tugged at his cheeks. Rambling a little, she mused that the Cantwells were "very nice people to work for" and Chambers "a very nice man." Sick with the effect she was having on the jury, Cross went over and over her story. Her truth would not be budged.

Late that afternoon, Senator John Foster Dulles put the finishings touches on the government's case. As he mounted the stand, he gave Hiss one cold look. Then, throughout his testimony, he pointedly kept his eyes away from his ex-colleague. Forthrightly, the man who had helped make Hiss president of the Carnegie Endowment put his finger on five lies the defendant had told about their relations. He told of warnings he had received in 1946 from various people that Hiss was a Communist. And he showed that Hiss had been virtually asked to resign from the Endowment in 1948 but had stalled until the documents were produced. With this, Murphy rested.

The summation and the charge to the jury were, in a sense, symbolic. Cross eternally pleaded his client's innocence. Murphy employed a combination of pointed exposition, legal histrionics, and honest indignation. Judge Goddard's charge was lucid, impartial to a fault, and stern. Cross demonstrated what had been increasingly apparent as the case moved along—that his strategy had been to weigh down the jury with irrelevant detail, to read long lists of cancelled checks and minutes of meetings into the record. He had also tried to throw the blame anywhere but on his client. Clytie Catlett, his own witness, had been bribed by George Crosley, he hinted. "Hidden confederates" were responsible. Perhaps Leo Pasvolsky, a suspicious Russian name, had been the real culprit. Perhaps it might have been a frame-up. He told the jury, "The government has failed entirely to suggest a motive for Mr. Hiss to commit espionage, unless it be *this vague suggestion* that he was a Communist [Italics ours]." Chambers, he insisted, had told the truth about Wadleigh and the others, but he had lied about Hiss. Why he should have selected Hiss for this distinction was never demonstrated.

Murphy held up each argument as a beacon to the jury, earnestly emphasizing some points, driving others home with a sweep of humor, compassionate yet righteous. When he spoke of Chambers, there was a moving dignity to his words, a human understanding of this man who had sacrificed livelihood and reputation in defense of a cause. He was explaining, not debating, and his overwhelming earnestness was alive in the courtroom. Against his words, Goddard's charge to the jury was antiphonal, not contradictory.

The jury took just under twenty-four hours to arrive at a decision. Seventeen months and seventeen days after Chambers had made his first open statement in Washington, the eight women and four men filed back to the jury box. As they passed Hiss, he eagerly sought to catch their eyes. They looked away. The blood drained out of a reporter's face as if he himself were on trial.

"Madam Foreman, have you and the members of the jury agreed on a verdict?" the clerk asked. His voice sounded hollow in the hushed room.

"I have," said Mrs. Ada Condell nervously.

"How say you?"

"I find the defendant guilty on the first count and guilty on the second count," she said.

"You have rendered a just verdict," Goddard told the jury. Hiss turned pale. The nerves on Mrs. Hiss' neck twitched. Then the morbid rigidity of their faces hid all emotion. It

was over, all over. The great deception had failed. But Alger
Hiss did not give up. Perhaps he will never give up. On the
day of sentencing, January 24, 1950, his lawyer was still protesting that the whole truth had not yet been told. And just
before Judge Goddard imposed sentence—five years for each
perjury count, the sentences to run concurrently—Alger Hiss
rose to his feet. In a loud, clear, venom-filled voice, he
sounded an unregenerate's call, "I am confident that in the
future the full facts of how Whittaker Chambers was able to
carry out forgery by typewriter will be disclosed." In the
audience, a sentimental woman wept easily.

Down on his Westminster farm where he had remained
throughout most of the trial, Whittaker Chambers said, "My
work is finished . . ."

But was it finished? Was it even started? Even as the last
stories of the conviction and sentencing were appearing in
the newspapers, an atonal, antiphonal shouting began as
Hiss' supporters retired to prepared positions. Here was the
chorus of sentimentality, the parade of the weeping, the
applause of the innocents who believe in Tinker Bell, the bil-
lowing of the wide skirts behind which the cynical and per-
fidious hide. Yet to come was Hiss' appeal to the higher
courts. Would this still the clamor?

In two long trials, the tally of treason had been made. The
evidence had been clear and damning, the proof of wide-
spread espionage incontrovertible. Against this was one thing
—Alger Hiss' *beaux yeux*. A spy is a spy is a spy, unless he can
stand up in a well-tailored suit and point to an ill-dressed
accuser. Then, to the Washington and Park Avenue theor-
izers, the accusation vanishes. More than three million words
of testimony, pinning the lie on Hiss, become just a gentle
zephyr rumpling his hair.

The reaction of the Harvard cheering section which rooted
for Hiss, of the Columbia University intellectuals who

gnashed their teeth at the prosecution, might well have been subject matter for serious study by Doctors Binger and Murray. It explains much, including the State Department's suicidal China policy which turned over half of Asia to the Communists. The parallel is almost too simple: Alger Hiss is an innocent man, despite his conviction; and the Chinese Communists are "agrarian reformers," despite their words and deeds. In this never-never land, there is no evil and the three little monkeys reign supreme.

This is the meaning and the message of the Hiss-Chambers case. Put aside the convulsive struggle of the two men. Dramatic though it is, their duel represents the flush of action which launches a Shakespearean tragedy. The argument of the play is more profound. There is the "concealed enemy" burrowing feverishly. And there is the pushing phalanx of sympathizers who have come to the defense of Hiss because they are subconsciously aware that his guilt is theirs. Who is the more guilty, the man who passes documents to a Soviet spy ring or the man who, for whatever reason, sponsors the culprit?

Hiss is one man, caught in a tragedy of arrogance and self-deception. But there are those who aided and abetted him in their blindness; and their name is legion. Instead of crushing the seeds of treason, they scattered them in the good American earth. The conviction of Alger Hiss is a flare, lighting up their sordid pasture. In a warring world, with the United States facing the greatest threat in its history, they refuse to see. This is the tragedy of history. Before it, the fate of Whittaker Chambers, the accuser, and Alger Hiss, the accused, pales into insignificance. The Hiss-Chambers drama can be a curtain raiser of a new steadfastness. Or it can be the last whimper of a tired and demoralized world.

Whittaker Chambers' work is finished. He has been liberated from some of the indignities forced on him by an unthinking and unthankful public. There are men of good will everywhere, but when the time came for them to stand up and be counted, they were elsewhere detained. Those who should have struck out for him were otherwise occupied. Fortunately, the real work has barely begun. Though the field lies fallow, it can yet be brought into cultivation. There is a time to plant and a time to pluck up what is planted. The time is now.